"Call upon Me, I will respond to you."
[Ghāfir 40:60]

A Handbook of ACCEPTED PRAYERS

Ibn Daud

A Handbook of Accepted Prayers

Comments & Suggestions
Allāh ﷻ says, "(The believers pray,) Our Lord! Do not punish us if we forget or make a mistake." [Al-Baqarah 2:286]

The author would appreciate hearing comments and suggestions from any readers. If you find any errors in this book, these are solely due to his shortcomings. Please email the author directly and he will do his best to correct them in the next edition inshā'Allāh.

British Library
A catalogue record for this book is available from the British Library.
www.bl.uk

Publishing
Published by Ibn Daud Books, Leicester, UK and printed by IMAK, Istanbul, Turkey.

Ibn Daud Books
theauthor@ibndaudbooks.com
www.ibndaudbooks.com
Leicester, UK

ISBN 978-1-8380492-3-2

TABLE OF CONTENTS

GLOSSARY OF EMOTIONS

Emotions aren't always the easiest things to put your finger on, but we must start with the basics: recognising that our emotional flare-ups can often push us into undesirable situations or precipitous events that don't offer spiritual benefit. Some people are more 'in control' of their emotions than others. The positive approach will always be to seek reorientation towards Allāh ﷻ and clarification within one's own mind as to how to avoid negative emotional reactions in general.

The author has identified a number of emotions related to each chapter (i.e. each spiritual disease) that the reader may more closely associate with, alongside definitions and explanations. It is hoped that this approach may help to navigate the reader directly to those chapters and the associated du'ā's that will be of most benefit inshā'Allāh.

The definitions below are short attempts at clarification that have been taken from a number of standard dictionaries, including the New Oxford Dictionary of English, Cambridge Dictionary, Merriam-Webster (online), Collins Online Dictionary, and Dictionary.com. Some use of a book by Patrick Michael Ryan entitled 'Dictionary of Emotions' (2014, Kindle Edition) has also been made.

A

Emotion	Definition	Disease	Page
Addicted	Physically and mentally dependent on something; unable to stop taking something (e.g. drugs), or doing something as a habit	Extravagance	160
		Fantasizing	176
		Love of the World	250
		Mockery	268
		Ostentation or Showing Off	304
		Seeking Reputation	322
		Vanity	330
Aggressive	Energetic and determined pursuance of one's goal(s); behaving in an angry and violent way, often towards other people	Anger	102
		Hard-Heartedness	208
		Hatred	218
		Vanity	330
Agitated (see Annoyed, Bitter, Frustrated)	Worried or nervous, distracted by troubles	Anger	102
		Iniquity	238

GLOSSARY OF EMOTIONS

Emotion	Definition	Disease	Page
Annoyed	Displeased and irritated; exasperated and angry	Anger	102
		Antipathy Towards Death	110
		Displeasure with Blame or Disapproval	134
		Displeasure with the Divine Decree	142
		Envy	150
		Iniquity	238
		Negative Feelings	276
Anxious	Fearful or worried about some a future event or circumstance, uneasy in the mind; troubled, fretful and impatient; any person who is anxious might become inconsiderate to others, because they might prioritise their own welfare	Antipathy Towards Death	110
		Displeasure with Blame or Disapproval	134
		Displeasure with the Divine Decree	142
		Fear of Poverty	186
		Fraud	198
		Iniquity	238
		Miserliness	258
		Negative Feelings	276
Apathetic (see Indifferent)	Indifferent and unconcerned, lacking motivation to do anything or to care for anything that is going on around you	Hard-Heartedness	208
Apprehensive	Fearful expectation or anticipation; feeling worried about something that you are going to do or that could potentially happen	Antipathy Towards Death	110
		Blameworthy Modesty	118
		Fear of Poverty	186
		Miserliness	258
		Relying on Other than Allāh ﷻ	312
Argumentative	Quarrelsome and happy to be opposed to others' views; often arguing or wanting to argue	Anger	102
		Displeasure with Blame or Disapproval	134
		Hard-Heartedness	208
		Hatred	218
		Relying on Other than Allāh ﷻ	312

GLOSSARY OF EMOTIONS

Emotion	Definition	Disease	Page
Arrogant	Haughty and feeling overbearing pride; unpleasantly proud and behaving as if you are more important than, or know more than, other people	Boasting, Arrogance and Pride	126
		Displeasure with the Divine Decree	142
		Hard-Heartedness	208
		Iniquity	238
		Obliviousness to Blessings or Ingratitude	292
		Ostentation or Showing Off	304
		Relying on Other than Allāh	312
Ashamed	Feeling humiliation, guilt, embarrassment, and/or remorse about something you have done, or about a quality in your character, or associations	Blameworthy Modesty	118
		Fear of Poverty	186
		Fraud	198
		Relying on Other than Allāh	312
Astray	Away from the correct path or correct way of doing something, falling into error or confusion	Antipathy Towards Death	110
		Heedlessness	228
		Relying on Other than Allāh	312

B

Emotion	Definition	Disease	Page
Bitter (see Agitated)	Someone who is bitter is angry, unhappy, hurt, and strongly resentful or cynical, because they cannot forget (or refuse to forget) bad things that happened in the past	Anger	102
		Displeasure with the Divine Decree	142
		Envy	150
		Hatred	218
		Negative Feelings	276
		Obliviousness to Blessings or Ingratitude	242
Brooding	Preoccupied with depressing, morbid, or painful memories or thoughts; prone to thinking deeply about the way someone or something presented you with obstacles; making you feel uncomfortable or worried, as if something bad is going to happen	Displeasure with Blame or Disapproval	134
		Relying on Other than Allāh	312

GLOSSARY OF EMOTIONS

C

Emotion	Definition	Disease	Page
Callous	Insensitive, cruel, unkind and without sympathy or feeling for other people	Boasting, Arrogance and Pride	126
		Iniquity	238
		Miserliness	258
		Wantonness or Greed	338
Careless	Heedless, negligent and not paying enough attention to what one does; lacking consideration, forethought or thoroughness	Boasting, Arrogance and Pride	126
		Mockery	268
		Heedlessness	228
Contemptuous	Scornful and disrespectful with an intense and cynical dislike; characterised by extreme contempt	Anger	102
		Boasting, Arrogance and Pride	126
		Iniquity	238
		Mockery	268
Covetous	Painfully desirous of another's advantages; wanting to have something too much, especially something that belongs to someone else	Envy	150
		Love of the World	250
		Obliviousness to Blessings or Ingratitude	292
		Seeking Reputation	322
		Wantonness or Greed	338
Cruel	Savage and heartless; extremely unkind and unpleasant and causing pain to people or animals intentionally	Boasting, Arrogance and Pride	126
		Fraud	198
		Hard-Heartedness	208
		Iniquity	238
		Miserliness	258
		Mockery	268
		Wantonness or Greed	338
Cynical (see Pessimistic)	Sceptical and/or doubtful of someone or something; believing that people are only interested in themselves and are not sincere	Antipathy Towards Death	110
		Displeasure with the Divine Decree	142
		Hard-Heartedness	208
		Miserliness	258
		Mockery	268
		Negative Feelings	276
		Obliviousness to Blessings or Ingratitude	292
		Relying on Other than Allāh ﷻ	312

GLOSSARY OF EMOTIONS

D

Emotion	Definition	Disease	Page
Deceitful	The act of keeping the truth hidden, especially to get an advantage; deliberately deceptive, especially by pretending one set of feelings ('fronting') and acting under the influence of another; deceptive or fraudulent; not worthy of trust or belief (i.e. dishonest)	Displeasure with the Divine Decree	142
		Fraud	198
		Iniquity	238
		Love of the World	250
		Relying on Other than Allāh ﷻ	312
		Seeking Reputation	322
		Wantonness or Greed	338
Deluded	Believing things that are not real or true	False Hope	168
		Fantasizing	176
		Love of the World	250
		Relying on Other than Allāh ﷻ	312
		Vanity	330
		Antipathy Towards Death	110
		Displeasure with Blame or Disapproval	134
		Displeasure with the Divine Decree	142
Depressed	Disheartened, typically with oneself or one's condition; without hope	Envy	150
		Extravagance	160
		Fear of Poverty	188
		Iniquity	238
		Mockery	268
		Negative Feelings	276
		Wantonness or Greed	338
Disappointed	Discouraged or displeased due to the failure to fulfil one's hopes or expectations; unhappy because someone or something was not as good as you hoped or expected, or because something did not happen	Displeasure with Blame or Disapproval	134
		Displeasure with the Divine Decree	142
		Iniquity	238
		Relying on Other than Allāh ﷻ	312
		Seeking Reputation	322
		Vanity	330
		Wantonness or Greed	338

GLOSSARY OF EMOTIONS

Dismissive	Indicating that you do not think something is worth considering; tending to criticise or belittle someone or something in a way that shows you do not respect or value him, her, or it (i.e. disparaging)	Mockery	268
Distracted (see Astray)	Unable to concentrate; preoccupied, anxious, and/or disturbed; nervous or confused because you are worried about something	Love of the World	250
Distressed	Anxiously uneasy, troubled, or grieved; upset or worried	Antipathy Towards Death	110
		Displeasure with Blame or Disapproval	134
		Displeasure with the Divine Decree	142
		Envy	150
		Fear of Poverty	186
		Iniquity	238
		Mockery	268
		Negative Feelings	276
Doubtful	Unsettled in opinion or belief; affected by uncertainty or doubt	Antipathy Towards Death	110
		Displeasure with the Divine Decree	142
		False Hope	168
		Fear of Poverty	186
		Miserliness	258
		Relying on Other than Allāh ﷻ	308

E

Emotion	Definition	Disease	Page
Egotistic	Excessively conceited or absorbed in oneself; self-centred; considering yourself to be better or more important than other people	Boasting, Arrogance and Pride	126
		Iniquity	238
		Mockery	268
		Ostentation or Showing Off	304
		Seeking Reputation	322
		Vanity	330
Embarrassed	Feeling uncomfortable due to shame or wounded pride; self-conscious; feeling shy	Blameworthy Modesty	118
		Relying on Other than Allāh ﷻ	308

GLOSSARY OF EMOTIONS

Excessive	Unrestrained; going beyond the usual, necessary, or proper limit or degree; an amount that is over and above what is acceptable, expected, or reasonable	Extravagance Fantasizing Love of the World Miserliness Mockery Ostentation or Showing Off Vanity Wantonness or Greed	160 176 250 258 268 304 330 338

F

Emotion	Definition	Disease	Page
Fearful (or Cowardly)	Feeling dread or anxiety about a possible or probable situation or event; frightened or worried about something	Antipathy towards Death Blameworthy Modesty Displeasure with the Divine Decree Iniquity Miserliness Relying on Other than Allāh ﷻ	110 118 142 238 258 312
Forgetful	Neglectful; unable to or not wanting to remember; often forgetting things	Heedlessness Love of the World Obliviousness to Blessings or Ingratitude Vanity	228 250 292 330
Frustrated	Distressed and annoyed; feeling annoyed or less confident because you cannot achieve what you want	Anger Antipathy towards Death Displeasure with Blame or Disapproval Displeasure with the Divine Decree Envy Iniquity Negative Feelings	102 110 134 142 150 238 276
Furious	Extremely angry and violently energetic	Anger Displeasure with the Divine Decree Hatred Iniquity	102 142 218 238

GLOSSARY OF EMOTIONS

G

Emotion	Definition	Disease	Page
Grudging	Displaying or reflecting reluctance or unwillingness to act pleasantly or to give (material) assistance; reluctant or unwilling to accept, admit, or give something	Antipathy towards Death	102
		Envy	150
		Displeasure with Blame or Disapproval	134
		Displeasure with the Divine Decree	142
		Hatred	218
		Miserliness	258
		Obliviousness to Blessings or Ingratitude	292
		Wantonness or Greed	338
Guilty	Feeling responsible for a specified wrongdoing, particular fault or error	Fraud	198
		Negative Feelings	276

H

Emotion	Definition	Disease	Page
Harsh	Ungentle or unpleasant in action or effect; unkind, cruel, or more severe than is necessary	Anger	102
		Boasting, Arrogance and Pride	126
		Hard-Heartedness	208
		Mockery	268
		Seeking Reputation	322
Helpless	Deprived of strength or power; incapacitated; unable to do anything to help yourself or anyone else	Fear of Poverty	186
		Iniquity	238
Hostile	Unfriendly and antagonistic or angry; not liking something	Anger	102
		Antipathy towards Death	110
		Displeasure with the Divine Decree	142
		Envy	150
		Hatred	218
		Iniquity	238
		Mockery	268
		Obliviousness to Blessings or Ingratitude	292

GLOSSARY OF EMOTIONS

I

Emotion	Definition	Disease	Page
Ignorant	Not having enough knowledge, understanding, or information about something	Antipathy towards Death	110
		Blameworthy Modesty	118
		Displeasure with the Divine Decree	142
		False Hope	168
		Heedlessness	228
		Love of the World	250
		Mockery	268
		Relying on Other than Allāh ﷻ	312
		Vanity	330
Immature	Not fully developed emotionally or intellectually; not behaving in a way that is as calm and wise as people expect from someone of your age	Fantasizing	176
		False Hope	168
		Love of the World	250
		Mockery	268
		Obliviousness to Blessings or Ingratitude	292
		Ostentation or Showing Off	304
		Vanity	330
Immoderate	Exceeding just or reasonable limits	Extravagance	156
		Love of the World	250
		Seeking Reputation	322
Impatient	Restless and/or eager; short-tempered under delay or opposition; easily annoyed by someone's mistakes or because you have to wait	Displeasure with the Divine Decree	142
Inadequate	Lacking requisite qualities or resources to meet a task; not good enough or too low in quality	Extravagance	160
		Love of the World	250
		Relying on Other than Allāh ﷻ	312
		Seeking Reputation	322
		Vanity	330
Indifferent (see Apathetic)	Completely lacking concern or interest; not thinking about or interested in someone or something; unaffected by strong emotion (i.e. dispassionate); without care or interest in knowing (i.e. uninterested)	Extravagance	160
		False Hope	168
		Hard-Heartedness	208
		Heedlessness	228
		Miserliness	258
		Obliviousness to Blessings or Ingratitude	292

GLOSSARY OF EMOTIONS

Insecure	Lacking self-confidence; the state (emotional) of lacking the certainty to carry out a task or to put oneself forward; insecure people have little confidence and are uncertain about their own abilities or if other people really like them	Antipathy towards Death	110
		Blameworthy Modesty	118
		Displeasure with the Divine Decree	134
		Envy	150
		Extravagance	160
		Fear of Poverty	186
		Iniquity	238
		Love of the World	250
		Miserliness	258
		Obliviousness to Blessings or Ingratitude	292
		Seeking Reputation	322
		Vanity	330
Insensitive	Deficient in human sensibility, acuteness of feeling, or consideration; unfeeling; callous	Hard-Heartedness	208
		Heedlessness	228
		Mockery	268
		Seeking Reputation	322
Insincere	Lacking sincerity; pretending to feel something that you do not really feel, or not meaning what you say	Boasting, Arrogance and Pride	126
		Fraud	198
		Mockery	268
		Negative Feelings	276
		Ostentation or Showing Off	304
		Relying on Other than Allāh ﷻ	312
		Seeking Reputation	322
		Vanity	330
Irrational	Without normal mental clarity or sound judgement	False Hope	168
		Fantasizing	176

J

Emotion	Definition	Disease	Page
Judgemental	Having an excessive or strong point of view; too quick to criticise people	Boasting, Arrogance and Pride	126
		Envy	150
		Mockery	268
		Ostentation or Showing Off	300
		Relying on Other than Allāh ﷻ	312

GLOSSARY OF EMOTIONS

L

Emotion	Definition	Disease	Page
Lazy	Disinclined or not willing to work or use any effort	Antipathy Towards Death	110
		False Hope	168
		Heedlessness	228
		Love of the World	250
Lustful	Driven by, feeling or connected with strong desire	Fantasizing	176
		Love of the World	250
		Ostentation or Showing Off	304
		Seeking Reputation	322
		Vanity	330
		Wantonness or Greed	338

M

Emotion	Definition	Disease	Page
Malicious	Intending to do harm or upset other people; cruel	Envy	150
		Iniquity	238
		Mockery	268
		Negative Feelings	276
		Seeking Reputation	322
		Wantonness or Greed	338
Manipulative	Influencing or attempting to influence the behaviour or emotions of others for one's own purposes	Fraud	198
		Hard-Heartedness	208
		Iniquity	238
		Seeking Reputation	322
		Wantonness or Greed	338

N

Emotion	Definition	Disease	Page
Neglectful	Not caring properly for someone or something; not giving enough care and attention	Antipathy Towards Death	110
		False Hope	168
		Hard-Heartedness	208
		Heedlessness	228
		Iniquity	238
		Miserliness	258
		Obliviousness to Blessings or Ingratitude	292
		Relying on Other than Allāh ﷻ	312

GLOSSARY OF EMOTIONS

O

Emotion	Definition	Disease	Page
Oblivious	Unmindful; unconscious; unaware	Antipathy Towards Death	110
		Extravagance	160
		Heedlessness	228
		Love of the World	250
		Obliviousness to Blessings or Ingratitude	292
		Seeking Reputation	322
		Vanity	330
Obstinate	Firmly or stubbornly adhering to one's purpose, opinion, etc.; not yielding to argument or persuasion; showing inflexibility and persistence in attitude	Boasting, Arrogance and Pride	126
		Displeasure with Blame or Disapproval	134
		Envy	150
		Heedlessness	228
		Miserliness	258
		Negative Feelings	276
Offended	Hurt, upset, or annoyed; resentful or indignant; insulted by someone or something, often because someone has been rude	Anger	102
		Displeasure with Blame or Disapproval	134
		Hard-Heartedness	208
		Mockery	268
Overwhelmed	Feeling overcome or engulfed by something, such as an emotion	Displeasure with the Divine Decree	142
		Fear of Poverty	186
		Love of the World	250
		Seeking Reputation	322
		Wantonness or Greed	338

P

Emotion	Definition	Disease	Page
Pessimistic (see Cynical)	Expecting the worst possible outcome; thinking that bad things are more likely to happen or emphasising the bad part of a situation	Fear of Poverty	186
		Mockery	268
		Negative Feelings	276
		Relying on Other than Allāh ﷻ	312

Pretentious	Creating and maintaining an appearance of undeserved importance or distinction; trying to appear or sound more important or clever than you are	Boasting, Arrogance and Pride	126
		Ostentation or Showing Off	304
		Relying on Other than Allāh	312
		Seeking Reputation	322
		Vanity	330

R

Emotion	Definition	Disease	Page
Reckless	Utterly unconcerned about the consequences of some action; without caution; careless	Heedlessness	228
		Wantonness or Greed	338
Reluctant	Unwilling, disinclined, uncertain, or doubtful about something and therefore slow to do it, especially something contrary to one's custom	Antipathy Towards Death	110
		Blameworthy Modesty	118
		Displeasure with Blame or Disapproval	134
		Displeasure with the Divine Decree	142
		Miserliness	258
Resentful	Embittered or angry because you have been forced to accept someone or something that you do not like	Displeasure with Blame or Disapproval	134
		Displeasure with the Divine Decree	142
		Envy	150
		Hatred	218
		Negative Feelings	276
Resistant	Not wanting to accept something, especially changes or new ideas	Miserliness	258
		Obliviousness to Blessings or Ingratitude	292

GLOSSARY OF EMOTIONS

S

Emotion	Definition	Disease	Page
Self-absorbed	Preoccupied with your own thoughts and activities	Boasting, Arrogance and Pride	126
		Love of the World	250
		Miserliness	258
		Seeking Reputation	322
		Vanity	330
Self-righteous	Excessively or hypocritically pious; believing that your ideas and behaviour are morally better than those of other people	Boasting, Arrogance and Pride	126
		Ostentation or Showing Off	304
		Vanity	330
Shy	Lacking self-confidence; nervous and uncomfortable with other people; shy and nervous; without much confidence; easily frightened (i.e. timid)	Blameworthy Modesty	118
Superstitious	Belief that is not based on human reason or scientific knowledge, but is connected with old ideas about magic, chance, etc.	False Hope	168
		Relying on Other than Allāh	312
Suspicious	Openly distrustful and unwilling to confide; inclined to feel that something illegal is happening or that something is wrong	Negative Feelings	276
		Relying on Other than Allāh	312

T

Emotion	Definition	Disease	Page
Thoughtless	Lacking in consideration for others; inconsiderate; tactless	Heedlessness	228
		Iniquity	238
		Mockery	268
		Obliviousness to Blessings or Ingratitude	292
Threatened	Feeling that something bad might happen, or that someone might do something bad to you	Antipathy Towards Death	110
		Blameworthy Modesty	118
		Iniquity	238

GLOSSARY OF EMOTIONS

U

Emotion	Definition	Disease	Page
Uncertain	Lacking confidence or assurance; not knowing what to do or believe, or not able to decide about something	False Hope	168
		Fear of Poverty	186
		Relying on Other than Allāh ﷻ	312
Uncharitable	Unkind and unfair	Hard-Heartedness	208
		Miserliness	258
		Relying on Other than Allāh ﷻ	312
Undignified	In the habit of making oneself look silly and losing people's respect in doing so, especially because of not being controlled, serious, or calm	Mockery	268
		Ostentation or Showing Off	304
		Vanity	330
Uneasy	Discomforted; anxious; slightly worried or uncomfortable about a particular situation	Blameworthy Modesty	118
		Displeasure with Blame or Disapproval	134
		Displeasure with the Divine Decree	142
		Fear of Poverty	186
		Relying on Other than Allāh ﷻ	312
Uninspired	Without intellectual, emotional, or spiritual excitement; not exciting or interesting	Relying on Other than Allāh ﷻ	312
Unkind	Not treating someone very well; to be inconsiderate of another's feelings	Boasting, Arrogant & Pride	126
		Hard-Heartedness	208
		Miserliness	258
		Mockery	268
		Negative Feelings	276

GLOSSARY OF EMOTIONS

V

Emotion	Definition	Disease	Page
Vain	Characterised by false pride; having an exaggerated sense of self-importance	Boasting, Arrogance and Pride	126
		Love of the World	250
		Ostentation or Showing Off	304
		Seeking Reputation	322
		Vanity	330
Vindictive	Having a strong or unreasoning desire for revenge; having or showing a wish to harm someone because you think that they harmed you; unwilling to forgive	Envy	150
		Hard-Heartedness	208
		Hatred	218
		Negative Feelings	276
		Relying on Other than Allāh	312
Vulgar	Objectionable, obnoxious; not suitable, simple, dignified or beautiful	Boasting, Arrogance and Pride	126
		Fantasizing	176
		Ostentation or Showing Off	304
Vulnerable	Exposed, unprotected; able to be easily physically or mentally hurt, influenced, or attacked	Blameworthy Modesty	118
		Fear of Poverty	186
		Iniquity	238
		Relying on Other than Allāh	312

W

Emotion	Definition	Disease	Page
Worthless	Hopeless, insignificant, useless, nothing to offer	Fear of Poverty	186
		Love of the World	250
		Negative Feelings	276
		Relying on Other than Allāh	312
		Seeking Reputation	322
Wound up	You have allowed teasing or irritation to push you into tension or anger; very worried or nervous	Anger	102
		Displeasure with Blame or Disapproval	134
		Mockery	268
		Relying on Other than Allāh	312

THE AUTHOR'S JOURNEY

It's supremely true that the best advice often comes in the most profoundly simple of places. My first book, the 'Handbook of Spiritual Medicine' was a book that was attentive to the spiritual illnesses that beset us all. As the cover notes stated, it was an attempt to provide antidotes through practical treatments as offered to us in the Qur'ān and the authentic aḥādīth (Prophetic sayings).

In late 2020, one very astute customer made a suggestion that a du'ā' book would be an excellent complement to these 'spiritual medicines'. With the global pandemic at its height, there was a great deal of theorising about social well-being within the media and among friends. There was much rewording and repackaging of the simple notion that 'talking things through' was a worthwhile activity to calm the wavering mind. Reflecting on this and asking myself: 'who better to talk to than Allāh ﷻ?' a nugget of an idea started to gain weight in my own mind.

Remembering all the excellent and essential du'ā' books that I had laid my hands on over the years, and scribbling down notes on my personal preferences for a handbook of du'ā's that would help me, things began to unfold. Firstly, I saw one thing that was lacking in the other du'ā' books: I struggled to find du'ā's related to emotions other than the typical few such as anger and envy. Secondly, I saw two benefits of crafting a new book, and the two of these seemed to complement each other. Obviously, there is the fact that du'ā' (or supplication, begging to one's Lord) is a core practice and meritorious act within worship and it never fails to get us closer to Allāh ﷻ. Secondly, the twenty-first century environment tends to distract us from our higher purpose. Our intentions, yes, they can be noble. But there is much mischief around us! Those of us who have even the weakest sympathy for the faithful declaration 'lā ilāha illallāh' (there is none worthy of worship besides Allāh ﷻ) know the wisdom and truth behind the ḥadīth: 'A person will wake up in the morning as a believer and may reach the evening as an unbeliever' [Ṣaḥīḥ Muslim 118]. We can all appreciate just how easily our inspirations and hopes that come to us at the beginning of the day can become warped, bent and battered on account of the distractions that this modern world tends to generate (particularly during times of great trials and tribulations).

I wanted to put forward to any person willing to cut free from these distractions, to that person seeking a clearing amongst the crooked branches of the bewildering forest of the everyday, that we can do this successfully by grabbing hold of the 'mukh' (an Arabic word usually translated as 'essence' but there are alternatives that I would like to explore: please bear with me), the core of worship.

Let me now focus on my Muslim brothers and sisters for a moment. That's not to disregard my universal siblings in humanity, but there's something I'd like to say about the five daily prayers that the Muslims are obliged to offer. Looking at ourselves in these acts that we call 'devotion', just how devoted are we? Just how regularly does the average Muslim 'muṣalli' (one who offers the ṣalāh), having taken time for the standing, bending and kneeling of their ritual prayer and then (to their credit) having offered their shorter supererogatory prayer, feel pleased that they are 'done and dusted'? Is it all too easy to get up from our knees and leave the place of prayer with this sense of fulfilment to rejoin the office workers, sitting room, dining space, or friends in the sports lounge? Do we not often get the feeling that the prayer 'duties' are sufficient?

I won't deny that many of my Muslim brothers and sisters recite 'astaghfirullāh' at the end of the congregational prayer. This is a wonderful thing, because it shows there is an understanding that we can never perfect the act of prayer in the way that Allāh ﷻ deserves to see it.

But is 'astaghfirullāh' enough? Another translation of 'mukh', taken from the well-known ḥadīth that 'du'ā' is mukh-ul 'ibādah' is 'brain' (Jāmi` At-Tirmidhī 3371). From this meaning, we can start to put ourselves in a critical position, in both senses of the word. We might like to jump to the quick conclusion that, by intensifying or improving on the du'ā' that we make, by refining the requests and pleas that you or I make to Allāh ﷻ, there is an intellectual improvement going on. It's certainly an attractive idea. In supplication, in begging Allāh ﷻ, laying your heart open to Him, you are doing the spiritual equivalent of completing cryptic crosswords. Perhaps that is not the best example to give, since cryptic crosswords aren't to everyone's benefit or liking, but the point is that there is stimulation of the cerebral. A more holistic understanding of the word 'mukh' might occur to us if we think of the nature of the action of du'ā'. What we are doing is using our best ideas, expressed as words on the tongue, which show - even if we aren't focusing on this notion particularly at the time - that we are in a state of servitude and dependence upon Allāh ﷻ.

The ḥadīth 'du'ā' is mukh-ul 'ibādah' is an important instance of Allāh ﷻ, through the words of the Prophet Muḥammad ﷺ, letting us in on some special wisdom: the person that offers du'ā' is intellectual; the person who is without any du'ā' is brainless. I could have toned that sentence down, but it seems good in that it strikes home to me.

Let me not denigrate too much here, though: I want to offer encouragement not criticisms. With this new 'Handbook of Accepted Prayers', I'm of a mind to 'raise the bar' somewhat. It was the stated intention of 'A Handbook of Spiritual Medicine' to provide a definitive plan, a structured guidance for my own self, to encourage me to lean towards good manners as exemplified in the most noble character of our beloved Prophet Muḥammad ﷺ. Seeking goodness is an improvement of course. This second handbook is in entirely the same direction, continuing with the theme of spiritual diseases of the heart, to make du'ā' to help better manage associated emotions. But this second book is different in that it shows more clearly that the prescription for the medication must be applied for directly, from the highest authority. There are terms of acceptance that we must be aware of and common rules that we need to keep to.

The 'Du'ā' Framework' section puts forward these common rules.

These are what we must necessarily 'put into' our du'ā's. However, it makes total sense to look to get something out of it. Allāh ﷻ has decreed that we should recognise Him as 'Ar-Raḥmān' and 'Ar-Raḥīm': indeed we use these names repeatedly in the daily prayer 'opener', 'Al-Fātiḥah'. Their meaning is that He is All Compassionate and The All Merciful, so it is entirely fitting that we look to beg results and improvement from Him. For me, in particular, I want to come away from the unimportant tittle-tattle and help myself to gain favour with Allāh ﷻ the Creator, above the crooked imperfections of the everyday world. I want there to be a preferred place for me, a place of near-satisfaction if not perfect satisfaction (and definitely not smugness!) that I can find in my time on this Earth, before I am buried within the earth. I desire to improve the sincerity of my own du'ā's, away from being mostly ritualistic and mechanistic, towards a way that is more appealing, heartfelt, sincere and pleasing to Allāh ﷻ, based on the methodology of the Qur'ān and Sunnah. I would like to invite every person who picks up this handbook to join me towards those aims and that destination: a gentle, brighter mental and emotional setting that is reached by exploring the nature of du'ā' as the essence, the pivot, the centre of worship. Or the brain.

Who will be reading this book? Very broadly, the willing reader is, therefore like me, the person who would like to cultivate a better relationship with Almighty Allāh ﷻ. It is highly probable that you have read something very similar to these words of intent somewhere before. The new or (I hope) inspiring thing about this du'ā' handbook is that you will find within it a structure. I've set out, and it is a patently obvious fact that you understood already, that the lack of harmony in modern life, the tendency toward the unwholesome or anti-social, means that we could definitely benefit from a stronger commitment to regular close conversations with Allāh ﷻ: but how exactly do we get started and what sort of conversation suits our needs? Certainly, there will be very many common goals, shared requests that we will lay at Allāh's ﷻ door: You want pious children and a caring spouse. I want the same. Uncle Ahmed wants the chance to go for a Hajj at Allāh's ﷻ house in Makkah, and he wants it to be an accepted Hajj, just as you do. But, when I sit down and look at my personal state, my character and emotions, there are going to be a variety of attributes and faults that are different from the next person's. Therefore, I will perhaps beg Allāh ﷻ to grant me pious children and a caring spouse who are capable of forgiving me for my hard-heartedness. And Uncle Ahmed could well ask for a Hajj in a state of good health, whereby he begs Allāh ﷻ (as the One who grants health and well-being) not to make it a journey that is too great a test for him. It is the structure and layout of this handbook that I intend, by the grace of Allāh ﷻ, will enable each reader and myself to find personal routes to enlightening conversations with Allāh ﷻ, routes that suit one's unique character.

Finding this route and this enlightenment will require that we push ourselves to see that the time we have been given in this world is the only time during which our own du'ā' can have an effect on our condition. This applies to our state in this world and the hereafter: with this purpose in mind, I pray that Allāh ﷻ gives you ease, a joyous and long life in this world with excellent deeds and character, where the tests upon you are not so burdensome that you cannot deal with them. I pray that you will remember me in your du'ā's, such that you will ask for me as I ask for you:

O Allāh ﷻ! Grant us the highest station in Jannah, the most unimaginably blessed dwelling place, and (O, Allāh ﷻ!) do not allow us to taste or touch the fire of Hell for even the shortest of moments.

O Allāh ﷻ! You created our bodies from clay and mud, earthly matter. You have given us ointments and balms to ease our physical ailments. Our souls, however, were created by You in the heavens and when our emotions feel disturbed or uncomfortable, we ask that You allow us to cry to You, for we understand that You are the Supreme Lover, and will not fail to hear our prayers. You are the controller of the hearts and souls.

O, Allāh ﷻ! You are the true King, Owner and Sustainer of all things seen and unseen.

اللَّهُمَّ إِنِّي أَعُوذُ بِكَ مِنْ عِلْمٍ لاَ يَنْفَعُ وَمِنْ قَلْبٍ لاَ يَخْشَعُ وَمِنْ نَفْسٍ لاَ تَشْبَعُ وَمِنْ دُعَاءٍ لاَ يُسْمَعُ

Allāhumma innī a'ūdhu bika min 'ilmin lā yanfa' wa min qalbin lā yakhsha' wa min nafsin lā tashba' wa min du'ā'-in lā yusma'

O Allāh, I seek refuge with You from knowledge that is of no benefit, a heart that is not humble, a soul that is not satisfied and a supplication that is not heard. [Sunan An-Nasaī 5536]

Āmīn.

Ibn Daud

Leicester, UK
Jumādā Al-Ākhirah 1444 (January 2023)

RECOMMENDATIONS

Although many works have been written on this subject of du'ā', the author Ibn Daud has written and presented this book in a systematic and very accessible manner.

Furthermore he has linked the du'ā's and supplications to emotions and spiritual ailments, which I believe is one of the unique aspects of this work. The author provides several du'ā's for each particular ailment with appropriate headings and references to original sources.

He has also referenced these ailments to 'Al-Asmā Al-Ḥusnā' as well as 'Aṣ-Ṣalāh Al-Ibrāhīmiyyah'. In my humble opinion this is a 'must-read' book and one to have as a point of reference for understanding and memorising much-needed du'ā's from the Qur'ān and Sunnah during times of extreme difficulties and challenges.

Dr Shaykh Ashraf Makadam
Director of Trust, Madani Schools Federation

Leicester, UK
Jumādā Al-Ākhirah 1444 (January 2023)

MāshāAllāh the 'Handbook of Accepted Prayers' by Ibn Daud is a well-organised compilation of du'ā's.

Fully referenced and categorised according to various emotions and feelings, this du'ā' book is definitely one to treasure. May Allāh ﷻ accept this effort of Brother Jamal and make it a means of ṣadaqah jāriyah for all those who have been part of this publication. Āmīn.

(Mawlānā) Muhammad Yahya
(Director) An Nasihah Publications

Leicester, UK
Jumādā Al-Ākhirah 1444 (January 2023)

RECOMMENDATIONS

MāshāAllāh this book highlights the key values and practices which most Muslims living in the modern era tend to neglect.

The reader can efficiently search for the illness which he wishes to remove and the author has it made it incredibly engaging by mentioning ad'iyah and adhkār.

Shaykh Imran bin Adam
Principal, Jame'ah Uloom Al Qur'ān

Leicester, UK
Jumādā Al-Ākhirah 1444 (January 2023)

RECOMMENDATIONS

In the Name of Allāh, The All Compassionate and The All Merciful.

Praise be to Allāh Ta'ala who constantly bestows upon us His grace, continuously grants us His blessings and mentions in the Qur'an:

"Call upon Me, I will respond to you." [Ghāfir 40:60]

Peace and blessings be upon Muḥammad, the best of creation, whose goodness and beauty were perfect and his family and companions and upon those who follow him with excellence until the Day of Judgement.

'A Handbook of Accepted Prayers' provides an invaluable source of practical advice, offering a range of du'ā's to suit any circumstance or emotion. It offers words of comfort and hope, helping the reader to strengthen their relationship with Allāh ﷻ in times of difficulty, fear and sadness. This book is a valuable tool for all those who seek a deeper connection with Allāh ﷻ and the assurance of His ever-present love and support. It is an indispensable resource to be used for inspiration and prayer.

After reviewing the book I was impressed by the clear format, along with its English translation and transliteration making this book easily accessible and beneficial for one and all. Praise be to Allāh Ta'ala for what He has enabled my dear brother Jamal to achieve.

I ask Allāh Ta'āla to accept his efforts, keep him with 'āfiyah and grant him unceasing success in both worlds. Āmīn.

Shaykh Faheem bin Ismaeel
Principal, The Imam Muhammad Adam Institute

Leicester, UK
Jumādā Al-Ākhirah 1444 (January 2023)

ACKNOWLEDGEMENTS

The Prophet ﷺ said, "He who does not thank the people is not thankful to Allāh." [Sunan Abī Dawūd 4811]

All praise be to Allāh ﷻ, Lord and Sustainer of the universe, for helping me fulfil this work, and salutations and peace be upon the Messenger of mercy and guidance, and upon his family, righteous Companions and those that follow him.

This work is the result of the encouragement and guidance of many special people from amongst the respected 'Ulamā of Leicester and further afield, to whom I wish to express my deepest gratitude: Dr Shaykh Ashraf Makadam, Director of Trust, Madani Schools' Federation, Mawlānā Imran bin Adam, Principal of Jame'ah Uloom Al Qur'an, Shaykh Faheem Ibn Ismaeel, Principal of The Imam Muhammad Adam Institute School and Mawlānā Yahya ibn Faruq, Director of An Nasihah Publications. May Allāh ﷻ protect and elevate their positions. Āmīn.

I am also indebted to my editing team, Mawlānā Amaan Muhammad, Mustafa Abid Russell, Irfan Chhatbar and Khaleel Kassim, without whom I would not have had the support, patience, skills and expertise to bring this book to fruition. I am truly honoured and deeply grateful to have found the company of such kind, patient and God-conscious individuals.

I would also like to express my gratitude to my sweet children, Ammaarah, Hafsah and Muhammad Ali, for helping me gain valuable insights into 'what good may look like', and my kind and loving sisters, Tehmina and Mashal, for passionately reviewing early drafts and for their ongoing encouragement.

Along my journey, I have received invaluable support from many other kind and generous individuals. May Allāh ﷻ compensate them with the best of rewards in both worlds. Āmīn.

My immense gratitude also goes to my wife, Sana, whose utmost patience in times of strain, and guidance and wisdom during this journey, have been a great source of strength for me.

And finally, I am extremely indebted to my loving parents, Hameeda Parekh and the late Mohammed Daud Parekh for their teaching and my upbringing. They led by example.

I pray to Allāh ﷻ for the best of rewards for our Prophet ﷺ, his inheritors, the scholars of Islām, and those who follow their path to happiness and salvation in this life and in the Hereafter. Āmīn.

Ibn Daud

Leicester, UK
Jumādā Al-Ākhirah 1444 (January 2023)

TRANSLITERATION KEY

Vowels

A	Short Vowel as in "Ago"	I	Short Vowel as in "Sit"
Ā	Long Vowel as in "Heart"	Ī	Long Vowel as in "See"
AY	Diphthong as in "Page"	AW	Diphthong as in "Home"
'	Abrupt start or pause	U	Short vowel as in "Put"
Ū	Long Vowel as in "Food"		

Consonants

ب	B	"B" no "H" attached	ص	Ṣ	"S" with full mouth
ت	T	Soft "T", no "H" attached	ض	Ḍ	"D" with full mouth, using sides of tongue
ث	TH	"TH" as in "Thin"	ط	Ṭ	"T" with full mouth
ح	Ḥ	"H" Guttural sound	ظ	Ẓ	"DH" as in "Dhuhr" with full mouth
خ	KH	"KH" Very guttural, no usage of tongue	ع	'	Guttural sound - accompanies vowel
د	D	Soft "D", no "H" attached	غ	GH	"GH" Very guttural, no usage of tongue
ذ	DH	"DH" as in "Adhān"	ق	Q	"K" with back of the tongue raised
س	S	"S" only, not "Z"	و	W	"W" read, not silent
ش	SH	"SH" as in "Shin"	ي	Y	"Y" only, not "I"

NOTE: Double consonants must be pronounced with emphasis on both letters without pause, e.g. Allāhumma should be read al-lāhum-ma.

Allāh is the Arabic word for God, the One True God shared by all classical monotheistic faiths, such as Judaism, Christianity and Islām. Throughout this book the Arabic word for God, Allāh, will be used.

Subhānahū wa ta'āla - May He be glorified

Ṣallalāhu 'alayhi wa sallam - Allāh's peace and mercy be upon him

'Alayhis salām - Peace be upon him

Radiyallāhu 'anhu - May Allāh be pleased with him

Rahimahullāh - May Allāh have mercy on him

HOW TO USE THIS BOOK

Key Steps to Using this Book

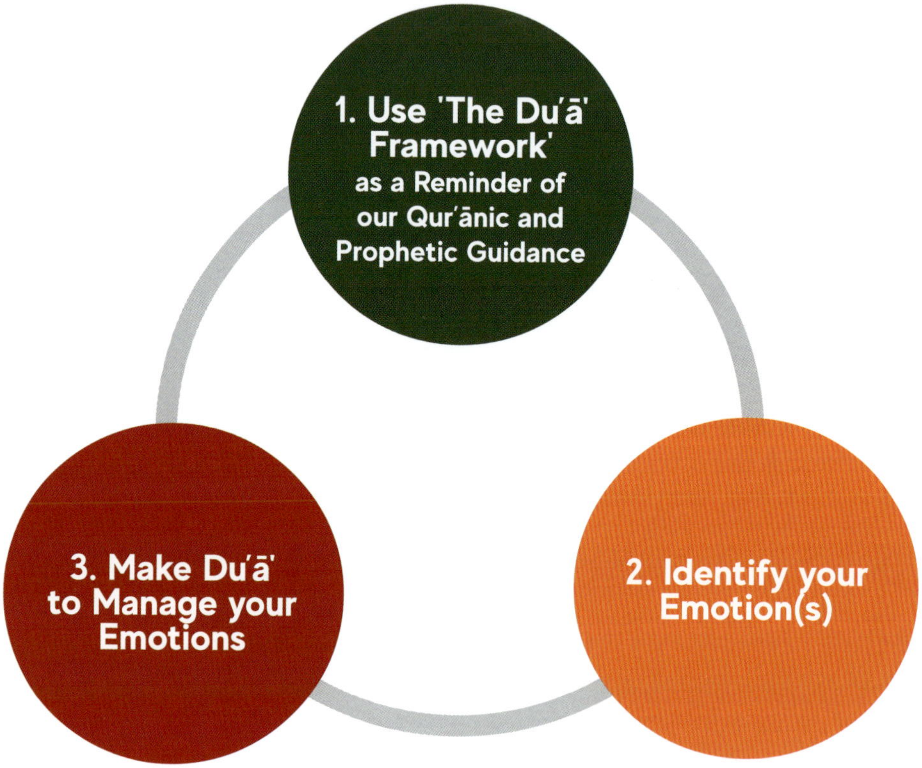
1. Use 'The Du'ā' Framework'
as a Reminder of
our Qur'ānic and
Prophetic Guidance
2. Identify your Emotion(s)
3. Make Du'ā' to Manage your Emotions

Step 1: Use 'The Du'ā' Framework' as a Reminder of our Qur'ānic and Prophetic Guidance

- **An Introduction** to 'The Du'ā' Framework'
- **What** is du'ā'? Its definition and rationale
- **Why** is it important? Life is a test and that du'ā' is worship
- **What** are its virtues? The benefits of du'ā'
- **What** are the prerequisites of du'ā'? How we prepare for du'ā'
- **When** is it best to make du'ā'? Those times or contexts in which du'ā' is accepted
- **What** is the etiquette of making du'ā'? The best approach to making du'ā'
- **How** do we achieve acceptance? Key reminders to ensure our du'ā's are accepted

Step 2: Identify your Emotion(s)

It is important that we understand and identify our emotional states if we are to make the most of the rich range of du'ā's prescribed in the Qur'ān and aḥādīth.

The Qur'ān and aḥādīth directly or indirectly reference human emotional states numerous times, so it should not come as a surprise that our lives take twists and turns based on our feelings and sentiments. We are social beings with complex behavioural patterns, as any anthropologist will tell you. If we can become steadily aware of the way our (perhaps deeper) feelings change, then we can feed this knowledge into the supplications we make when we turn to Allāh ﷻ, with a confidence that we can gain a 'grounded' balance if we ask in the right way.

Allāh ﷻ says, "Moreover, He is the One Who brings about joy and sadness" [An-Najm 53:43]. Allāh ﷻ created in his creatures the ability to laugh and cry and the causes for each of these opposites [Tafsīr Ibn Kathīr 7:466 under verse 53:43].

1. **Table of Contents (Spiritual Diseases):** You may relate directly to one or more of these 'spiritual diseases' (also regarded as emotional states), each of which has been defined at the start of each chapter to help the reader understand and recognise its characteristics.

2. **Glossary of Emotions:** The author has identified a number of chapters (i.e. each spiritual disease) associated with each emotion as another way to navigate directly to those chapters and the associated du'ā's that will be of most benefit inshā'Allāh. A set of 'industry standard' definitions have been provided to help you recognise and perhaps relate to the characteristics of each emotion.

Step 3: Make Du'ā' to Manage your Emotions

Making du'ā' is about effectively managing your own and other people's emotions, which is referred to as emotional intelligence, and as a result making heartfelt du'ā' for yourself and others.

Making du'ā' is about either leaving or attaining an emotional state. On a practical level, it is about using the treasures from the Qur'ān and Sunnah to initiate a dialogue with our Creator ﷻ so that we can move from a negative to a positive state.

Our Prophet ﷺ would often ask Allāh ﷻ for patience, compassion and contentment, to relieve him in times of sadness, loneliness, worry and anxiety.

Navigating the book, the reader can initiate a conversation with their Creator ﷻ by making du'ā' and establishing an intimate relationship, believing that Allāh ﷻ is listening. For some, this can open up a new and transformative relationship entirely.

AN INTRODUCTION TO THE DU'Ā' FRAMEWORK

An Islāmic Methodology

In an effort to re-position du'ā' in the hearts and minds of the Ummah away from a 'ritual and final resort', the author has devoted time to defining 'The Du'ā' Framework', which essentially reminds himself first and then readers to take a step back, to revisit the Qur'ānic and Prophetic guidance explaining what du'ā' is, why it is so important, its benefits, how best to prepare for it, when best to make du'ā', the etiquette of du'ā' and how to ensure acceptance.

Du'ā' will change our inner and outer state if we make it as promised by Allāh ﷻ; "And whose word is more truthful than Allāh's?" [An-Nisā 4:87] The Messenger of Allāh ﷺ came across a community of people going through a tribulation. He advised, "Why don't they supplicate (make du'ā') to Allāh for assistance?" Indeed, du'ā', according to a ḥadīth, has the unique ability to change destiny [Sunan Ibn Majah 90].

The author has collated du'ā's from the Qur'ān and aḥādīth and associated them with both spiritual diseases of the heart for those readers who can immediately relate, as well as with numerous associated emotions, to give the reader every chance of ensuring that these blessed du'ā's are implemented as effectively as possible - at the right time, in the right way, for the right moment.

Du'ā' should be a whispering conversation with Allāh ﷻ, our Creator, our Lord and our Sustainer. By invoking His most appropriate names for the right moment, and by sending blessings upon His beloved Rasūl ﷺ, with a sincere and attentive heart, we then allow ourselves to enter the realms of acceptance.

We should ask Allāh ﷻ because only Allāh ﷻ can give. This is a powerful reminder of our inherent incapability, and Allāh's ﷻ unlimited powers. He has power over everything, whilst we have none. His knowledge encompasses everything, whilst we know little. He is the Lord and we are His slaves.

In such tribulating times, we are still in a position to utilise the most powerful 'weapon' at the disposal of every believer - du'ā' - to stand before Allāh Almighty ﷻ and to petition Him for His help.

اَللّٰهُمَّ اغْسِلْ خَطَايَایَ بِمَاءِ الثَّلْجِ وَالْبَرَدِ، وَنَقِّ قَلْبِي مِنَ الْخَطَايَا، كَمَا يُنَقَّى الثَّوْبُ الأَبْيَضُ مِنَ الدَّنَسِ، وَبَاعِدْ بَيْنِي وَبَيْنَ خَطَايَایَ كَمَا بَاعَدْتَ بَيْنَ الْمَشْرِقِ وَالْمَغْرِبِ

Allāhummaghsil khatāyāya bi mā-ith thalji wal-barad, wa naqqi qalbī minal khatāyā kamā yunaqqath thawbul abyaḍu minad danas, wa bā'id baynī wa bayna khatāyāya kamā bā'adta baynal mashriqi wal maghrib

O Allāh! Wash away my sins with the water of snow and hail, and cleanse my heart from the sins as a white garment is cleansed of filth, and let there be a far away distance between me and my sins as You have set far away the East and the West from each other.

[Ṣaḥīḥ Al-Bukhārī 6375]

Ibn Daud

THE DU'Ā' FRAMEWORK

An Islāmic Methodology

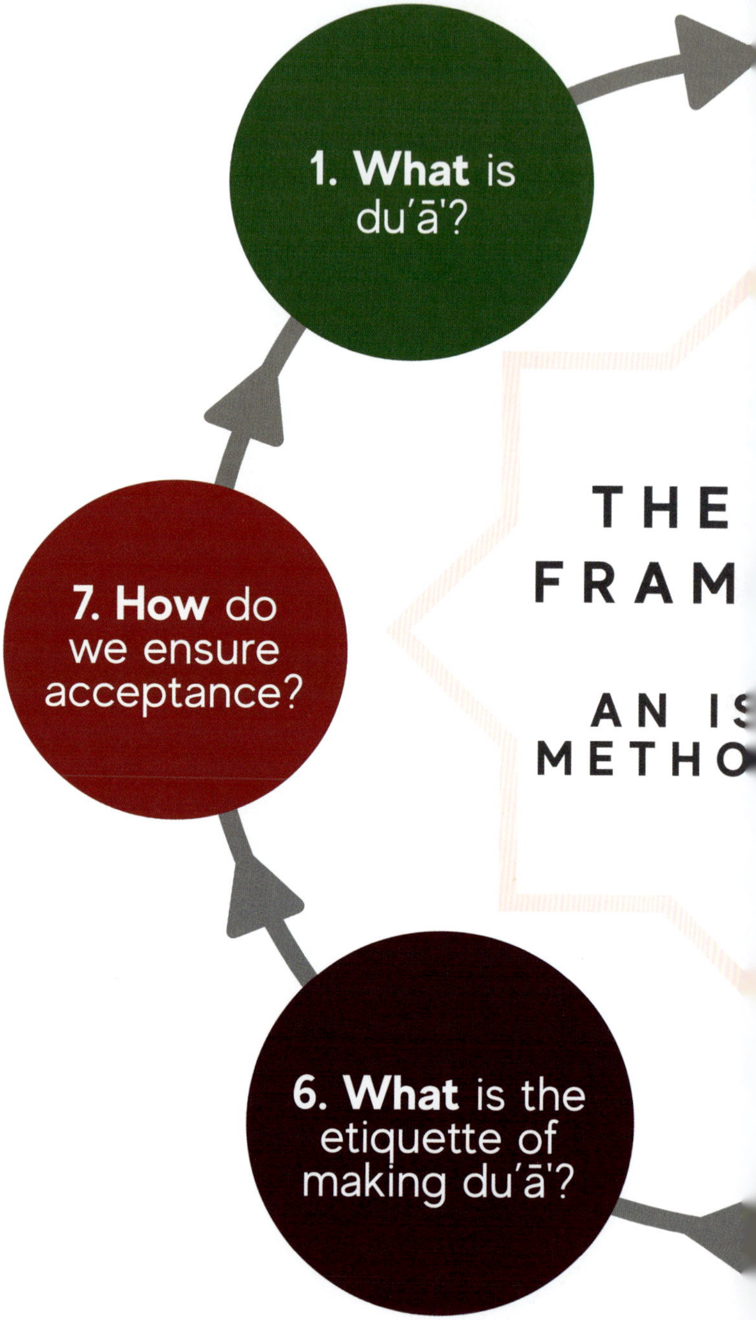
1. What is du'ā'?
7. How do we ensure acceptance?
6. What is the etiquette of making du'ā'?
THE
FRAM
AN IS
METHO

2. Why is du'ā' important?
3. What are the virtues of du'ā'?
4. What are the prerequisites of du'ā'?
5. When is du'ā' readily accepted?
U'Ā'
WORK
AMIC
OLOGY

1. WHAT IS DU'Ā'?

Du'ā' is a whispering conversation with Allāh ﷻ, our Creator, Lord and Sustainer. We ask Him because only He can fulfil our needs. Looking at supplication in this way, where the relationship is clearly one of the needy servant calling on the all-Providing Master, we gain a powerful reminder of man's inherent incapability, and Allāh's ﷻ unlimited powers. He has power over everything, whilst we have none. His knowledge encompasses everything, whilst we know little. He is the Lord and we are His slaves.

The Messenger of Allāh ﷺ said, "There is nothing more honourable to Allāh than du'ā'." [Jāmi` At-Tirmidhī 3370] He also said, "Allāh is angry with those who do not make du'ā' to Him." [Jāmi` At-Tirmidhī 3373]

The action or habit of making du'ā' forces a person to consider their position in the Universe, thereby increasing their īmān (faith). It demonstrates:

- A person has absolutely no control over his destiny.
- A person has the power neither to benefit himself nor to avert any evil.
- The neediness and helplessness that a person should feel in relation to their Lord.
- An expression of our complete submission and 'ubūdiyyah (servitude) to Him.
- That one making du'ā' sincerely believes that Allāh ﷻ hears his du'ā', and will respond to it.
- That such a person affirms Allāh's ﷻ Infinite Mercy, Beneficence and Generosity.
- That a person knows he must cultivate the realisation that he is poor in all senses when he compares himself to the Mercy of his Lord.
- That the servant must feel constantly humble; his 'outpourings' in his conversations with his Lord will be in accord with this humility.
- An appreciation of the perfection of Allāh's ﷻ names and attributes.

If we take a journey to the very heart and basics of the monotheistic way of Islām, we see that the word itself is Arabic. 'Islām' translated into English means 'submission to God's will'. The word 'īmān' is usually translated as 'faith' within a believer's heart; yet this is inadequate, since the Qur'ānic version of 'īmān' is that it is a conviction based upon reason and knowledge; a conviction that results from full mental acceptance. Īmān in its full form renders the believer fully satisfied.

The thoughtful process of turning towards Allāh ﷻ in du'ā' gives illustration to the term 'īmān'. The believer knows that he needs Allāh ﷻ in every matter and has sought Allāh's ﷻ attention. The contemplative believer is also actively aware of Allāh's ﷻ perfect nature. These combine in tandem as the essence of īmān and servitude to Allāh ﷻ.

This is why the Messenger of Allāh ﷺ said:

- "Du'ā' is worship" [Jāmi' At-Tirmidhī 2969]
- "Supplication is the essence of worship" [Jāmi' At-Tirmidhī 3371]

By making du'ā' we speak to Allāh ﷻ directly. We do not need intermediaries or special permission. Neither must we wait to access the court of Allāh ﷻ. We can ask Allāh ﷻ instantly, anywhere, anytime. This intimacy and bond that we share is outlined in the āyah:

"When My servants ask you (O Prophet) about Me: I am truly near. I respond to one's prayer when they call upon Me. So let them respond (with obedience) to Me and believe in Me, perhaps they will be guided (to the Right Way). [Al-Baqarah 2:186]

Du'ā' is truly a gift and we should make full use of it, forming it into an indispensable component in our everyday life. The heart of the believer shouldn't require too much persuasion of the benefits.

2. WHY IS DU'Ā' IMPORTANT?

Life is a Test

Allāh ﷻ says, "(He is the One) Who created death and life in order to test which of you is best in deeds. And He is the Almighty, All-Forgiving" [Al-Mulk 67:2].

As human beings, our life in this world is characterised by fluctuating conditions making us happy and sad. No one experiences perpetual bliss or misery. Our faith and belief is tested when we undergo difficulties and afflictions. These difficulties may be physical, emotional, financial and/or psychological. These adverse conditions may at times be upon an individual, a family, a community or upon a large section of the Ummah as is the current case across many countries of the world. Life, by its very nature, is a test.

This is borne out by the following verse: "We will certainly test you with a touch of fear and famine and loss of property, life, and crops. Give good news to those who patiently endure." [Al-Baqarah 2:155].

As believers we ought to believe that every condition is a manifestation of the will of Allāh ﷻ. What has passed us was not meant to befall us and what has befallen us was not meant to pass us. Pleasant and favourable conditions demand us to be grateful and humble or adverse conditions require us to be patient and to seek Allāh's ﷻ help.

The Prophet ﷺ said, "Assistance comes with patience, relief after affliction and ease after difficulty." [Musnad Aḥmad 2803].

Du'ā' is Worship

Making du'ā' or supplication before Allāh ﷻ is what we can encourage ourselves to consider as a solution to solve our problems, large and small. Unfortunately, however, for many of us du'ā' has become an empty ritual. So many of us only make thoughtful and contemplative du'ā's in the 'final' instance, as a last resort. All other options must have faded away, all other means exhausted before we engage. Our du'ā's have become half-hearted, uncertain of their acceptance and limited and restricted in their nature. However, Allāh ﷻ tells us in the Qur'ān:

- "And the bounty of your Lord can never be withheld" [Al-Isrā 17:20]
- "When He decrees a matter, He simply tells it, 'Be!' And it is!" [Āli 'Imrān 3:47]

So we should seize the opportunity to make du'ā' for ourselves as well as others. The Prophet ﷺ said, "There is no believing servant who supplicates for his brother behind his back (in his absence) except that the Angels say: 'The same be for you too.'" [Ṣaḥīḥ Muslim 2732]

The Messenger of Allāh ﷺ is very clear, definitive and absolute when he said, "Du'ā' is worship" [Jāmi' At-Tirmidhī 2969] and "Supplication is the essence of worship" [Jāmi' At-Tirmidhī 3371].

So how is it that we give so little attention to that described as both the 'essence' of worship as well as worship itself? Du'ā' is an act that should 'connect' the slave to his Master ﷻ. The slave lifts his hands as a beggar does, in all humility, with an attentive heart, having full hope in his Creator, Fashioner and Sustainer. Consider for a moment, please, the dilemma for the loving mother. Her demanding child is disobedient or errant: out of love she chooses not to neglect or wave a dismissive hand in the face of her offspring; it is in her nature to cherish and to have sympathy. In the same way, but for all time, across the whole of creation and with greater frequency and intensity, the Most Merciful Allāh ﷻ never abandons or leaves the beggar empty-handed. Furthermore, it is His love that inspires the worldwide motherly love that resolves this dilemma: His mercy ultimately breathes sweetness into the hearts of the forgiving mothers: within humans, mammals, insects, fish and birds.

3. WHAT ARE THE VIRTUES OF DU'Ā'?

The 10 Virtues of Making Du'ā'

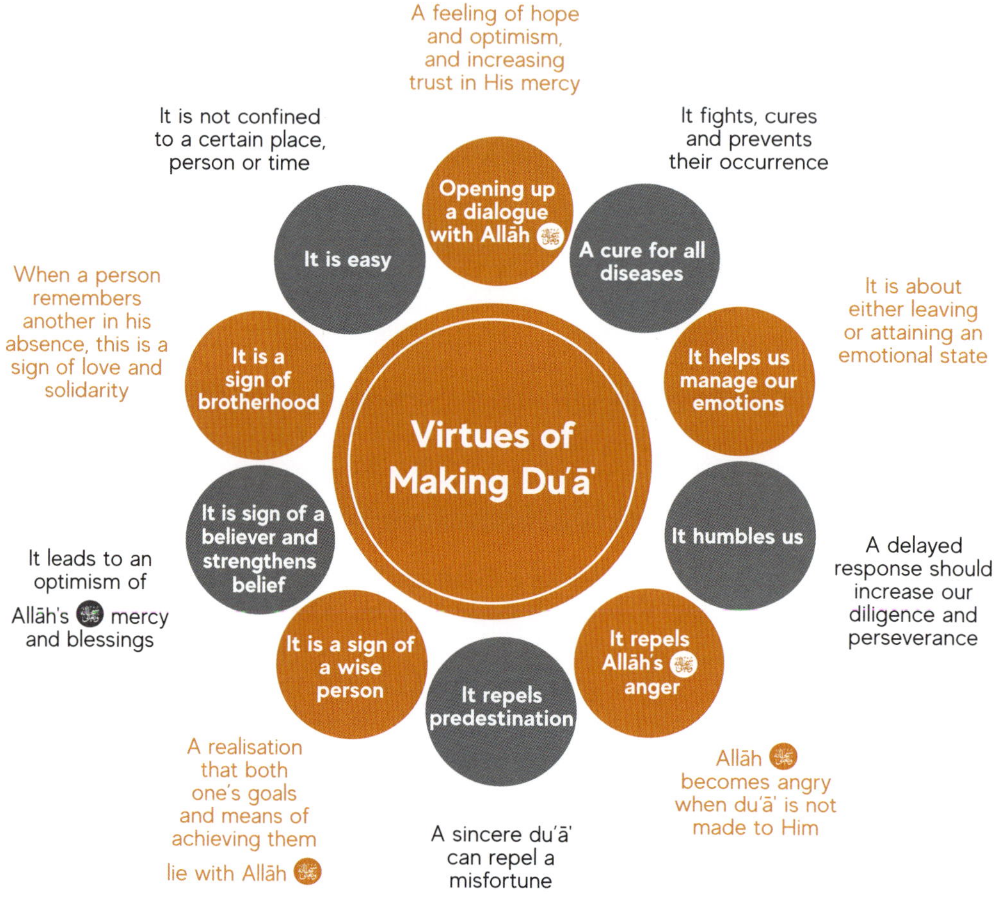
Virtues of Making Du'ā'
Opening up a dialogue with Allāh
A feeling of hope and optimism, and increasing trust in His mercy
A cure for all diseases
It fights, cures and prevents their occurrence
It helps us manage our emotions
It is about either leaving or attaining an emotional state
It humbles us
A delayed response should increase our diligence and perseverance
It repels Allāh's anger
Allāh becomes angry when du'ā' is not made to Him
It repels predestination
A sincere du'ā' can repel a misfortune
It is a sign of a wise person
A realisation that both one's goals and means of achieving them lie with Allāh
It is sign of a believer and strengthens belief
It leads to an optimism of Allāh's mercy and blessings
It is a sign of brotherhood
When a person remembers another in his absence, this is a sign of love and solidarity
It is easy
It is not confined to a certain place, person or time

Du'ā' opens up a dialogue with our Creator

Du'ā' results in a feeling of hope and optimism, and increasing trust in Allāh's ﷻ mercy. For some, this can open up a new relationship, believing that Allāh ﷻ is hearing him. His imān (faith) increases, as his love of Allāh ﷻ also increases. At the same time, he remembers his sins that may be preventing his du'ā' from receiving a positive response and he fears that because of these sins, his du'ā' will be rejected. So he repents to Allāh ﷻ, and begins to change his life, striving to please Allāh ﷻ, realising that only Allāh ﷻ can change his situation. This is the straightforward process of developing a new relationship with Allāh ﷻ.

Finally, a stage is reached, by a very select and blessed few, in which the pleasures of this communication become more pleasing to the soul than the actual response of the du'ā' would be!

Allāh ﷻ says, "When My servants ask you (O Prophet) about Me: I am truly near. I respond to one's prayer when they call upon Me." [Al-Baqarah 2:186]

Du'ā' is a cure for all diseases

Ibn Al-Qayyim رحمه الله said, "Du'ā' is of the most beneficial cures, and it is the enemy of all diseases. It fights them, and cures them, and prevents their occurrence, and causes them to be raised up or reduced after its occurrence. It is the weapon of the believer" [Ad-Dā' wa Ad-Dawā', p10]. Diseases referred to here are both physical (such as a headache or something more substantial such as cancer) and spiritual (such as anger, envy or love of the world).

Du'ā' helps us manage our emotions

For many of us, making du'ā' is about either leaving or attaining an emotional state. On a practical level, it is about using the treasures from the Qur'ān and Sunnah to initiate a dialogue with our Creator ﷻ so that we can move from a negative to a positive state.

Allāh ﷻ says, "And seek help through patience and prayer. Indeed, it is a burden except for the humble." [Al-Baqarah 2:45]

Du'ā' humbles us, and is a sign of diligence and perseverance

As the response to du'ā' is delayed, a person increasingly realises that there is no one besides Allāh ﷻ that can help him, or respond to his du'ā'. With this realisation comes the awe and meekness that is required in Allāh's ﷻ presence, as humility and humbleness set in, for a person realises his own weak and fragile nature.

A believer displays his contentment at the decree of Allāh ﷻ if there is (what he perceives as) any delay in Allāh's ﷻ response, not showing frustration or annoyance. Had the du'ā' been responded to (immediately), the servant might not feel such sincere humility, nor the will to develop humbleness in the presence of the Divine One.

Allāh ﷻ says, "Indeed, they used to race in doing good, and call upon Us with hope and fear, totally humbling themselves before Us" [Al-Anbiyā' 21:90]. The Qur'ān is replete with verses in which angels, prophets and believers make du'ā' to Allāh ﷻ.

The Prophet ﷺ said, "The most miserly is he who does not give salām and the most incapable (or lazy) person is he who does not make du'ā'." [Ibn Ḥibbān 4498]

There are select words that Allāh ﷻ has instructed us to recite daily as a reminder of our dependency on and relationship with Him. These include "You (alone) we worship and You (alone) we ask for help" [Al-Fātiḥah 1:5].

The many and varied tracts of interpretation explaining Surah Al-Fatiḥah agree, without exception, that the words represent a truly profound conversation and series of supplications put to Almighty Allāh ﷻ by the needy servant.

Du'ā's repel Allāh's ﷻ anger

The Prophet ﷺ said, "Allāh is angry with those who do not make du'ā' to Him." [Jāmi' At-Tirmidhī 3373] In addition, if one was to leave du'ā' out of arrogance, or a feeling of self-sufficiency, this would, in reality, be a type of disbelief in Allāh ﷻ, and a deification or worship of one's self.

Du'ā' repels predestination

The Prophet ﷺ stated, "Nothing repels predestination (qadr) except du'ā'." [Ibn Mājah 90] In other words, one could take a certain situation where a misfortune has been decreed for a person, yet, because of the sincerity and quality of his du'ā', Allāh ﷻ will repel that misfortune from him, and change what was previously fated.

Du'ā' is a sign of a wise person

One who calls to Allāh ﷻ, using du'ā' as the optimum means to achieve his goals, has made a wise decision that the goals of all of his desires lie with Allāh ﷻ, and that the means of achieving these goals also lies with Allāh ﷻ.

"(Are they better) or those who worship (their Lord) devoutly in the hours of the night, prostrating and standing, fearing the Hereafter and hoping for the mercy of their Lord? Say (O Prophet), "Are those who know equal to those who do not know?" None will be mindful (of this) except people of reason." [Az-Zumar 39:9]

Du'ā' is a sign of a believer and strengthens belief

Waiting on a delayed response to a du'ā' necessitates a strong hope in Allāh ﷻ, and an optimism of Allāh's ﷻ mercy and blessings. And the longer the response of the du'ā' is delayed, the stronger and more powerful this relationship and channel should become. In this way, continued du'ā' strengthens one's īmān.

Without a doubt, Shayṭān whispers the seeds of doubt into the hearts of humankind, and will try to make the best of the opportunity to amplify the negativity in the servant's heart when a du'ā' is not answered! For here is the servant, weak and humble in front of Allāh ﷻ, calling and crying out to him, 'O my Lord! O my Lord!' Yet, there is no response!

Yes, this type of occurrence is common, but the true believer turns the tables on the accursed Shayṭān, transforming embitterment to betterment.The believer, that person with the strength of faith that grants them diligent awareness of Shayṭān's persistent plots, sees the dangers and, instead of letting it cause him to turn away from Allāh's ﷻ worship, he seizes it as an opportunity to attack Shayṭān. He intensifies and remains regular in his worship of Allāh ﷻ, turning to Allāh ﷻ again and again, seeking refuge from his nemesis, for he realises that his only hope for safety is through Allāh ﷻ, and his only refuge and safe haven is with Allāh Almighty ﷻ. So in this intense battle between Shayṭān and the son of Adam, the weapon that is used is du'ā' to Allāh ﷻ, and the armour that is worn is the shielding refuge sought in Allāh ﷻ.

The Prophet ﷺ said, "The supplication of the servant is granted as long as he does not supplicate for sin or for severing the ties of blood, or he does not become impatient." It was said, "Allāh's Messenger, what does, 'If he does not grow impatient' imply?" He ﷺ said, "That he should say like this, 'I supplicated and I supplicated but I did not find it being responded to.' Then he becomes frustrated and abandons supplication." [Ṣaḥīḥ Muslim 2735]

Du'ā' is a sign of brotherhood

It has been guaranteed a response. It is a clear sign of love and solidarity, and the fact that a person remembers another Muslim in his absence clearly demonstrates his concern and care.

The Prophet ﷺ said, "There is no believing servant who supplicates for his brother behind his back (in his absence) except that the Angels say: 'The same be for you too.'" [Ṣaḥīḥ Muslim 2732]

Du'ā' is easy

Du'ā' is not confined to a certain place, person or time. Rather, all persons, whether male or female, old or young, rich or poor, scholar or worshipper, can make du'ā' at any time and in any place. Fundamentally, all that is needed is an attentive heart and a humble soul.

'Ā-ishah ؓ reports that the Messenger of Allāh ﷺ used to remember Allāh at all moments. [Ṣaḥīḥ Muslim 373]

4. WHAT ARE THE PREREQUISITES OF DU'Ā'?

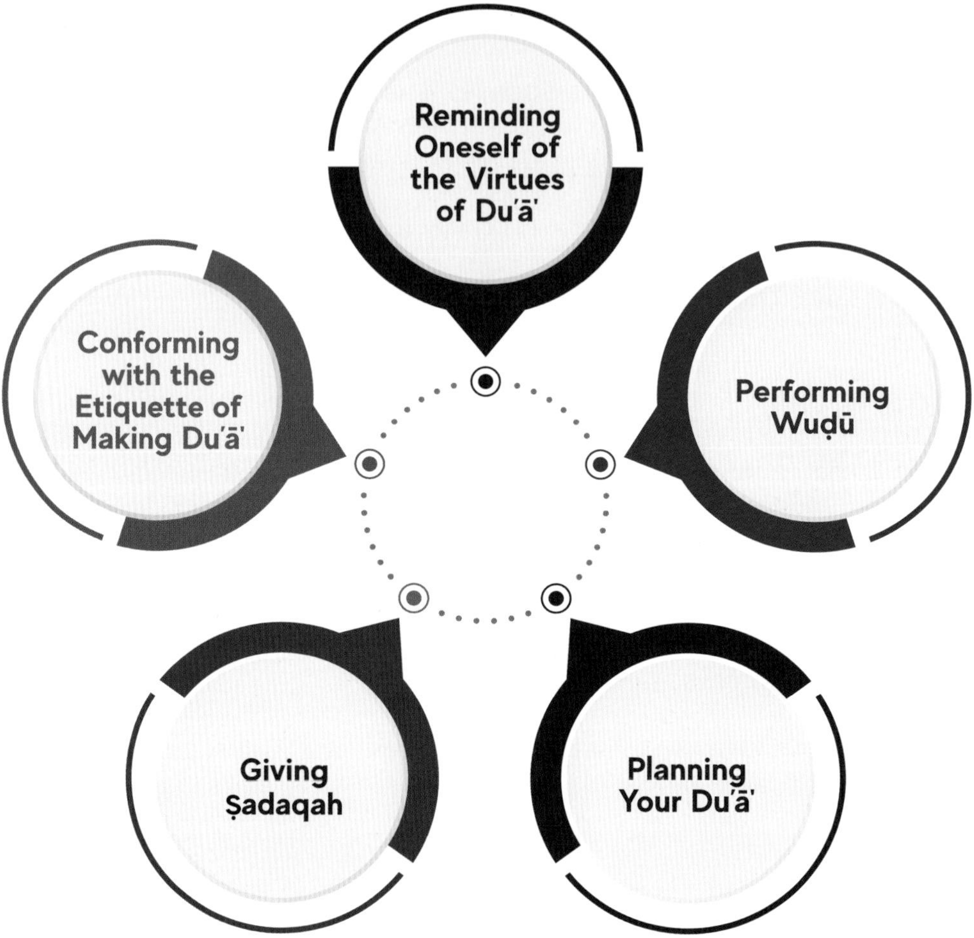

Reminding yourself of some of the key virtues of du'ā'
The previous section outlines the 10 virtues of making du'ā'. The Prophet ﷺ said, "There is nothing more honourable to Allāh than du'ā'" [Jāmi' At-Tirmidhī 3370]. This is due to the fact that du'ā' is a means of showing one's poverty and incapacity in comparison to Allāh's ﷻ controlling might and power.

Performing wuḍū
The Prophet ﷺ said, "I disliked remembering Allāh except in the state of purification." [Sunan Abī Dawūd 17]

Planning your du'ā'
You should choose a time in which du'ā' is readily accepted (see next chapter). Imām Al-Ghazāli exhorted on the importance of routines, "Your time should not be without structure, such that you occupy yourself arbitrarily with whatever comes along. Rather, you must take account of yourself and order your worship during the day and the night, assigning to each period of time an activity that must not be neglected nor replaced by another activity. By the ordering of this time, the blessing will show in itself." [The Beginning of Guidance/Bidāyah Al-Hidāyah, p.60- 61]

'Abdullāh ibn 'Amr said, "For your worldly affairs, construct your plans based on the assumption that you will live forever, and as for the work reserved for the Hereafter, create your programs based on the assumption that you are going to die tomorrow." [Gharīb Al-Ḥadīth v.1 p.286]

Giving ṣadaqah
The Prophet said:

- "Charity is a proof" [Ṣaḥīḥ Muslim 223]
- "Indeed charity extinguishes the Lord's anger and it protects against an evil death" [Jāmi' At-Tirmidhī 664]

Allāh says:

- You will never achieve righteousness until you donate some of what you cherish. And whatever you give is certainly well known to Allāh [Āli 'Imrān 3:92]
- Allāh's mercy is always close to the good-doers [Al-A'rāf 7:56]

Scholars have unanimously agreed that prefacing one's supplication with a good deed is beneficial to one's prayer.

Conforming with the etiquette of making du'ā'
Naturally you should try to call upon Allāh in a manner that is pleasing to Him, as taught to us by our Prophet. Part 6 of 'The Du'ā' Framework' reminds us of the etiquette of making du'ā'.

5. WHEN IS DU'Ā' READILY ACCEPTED?

SPECIAL TIMES RELATED TO ṢALAH

These are specific times, situations or conditions when making du'ā' is most praiseworthy and profitable.

- Du'ā' after performing Wuḍū
- Du'ā' when the Adhān is called
- Du'ā' between Adhān and Iqāmah
- Du'ā' before Zuhr
- Du'ā' while reciting Al-Fātiḥah
- Du'ā' while prostrating
- Du'ā' before the end of Ṣalah
- At the end of the obligatory/farḍ prayers
- On the day of Jumu'ah
- Last third of the night
- An hour of the night

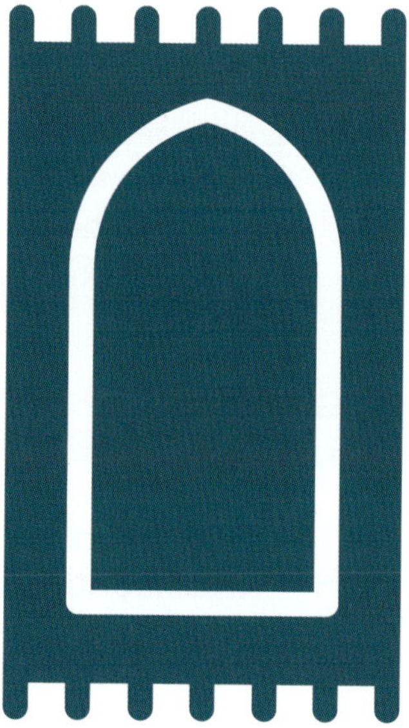

- **Du'ā' after performing Wuḍū**
  The Prophet ﷺ said, "There is no one amongst you that makes wuḍū and does so perfectly, and then says, 'I testify that there is no deity worthy of worship except Allāh. He is alone, having no partners. And I bear witness and testify that Muhammad is His slave and messenger', except that all eight doors of Paradise are opened for him, and he can enter into it through whichever one he pleases." [Ṣaḥīḥ Muslim 234]

In this ḥadīth, there is an indication that du'ā' at this time has a greater chance of being responded to, as all the doors of Paradise are opened to the believer.

- **Du'ā' when the Adhān is called**
  The Prophet ﷺ said, "When the call to prayer is made, the doors of the skies are opened, and du'ā' is answered." [Musnad Abī Dāwūd Aṭ-Ṭayālisī 2220]

- **Du'ā' between Adhān and Iqāmah**
  The Prophet ﷺ said, "The supplication is not rejected between the Adhān and the Iqāmah" [Jāmi' At-Tirmidhī 3595]. Five times every day, while a worshipper is waiting to offer his prayers to Allāh ﷻ, he is given the opportunity to ask from Him his needs of this world and the Hereafter. The Prophet ﷺ said, "Supplication is not rejected between the Adhān and the Iqāmah, therefore offer your supplication (at this time)." [Musnad Aḥmad 12584]

- **Du'ā' before Zuhr**
  The Prophet ﷺ said of the time after the sun reaches its zenith (solar noon) before zuhr, "It is an hour in which the gates of the heavens are opened." [Jāmi' At-Tirmidhī 478]

- **Du'ā' while reciting Al-Fātiḥah**
  The Prophet ﷺ said that "Allāh the Exalted had said, 'I have divided the prayer into two halves between Me and My servant, and My servant will receive what he asks.' When the servant says, 'All praise is for Allāh, Lord of all worlds', Allāh the Most High says: 'My servant has praised Me.' And when he (the servant) says, 'The Most Compassionate, Most Merciful', Allāh the Most High says, 'My servant has lauded Me.' And when he (the servant) says, 'Master of the Day of Judgement', He remarks, 'My servant has glorified Me.' And when he (the worshipper) says: 'You (alone) we worship and You (alone) we ask for help', He (Allāh) says, 'This is between Me and My servant, and My servant will receive what he asks for.' Then, when he (the worshipper) says, 'Guide us along the Straight Path, the Path of those You have blessed, not those

You are displeased with, or those who are astray.' **He (Allāh) says,** 'This is for My servant, and My servant will receive what he asks for.'" [Ṣaḥīḥ Muslim 395]

There is therefore great incentive for us to recite Al-Fātiḥah in every prayer with great humility and reflection, so that it is possible that we are given what we ask for.

- **Du'ā' while prostrating**
  The Prophet ﷺ said "The nearest a servant comes to his Lord is when he is prostrating himself, so make supplication (in this state)." [Ṣaḥīḥ Muslim 482] When a person in prostration lowers the most noble and sacred part of his body to the dust, seeking the pleasure and forgiveness of his Lord, this noble posture is the epitome of humility and submissiveness. This is why this posture is the most beloved by Allāh ﷻ.

- **Du'ā' before the end of Ṣalah**
  'Abdullāh ibn Mas'ūd ؓ narrates, "I was once praying, and the Prophet, Abū Bakr, and 'Umar (were all present). When I sat down (in the final tashahhud), I praised Allāh, then sent blessings on the Prophet, then started praying for myself. (At this,) the Prophet ﷺ said, 'Ask, and you shall be given it! Ask, and you shall be given it!'" [Jāmi' At-Tirmidhī 593]

- **At the end of the obligatory/farḍ prayers**
  "It was said, 'O Messenger of Allāh, which supplication is most likely to be listened to?' He ﷺ said: '(During) the last part of the night, and at the end of the obligatory prayers.'" [Jāmi' At-Tirmidhī 3499]

- **On the day of Jumu'ah**
  The Prophet ﷺ said, "There is an hour (opportune time) on Friday and if a Muslim gets it while praying and asks something from Allāh, then Allāh will definitely meet his demand" [Ṣaḥīḥ Al-Bukhārī 935]. And he (the Prophet ﷺ) pointed out the shortness of that time with his hands.

There are two main opinions as to when this time is:

1. It is said to be between the time when the Imam sits down and the end of the prayer. The Prophet ﷺ said "It is between the time when the Imam sits down and the end of the prayer" [Ṣaḥīḥ Muslim 853]
2. Or it is after 'Aṣr, i.e. during the last portion of the day of Jumu'ah. The Prophet ﷺ said, "Friday is divided into twelve hours. Amongst them there is an hour in which a Muslim does not ask Allāh for anything but He gives it to him. So seek it in the last hour after the afternoon prayer" [Sunan Abī Dawūd 1048]

- **Last third of the night**
  The Prophet ﷺ said, "Every night our Lord, the Blessed, the Superior, comes down on the nearest Heaven to us when the last third of the night remains, saying: "Is there anyone to invoke Me, so that I may respond to invocation? Is there anyone to ask Me, so that I may grant him his request? Is there anyone seeking My forgiveness, so that I may forgive him?" [Ṣaḥīḥ Al-Bukhārī 1145]

  Imām Al-Bukhārī mentions this ḥadīth in the chapter of tahajjud in his book, so there is a connection between the ḥadīth and this specific night prayer. However, it is not exclusive to tahajjud prayer, since (when describing the righteous) Allāh ﷻ says "they used to sleep only little in the night, and pray for forgiveness before dawn." [Ad-Dhāriyāt 51: 17-18]

  The Prophet ﷺ said, "The closest that the Lord is to a worshipper is during the last part of the night, so if you are able to be of those who remember Allāh in that hour, then do so." [Jāmi' At-Tirmidhī 3579]

- **An hour of the night**
  The Prophet ﷺ said, "There is an hour during the night in which no Muslim individual will ask Allāh for good in this world and the next without His giving it to him; and that applies to every night." [Ṣaḥīḥ Muslim 757]

PRAYING FOR OTHERS

When a person who is sick makes du'ā' for another
The Prophet ﷺ said, "When you enter upon one who is sick, tell him to pray for you, for his supplication is like the supplication of the angels." [Ibn Mājah 1441]

When a parent makes du'ā' for their child
The Prophet ﷺ said, "There are three supplications that will undoubtedly be answered: the supplication of one who has been wronged; the supplication of the traveller; and the supplication of a father for his child." [Ibn Mājah 3862]

When children make du'ā' for their parents
Children are encouraged to pray for their deceased parents. The Prophet ﷺ said, "When a person dies, all of his actions are cut off except from three (matters): recurring charity, or knowledge (by which people) benefit, or a pious son, who prays for him (for the deceased)." [Ṣaḥīḥ Muslim 1631]

The Qur'an itself commands this, for Allāh ﷻ says,

رَبِّ ارْحَمْهُمَا كَمَا رَبَّيَانِي صَغِيرًا

Rabbirḥamhumā kamā rabbayānī ṣaghīrā

"And lower unto them the wings of humility and mercy, and say, 'O My Lord! Have mercy on them, even as they took care of me while I was young.'"

[Al-Isrā 17:24]

When the soul of a person is taken

Whenever a person is in the presence of one who is about to die, he should pray to Allāh ﷻ for all that is good for the dying person, his family, and for himself. This is because the angels of death are waiting nearby to take the soul of the person and they say 'Āmīn' to every du'ā' made at this occasion.

The Prophet ﷺ came to Abū Salamah (as he died). His eyes were open, staring fixedly. He closed them, and then said, "When the soul is taken away the sight follows it." Some of the people of his family wept and wailed. So he said, "Do not supplicate for yourselves anything but good, for angels say 'Āmīn' to what you say." He then said: "O Allāh, forgive Abū Salamah, raise his degree among those who are rightly guided, grant him a successor in his descendants who remain. Forgive us and him, O Lord of the Universe, and make his grave spacious, and grant him light in it." [Ṣaḥīḥ Muslim 920]

For your absent brother

The Prophet ﷺ said, "There is no believing servant who supplicates for his brother behind his back (in his absence) except that the Angels say: 'The same be for you too.'" [Ṣaḥīḥ Muslim 2732]

VULNERABLE OR CHALLENGING/ DIFFICULT CONDITIONS

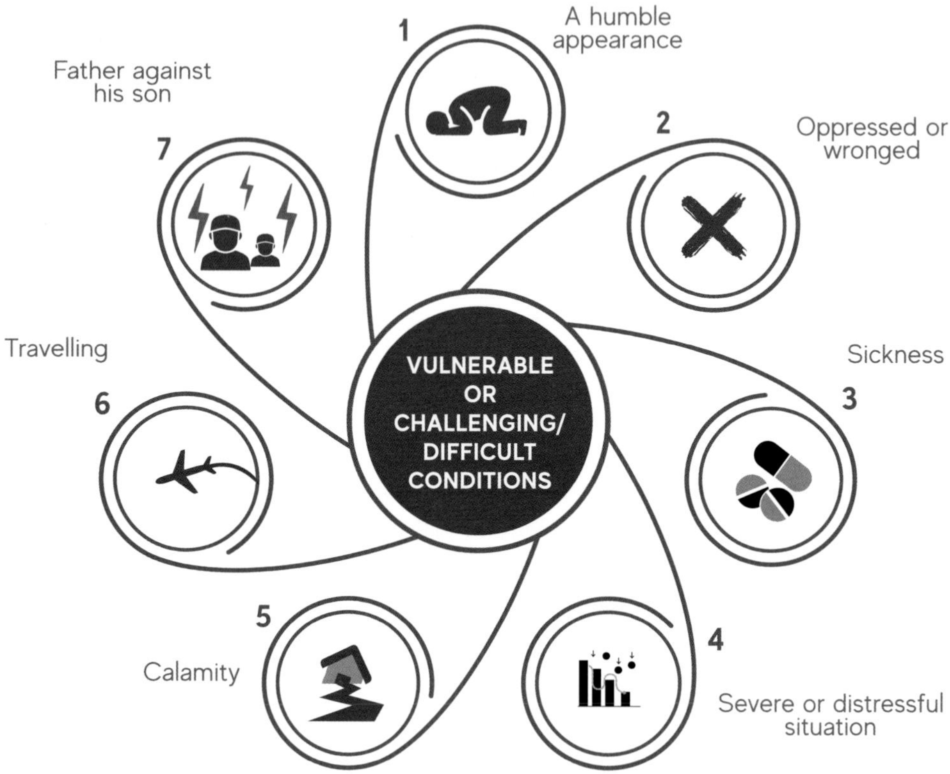

1 Having a humble appearance

One of the factors that speeds a person's du'ā' towards being answered is when one has become dishevelled, displaying a humbled appearance. When such a condition exists, the result of factors beyond the control of the person himself, then such a du'ā' is more likely to gain a response.

The Prophet ﷺ said, "How many are there with dishevelled hair, covered with dust, possessing only two cloths, whom no one pays any mind to; if he swears by Allāh then He shall fulfil it." [Jāmi' At-Tirmidhī 3854]

This is because it shows a person's poverty and need for Allāh ﷻ, and proves that he is not concerned about his appearance or looks, but rather about the response to his du'ā'.

2 When oppressed or wronged

The Prophet ﷺ said, "Be afraid of the curse of the oppressed as there is no screen between his invocation and Allāh." [Ṣaḥīḥ Al-Bukhārī 2448]

3 When sick

The Prophet ﷺ said, 'When you enter upon one who is sick, tell him to pray for you, for his supplication is like the supplication of the angels." [Ibn Mājah 1441]

4 When in a severe or distressful situation

Allāh ﷻ says, "Or (ask them,) 'Who responds to the distressed when they cry to Him, relieving (their) affliction?'" [An-Naml 27:62]

When a person finds himself in a grave crisis, and his heart is about to shatter with grief and fear, at this point he turns to Allāh ﷻ with a heart like that of no other person. The quality of sincerity that he displays, and the desperate need that he feels for the Mercy of his Lord, is so strong and pure that it is a du'ā' that is answered in all situations.

Imām Al-Qurṭubī ﵀ wrote, "Allāh has guaranteed the response of the du'ā' of the one in distress, as He Himself informed us of this (guarantee). And the reason for this is that the one in distress will turn to Him with a pure sincerity, cutting his hope off from all other sources. And sincerity to Him is the cause of (gaining) His protection, regardless of whether it emanates from a disbeliever or Muslim, evil or pious!" [Al-Jāmi' li Aḥkām al-Qur'ān 13/223]

5 After a calamity

The Prophet ﷺ said, "There is no Muslim that is afflicted with a calamity, and he says what Allāh has commanded him to say, 'To Allāh we belong and to Him we will return! O Allāh! Reward me due to this calamity, and grant me something better than it in exchange,' except that Allāh will give him something better than it in exchange." [Ṣaḥīḥ Muslim 918]

So it is necessary that the person display patience and satisfaction at Allāh's ﷻ decree, and not wail or lament over his misfortune.

6 When travelling

The Prophet ﷺ said, "Three supplications are accepted, there is no doubt in them (about them being accepted): the supplication of the oppressed, the supplication of the traveller, and the supplication of the father against his son." [Jāmi` At-Tirmidhī 1905]

7 The father against his son

The Prophet ﷺ said, "Three are the supplications that are responded to (one of them being)... the supplication of the father against his son." [Musnad Aḥmad 7510]

There is a risk that a father could make a du'ā' to the detriment of his son, if the son does not treat his father properly. In this, there is a strong encouragement to Muslims to treat their parents with kindness, and to avoid causing them distress in any way. This is also a warning to parents not to rush in making a du'ā' against their children, for they might make a du'ā' in a state of anger which they would later regret.

The Prophet ﷺ said, "Don't curse your own selves, nor your children, nor your belongings. There is the possibility that your curse may synchronise with the time when Allāh is about to confer upon you what you demand and thus your prayer may be readily responded to." [Ṣaḥīḥ Muslim 3009]

The du'ā' of the mother is also included in this ḥadīth, for the right of the mother is even greater than that of the father.

The du'ā' of the parents for their daughters comes under this ḥadīth as well, since the rulings applicable to men also apply to women unless there exists evidence to the contrary.

BLESSED TIMES OR CONDITIONS

- Fulfilling the rights of parents
- After doing good deeds
- Voluntary acts after the obligatory ones
- Remembering Allāh ﷻ frequently
- A just ruler
- During times of ease
- At the crowing of a rooster
- When it rains
- When drinking Zamzam water
- During Ramadan
- During Umrah or Hajj

- **Fulfilling the rights of parents**
  One of the most important and greatest acts of worship that a person can do after worshipping Allāh ﷻ is that he be dutiful to his parents.

  Allāh ﷻ says:
  - "For your Lord has decreed that you worship none but Him. And honour your parents. If one or both of them reach old age in your care, never say to them (even) 'ugh', nor yell at them. Rather, address them respectfully" [Al-Isrā 17:23]
  - "And We have commanded people to (honour) their parents. Their mothers bore them through hardship upon hardship, and their weaning takes two years. So be grateful to Me and your parents. To Me is the final return" [Luqman 31:14]

  The rights of parents are indeed very great, and it is because of this that the person who fulfils these rights earns a very high status with Allāh ﷻ. Of the blessings that such a person has is that his du'ā's are answered. [Ṣaḥīḥ Al-Bukhārī 3465]

- **After doing good deeds**
  This is about supplicating after doing good deeds, supported by the lengthy ḥadīth of the individuals trapped in the cave and who made du'ā' for the boulder blocking the entrance to move by mentioning their good deeds to Allāh ﷻ. [Ṣaḥīḥ Al-Bukhārī 2272]

  The Prophet ﷺ related famously that three men, trapped in a mountain cave by a boulder that had rolled down and blocked their exit, chose to turn to Allāh ﷻ for help. They agreed that they should mention their righteous deeds to gain Allāh's ﷻ pleasure.

  The first man had waited all night long by his parents' bedside with a bowl of sheep's milk.

  The second man told of how he had known a beautiful and

beloved woman, and how he had given her gold dinars to entice her towards sexual fulfilment. She was about to consent, but then said that it was forbidden to 'outrage her chastity' outside of wedlock. Hearing this, the man's good deed was to walk away and to leave the gold dinars with her.

The third man told of an employee to whom he had granted a large (and seemingly overgenerous) amount of sheep, camels and cows in lieu of some wages he had due to him because of a previous absence. Each man said 'O Allāh! If this deed was for Your sake only, please relieve us from the present suffering' after telling of their good deeds.

Each time, by Allāh's ﷻ will, the boulder inched away from the mouth of the cave, until it finally gave them room enough to escape.

The Prophet ﷺ said, "Make the orphan come close to you, and be nice to him, and wipe his head, and feed him from your food. That will cause your heart to be soft, and your needs to be fulfilled." [Tārīkh Dimashq 47:153]

Thus, the two aḥadith of the Prophet ﷺ are guidance toward making du'ā' having performed acts of charity or good will. It is interesting to see that there doesn't appear to be a time frame for this: the three men trapped in the cave were able to call on Allāh ﷻ successfully by recounting deeds that may have taken place many years ago.

- **Doing extra voluntary acts after the obligatory ones**
  This is one of the greatest ways that a person can increase his or her chances of du'ā' being answered.

  The Prophet ﷺ said that Allāh ﷻ said, "I will declare war against him who shows hostility to a pious worshipper of Mine. And the most beloved things with which My slave comes nearer to Me, is what I have enjoined upon him; and My slave keeps on coming closer to Me through performing voluntary acts till I love him, so I become his sense of hearing with which he hears, and his sense of sight with which he sees, and his hand with which he grips, and his leg with which he walks; and if he asks Me, I will give him, and if he asks My protection (Refuge), I will protect him." [Ṣaḥīḥ Al-Bukhārī 6502]

So when a person increases his voluntary good deeds, such as prayer, and fasting, and giving charity, then Allāh ﷻ loves him, and when Allāh ﷻ loves him, all his du'ā's are answered.

- **The one who remembers Allāh ﷻ frequently**
  The Prophet ﷺ said, "Three (people's) supplications are not rejected: the one who remembers Allāh frequently, and the one who has been wronged, and a just ruler." [Al-Bayhaqī in Shu'ab Al-Īmān 6973]

- **A just ruler**
  This is based on the above ḥadīth. When a person whom Allāh ﷻ has placed in a position of control and power over people is able to restrain his emotions and desires, and rules or governs them with justice and honesty, then Allāh ﷻ blesses him, and causes his du'ā' to be answered.

- **Make abundant du'ā' in times of ease**
  The true believer always remembers Allāh ﷻ, both in times of ease and hardship.

  The Messenger of Allāh ﷺ said:
  - "Whoever wishes that Allāh would respond to him during hardship and grief, then let him supplicate plentifully when at ease" [Jāmi` At-Tirmidhī 3382]
  - "O youth! Do you not wish that I should teach you some advice that Allāh will benefit you with? Protect (the commandments) of Allāh, and Allāh will protect you, protect (the commandments) of Allāh, and you will find Him ever in front of you. Know Him when you are in a state of contentment, and He will know you when you are in a state of need" [Musnad Aḥmad 2803]

- **At the crowing of a rooster:**
  The Prophet ﷺ said, "When you hear a rooster crowing, then ask Allāh for His Bounties, for it has seen an angel, and when you hear a donkey braying, then seek refuge in Allāh from Shayṭān, for it has seen a Shayṭān." [Ṣaḥīḥ Al-Bukhārī 3303]

- **When it rains**
  The Prophet ﷺ said, "Two (supplications) are not rejected: Supplication when the call to prayer is made, and in stress when people are locked in battle." There is a version of this ḥadīth that has the wording: "and when rain is falling." [Al-Ḥākim 2534]

- **When drinking Zamzam water**
  The Prophet ﷺ said, "The water of Zamzam is for whatever it is drunk for. So if you drink it seeking cure via it, Allāh will cure you. If you drink it seeking protection via it, Allāh will protect you. If you drink it so that your thirst is quenched, it will quench it." [Al-Ḥākim 1739]

- **During Ramadan**
  - During Ramadan
    The month of Ramadan is a blessed month, during which the Qur'an was revealed, and the process of inspiration started upon the Prophet ﷺ. Therefore, the du'ā' of Ramadan is a blessed du'ā' as it has a greater chance of being accepted, because the gates of paradise and mercy are opened.

    "When the month of Ramadan starts, the gates of the heavens are opened and the gates of Hell are closed and the devils are chained." [Ṣaḥīḥ Al-Bukhārī 1899]

  - **When breaking the fast**
    The Prophet ﷺ said, "Three persons, their supplication is not rejected: The just ruler, the fasting person when he breaks his fast, and the supplication of the wronged person. It is raised up above the clouds, and the gates

of Heaven are opened up for it, and the Lord, Blessed and Exalted, says: I shall surely come to your aid, even if after a time." [Jāmi' At-Tirmidhī 3598]

- **Du'ā' on 'The Night of Decree'**
  'Ā-ishah narrated "I said, 'O Messenger of Allāh, what is your view if I know when the Night of Decree is, then what should I say in it?' He said: 'Say: "O Allāh, indeed You are Pardoning, [Generous,] You love to pardon, so pardon me."'" [Jāmi' At-Tirmidhī 3513]

اَللّٰهُمَّ إِنَّكَ عَفُوٌّ كَرِيمٌ تُحِبُّ الْعَفْوَ فَاعْفُ عَنِّي

Allāhumma innaka 'afuwwun karīmun tuḥibbul 'afwa fa'fu 'annī

- **Du'ā' during Umrah or Hajj**
  - **People performing Hajj and Umrah**
    The Prophet said, "The one who fights in the cause of Allāh, and the pilgrim performing Hajj and 'Umrah are a delegation to Allāh. He invited them, so they responded to Him, and they asked Him and He gave to them." [Ibn Mājah 2893]

  - **Between the Black Stone and door of the Ka'bah**
    'Amr ibn Shu'ayb reported on the authority of his father, "I went round the Ka'bah along with 'Abdullāh ibn 'Amr. When we came behind the Ka'bah I asked: 'Do you not seek refuge?' He uttered the words: 'I seek refuge in Allāh from the Hell-fire.' He then went (farther) and touched the Black Stone, and stood between the corner (Black Stone) and the entrance of the Ka'bah. He then placed his breast, his face, his hands and his palms in this manner, and he spread them (while supplicating), and said: 'I saw the Messenger of Allāh doing this.'" [Sunan Abī Dawūd 1899]

- **Du'ā' inside the Ka'bah**
  Usamah ibn Zayd reported, "When the Prophet entered the House (Kabah), he made du'ā' at all of its corners." [Ṣaḥīḥ Muslim 1330]

  The hijr (the semi-circular attachment that is opposite the Yemeni corner and Blackstone wall) was originally actually a part of the Ka'bah, and prayer inside the hijr is exactly the same as praying inside the physical structure of the Ka'bah. Therefore, one should be eager to pray in the hijr, and make du'ā' in it as well, for it is equivalent to praying in the actual Ka'bah.

  'Ā-ishah narrated, "I wanted to enter the House (Ka'bah) and pray therein. The Messenger of Allāh caught me by the hand and admitted me to the hijr. He then said, 'Pray in the hijr when you intend to enter the House (the Ka'bah), for it is a part of the House (the Ka'bah). Your people shortened it when they built the Ka'bah, and they took it out of the House.'" [Sunan Abī Dawūd 2028]

- **The first ten days of Dhul-Ḥijjah**
  The Prophet said, "There are no days during which the righteous action is so pleasing to Allāh than these days (i.e. the first ten days of Dhul-Ḥijjah)" [Ṣaḥīḥ Al-Bukhārī 969]. This ḥadīth shows the general superiority of this time, and as du'ā' is one of the most beloved acts of worship, we are encouraged to make du'ā' during these ten days.

- **At Aṣ-Ṣafā and Al-Marwah**
  In brief and to the nearest meaning, Jābir ibn 'Abdullah reported that the Prophet first mounted Aṣ-Ṣafā till he saw the House, and facing the Qiblah he declared the Oneness of Allāh and glorified Him. He then supplicated. When he reached Al-Marwah, he did at Al-Marwah what he had done at Aṣ-Ṣafā. [Ṣaḥīḥ Muslim 1218]

- **After Stoning the Jamarāt**
  Ibn 'Umar reports that whenever Allāh's Messenger stoned the Jamrah near the Mina Masjid, he would pelt it with seven small pebbles and say Takbīr on throwing each pebble. Then he would go ahead and stand facing the Qiblah with his hands raised, and supplicate (to Allāh) and he used to stand for a long period. Then he would come to the second Jamrah and stone it with seven small stones, reciting Takbīr when throwing each stone. Then he would stand facing the Qiblah with raised hands to supplicate (to Allāh). Then he would come to the Jamrah near the 'Aqabah and pelt it with seven small pebbles, reciting Takbīr when throwing each stone. He then would leave and not stay by it. [Ṣaḥīḥ Al-Bukhārī 1753]

- **On the Day of 'Arafah**
  The Prophet said, "The best of supplications is the supplication of the Day of 'Arafah" [Jāmi' At-Tirmidhī 3585]. During this auspicious day, Allāh does not refuse the requests of His worshippers.

6. WHAT IS THE ETIQUETTE OF MAKING DU'Ā'?

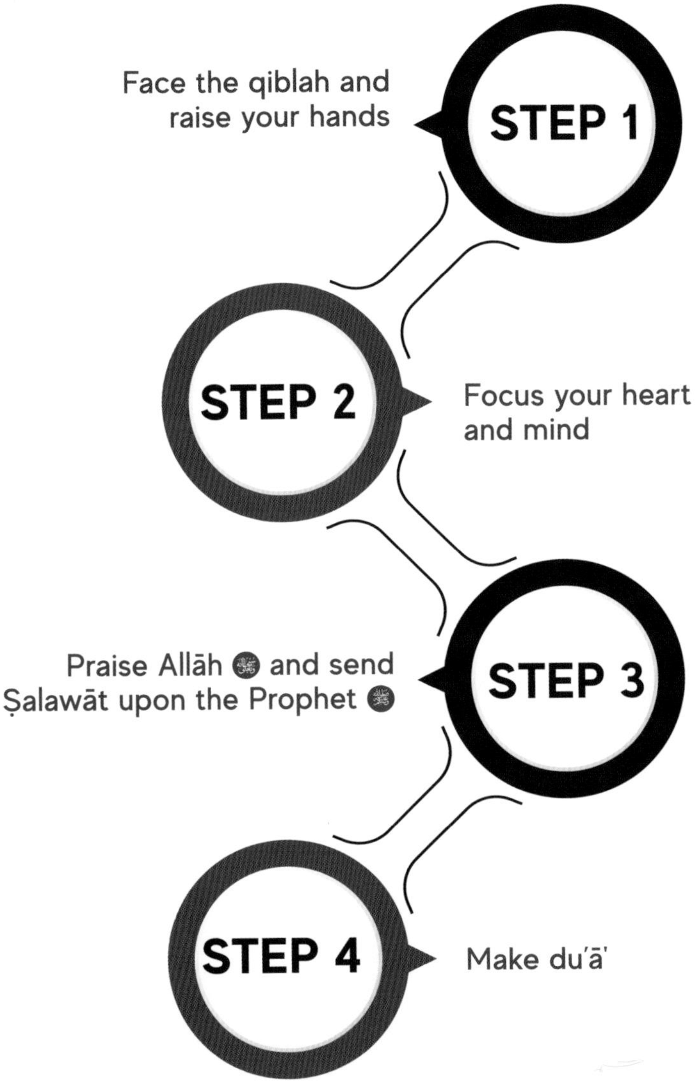
STEP 1
Face the qiblah and raise your hands
STEP 2
Focus your heart and mind
STEP 3
Praise Allāh and send Ṣalawāt upon the Prophet
STEP 4
Make du'ā'

STEP 1: Face the Qiblah and Raise Your Hands

Raising one's hands in du'ā' is beloved to Allāh ﷻ. It brings to mind Allāh's ﷻ complete power, and demonstrates that man is poor and desirous of His Lord's blessings, for he has humbled himself in front of the One full of honour, and raised his hands up to Him, indicating his poverty. In other words, it is a physical manifestation of all that this noble act of du'ā' embodies.

Ibn 'Umar ؓ reported that, "The Prophet would go ahead and stand facing the Qiblah with his hands raised, and invoke (Allāh) and he used to stand for a long period" [Ṣaḥīḥ Al-Bukhārī 1753]. This occurred during the time of Hajj.

'Ā-ishah ؓ said that "The Prophet ﷺ used to remember Allāh ﷻ at all moments." [Ṣaḥīḥ Muslim 373]

Abū Mūsā Al-Ash'arī ؓ reported that "The Prophet ﷺ asked for water, performed ablution and then raised his hands (and thereafter supplicated)." [Ṣaḥīḥ Al-Bukhārī 4323]

'Abdullāh ibn Mas'ūd ؓ reported that, "The Prophet ﷺ faced the Ka'bah and supplicated..." [Ṣaḥīḥ Al-Bukhārī 3960]

These conditions are not necessary for du'ā' but are praiseworthy nonetheless.

STEP 2: Focus Your Heart and Mind

Make your heart present
Completely focus on Allāh ﷻ, with earnestness, knowing exactly what you are asking for, remembering who you are asking.

The Messenger of Allāh ﷺ said, "Make du'ā' to Allāh whilst you are certain of a response, because Allāh does not accept a du'ā' from a heedless, distracted heart." [Jāmi' At-Tirmidhī 3479]

Be determined in your request
What is desired is that a person be firm in his du'ā', asking from Allāh ﷻ in a determined manner. It is inadvisable to use phrases such as 'if you wish' or 'if you might be so kind' in matters where a person is in absolute and unquestionable need. All people require Allāh's ﷻ forgiveness, His mercy, or blessings, etc. and the words 'if you wish' or 'if you could possibly' become redundant. We are instructed in this by the best of creation, the Prophet Muhammad ﷺ, who said, "None of you should say, 'O Allāh, forgive me if You wish; O Allāh, be merciful to me if You wish,' but he should always appeal to Allāh with determination, for nobody can force Allāh to do something against His will." [Ṣaḥīḥ Al-Bukhārī 6339]

Have good intentions
It is only acceptable for a Muslim to ask Allāh ﷻ for something with sincerity, and in order that he do good with it. It is the height of transgression to demand from your Creator those things that He has prohibited for you, either in this life or in the life Hereafter. And we should be careful what we say in a state of anger, so as not to cause pain and grief not only upon our loved ones, but also upon ourselves. And it is not in the character of a Muslim to curse others.

Allāh ﷻ says, "He is the Ever-Living. There is no god (worthy of worship) except Him. So call upon Him with sincere devotion, (saying,) 'All praise is for Allāh, Lord of all worlds.'" [Ghāfir 40:65]

The Prophet ﷺ said:

- "The du'ā' of any worshipper will continue to be responded to, as long as he does not ask for a sin or a breaking of the ties of kinship, and as long as he is not hasty" [Ṣaḥīḥ Muslim 2735]
- "Don't curse your own selves, nor your children, nor your belongings. There is the possibility that your curse may synchronise with the time when Allāh is about to confer upon you what you demand and thus your prayer may be readily responded to" [Ṣaḥīḥ Muslim 3009]
- "A true believer does not taunt or curse or abuse or talk indecently" [Jāmi' At-Tirmidhī 1977]
- "The supplication of the servant is granted as long as he does not supplicate for sin or for severing the ties of blood, or he does not become impatient." It was said, "Allāh's Messenger, what does: 'If he does not grow impatient' imply?" He said, "That he should say like this: I supplicated and I supplicated but I did not find it being responded to. Then he becomes frustrated and abandons supplication" [Ṣaḥīḥ Muslim 2735]

Praying du'ā' sincerely to Allāh ﷻ alone

By making du'ā' you speak to Allāh ﷻ directly. You do not need intermediaries or special permission. Neither must you wait to access the court of Allāh ﷻ. You pray only to Allāh ﷻ, and not to any of those things that constitute the Creation: from lifeless objects like idols or the sun to trees, animals, men, a pious person, a prophet, an angel, or any other object besides.

"Those (idols) you invoke besides Allāh are created beings like yourselves. So call upon them and see if they will answer you, if your claims are true!" [Al-A'rāf 7:194]

"O boy! Guard (the duties of) Allāh, and He will guard you! Guard (the duties of) Allāh, and you will find Him in front of you. And when you ask, ask only from Allāh, and when you seek help, seek help only from Allāh!" [Jāmi' At-Tirmidhī 2516]

Humble yourself and pray quietly
One of the ways in which sincerity is shown in du'ā' is crying, bringing about a feeling of humility in front of Allāh ﷻ, fearing your own shortcomings in your duty towards Him (that you are asking from the One whom you have disobeyed) and hoping for His reward. Making du'ā' quietly in a subdued and softened voice demonstrates respect and manners in front of Allāh ﷻ, and also enables him to show the closeness that a true believer feels to his Creator.

Allāh ﷻ says: "Call upon your Lord humbly and secretly... and call upon Him with hope and fear." [Al-A'rāf 7:55-6]

'Abdullāh ibn Ash-Shikhkhīr رضي الله عنه said "I saw the Prophet ﷺ praying and a sound came from his breast like the rumbling of a mill owing to weeping." [Sunan Abī Dawūd 904]

"Say, (O Prophet,) "Who rescues you from the darkest times on land and at sea? He (alone) you call upon with humility, openly and secretly: "If You rescue us from this, we will be ever grateful." [Al-An'ām 6:63]

The one making du'ā' should realise his lowly status, and be wise enough to contemplate his own many faults and shortcomings with regards to the rights that Allāh ﷻ has over him.

Be persistent
Repeating the du'ā' three times is a recommended action and demonstrates a sense of urgency in obtaining what one is asking for. 'Abdullāh ibn Mas'ūd رضي الله عنه narrates that when he (the Prophet ﷺ) supplicated, he supplicated thrice, and when he asked for Allāh's blessings, he asked thrice. [Ṣaḥīḥ Muslim 1794]

Be ambitious and ask for everything

Do not limit your supplications to just small matters in difficult times. Nothing is too big for the One being asked and nothing is too small for the one asking Him.

The Messenger of Allāh ﷺ said:

- "When one of you asks for something (from Allāh), then let him be plentiful (in what he asks for), for indeed he is asking his Lord" [Ibn Ḥibbān 889]
- "When you ask Allāh, ask for al-Firdaws (the highest level of Jannah)" [Jāmi` At-Tirmidhī 2531]
- "Let one of you ask his Lord for his every need, even until he asks Him for the strap of his sandal when it breaks" [Jāmi` At-Tirmidhī 3604]

Realise that only Allāh ﷻ responds to du'ā'

Part of the completeness of a person's tawḥīd is understanding that only Allāh ﷻ is capable of hearing your prayer and only He has the power to grant what you desire. Allāh ﷻ says:

- "Or (ask them,) 'Who responds to the distressed when they cry to Him, relieving (their) affliction, and (Who) makes you successors in the earth? Is it another god besides Allāh? Yet you are hardly mindful!'" [An-Naml 27:62]
- "Allāh is Ever Kind to His servants. He provides (abundantly) to whoever He wills. And He is the All-Powerful, Almighty" [Ash-Shūrā 42:19]
- "Or who is it that will provide for you if He withholds His provision?" [Al-Mulk 67:21]
- "Whatever blessings you have are from Allāh" [An-Naḥl 16:53]

Expect the best from Allāh ﷻ

Allāh ﷻ treats us with utmost beneficence and generosity. Indeed His mercy is all encompassing. Allāh ﷻ says, "But My mercy encompasses everything." [Al-A'rāf 7:156]

The Messenger of Allāh ﷺ said:

- "Verily your Lord is Generous and Shy. If a person raises their hands to Him, He becomes shy to return them empty and rejected" [Jāmi` At-Tirmidhī 3556]

- "Allāh has said, 'I live in the thought of My servant as he thinks of Me and with him as he calls Me'" [Ṣaḥīḥ Muslim 2675]

So if a person is not certain of the response of Allāh ﷻ, and he feels that he will not be responded to, then he will be treated the way that he feels.

The Prophet ﷺ said:
- "Indeed, having good thoughts concerning Allāh is from the perfection of the worship of Allāh" [Jāmi' At-Tirmidhī 3604]
- "Call upon Allāh while being certain of being answered" [Jāmi' At-Tirmidhī 3479]
- "Allāh has said, 'I live in the thought of My servant as he thinks of Me. If he thinks well of Me then that is his and if he thinks bad then that is his'" [9076 Musnad Aḥmad]

The life of a true believer is a blessing from Allāh ﷻ so, no matter what situation a person is in, he will be in a blessed situation.

The Prophet ﷺ proclaimed, "Wonderous indeed are the affairs of a believer, for every affair of his is good! And this applies only to a believer. If some good befalls him, he thanks Allāh, and that is good for him. And if some evil befalls him, he is patient, and that is good for him!" [Ṣaḥīḥ Muslim 2999]

Pray with concise du'ā's
'Ā-ishah ؓ narrates that the Prophet ﷺ "loved concise du'ās, and he would leave all (du'ās) besides those." [Sunan Abī Dawūd 1482]

The Prophet ﷺ used to pray frequently with concise du'ā's, and he was the one who had been given the most eloquent and concise of words. It was as if he were asking for all the good possible of both worlds, and seeking refuge in all evils, in the briefest and most eloquent of phrases, so that the people who heard him could memorise his du'ās easily, and understand what he said.

STEP 3: Start with the Praise of Allāh ﷻ and Send Ṣalawāt upon the Messenger of Allāh ﷺ

This is because the person who is making du'ā' is asking Allāh ﷻ for forgiveness, mercy and sustenance, so it behoves the worshipper to start his du'ā' with the praise and glorification of Allāh ﷻ.

The Messenger of Allāh ﷺ once heard a person making du'ā' during prayer. He did not glorify Allāh ﷻ nor invoke ṣalawāt upon the Messenger of Allāh ﷺ. The Messenger of Allāh ﷺ said, 'He was too hasty.' He called him and said: 'When one of you makes du'ā', he should start off with praising and glorifying His Lord, and should then invoke ṣalawāt on the Prophet. He should then make du'ā' for whatever he wishes.' [Sunan Abī Dawūd 1481]

Allāh ﷻ says, "Allāh has the Most Beautiful Names. So call upon Him by them." [Al-A'rāf 7:180]

Ibn Al-Qayyim (rahimahullah) said, "One should ask in every supplication via a suitable name (of Allāh) for that (supplication). Then the asker will be successful because of that name. He who analyses the supplications of the Prophets, especially the final and leader of them (the Prophet Muhammad ﷺ) will find them (all) like this." [Badā'i Al-Fawā-id, v.1 p289]

Upon analysis of the supplications of the Prophet Muhammad ﷺ, we can see that when supplicating to Allāh ﷻ with one of His beautiful names he would exclaim and use the name in the vocative case, e.g. "O Owner of Majesty and Honour". In Arabic this is achieved by adding the word 'yā' prior to the name of Allāh ﷻ. So the English 'O Bestower of Honour' becomes 'Ya Mu'izz' in Arabic.

فادعوه بها
ولله الأسماء الحسنى

THE BEAUTIFUL NAMES

اَلاسْمَاءُ الْحُسنٰى

AL-ASMĀ AL-ḤUSNĀ

He is Allāh ﷻ, the Creator, the Incomparable Originator, the Fashioner. He (alone) has the most beautiful names. Whatever is in the heavens and the earth (constantly) glorifies Him. And He is the Victorious, All-Wise. [Al-Ḥashr 59:24]

Allāh ﷻ says, "Say, (O Prophet,) "Call upon Allāh or call upon the All Compassionate, whichever you call, He has the Most Beautiful Names." Do not recite your prayers too loudly or silently, but seek a way between." [Al-Isrā 17:110]

Virtues of memorising the ninety-nine names of Allāh ﷻ

The Prophet ﷺ said, "Allāh has ninety-nine names, i.e. one-hundred minus one, and whoever knows them will go to Paradise." [Ṣaḥīḥ Al-Bukhārī 2736]

Throughout the verses of the Qur'ān and the words of the Prophet ﷺ we can find more than 99 names for Allāh ﷻ. So the above ḥadīth is not limiting. There is however a record of 99 specific names that have been used to explain the above ḥadīth. [Jāmi` At-Tirmidhī 3507].

Ibn Al-Qayyim Al-Jawzī رحمه الله has said "Whoever attains the ma'rifah (deep awareness) of Allāh through His Names, Attributes and Actions, he will undoubtedly love Him." [Madārij As-Sālikīn 3/18]

THE BEAUTIFUL NAMES

1	الرَّحْمَانُ	Ar-Raḥmān	The All Compassionate
2	الرَّحِيمُ	Ar-Raḥīm	The All Merciful
3	الْمَلِكُ	Al-Malik	The Absolute Ruler
4	الْقُدُّوسُ	Al-Quddūs	The Pure One
5	السَّلَامُ	As-Salām	The Source of Peace
6	الْمُؤْمِنُ	Al-Mu'min	The Inspirer of Faith
7	الْمُهَيْمِنُ	Al-Muhaymin	The Guardian
8	الْعَزِيزُ	Al-Azīz	The Victorious
9	الْجَبَّارُ	Al-Jabbār	The Compeller
10	الْمُتَكَبِّرُ	Al-Mutakabbir	The Supreme
11	الْخَالِقُ	Al-Khāliq	The Creator
12	الْبَارِئُ	Al-Bāri'	The Incomparable Originator
13	الْمُصَوِّرُ	Al-Muṣawwir	The Fashioner
14	الْغَفَّارُ	Al-Ghaffār	The Forgiving
15	الْقَهَّارُ	Al-Qahhār	The Ever-Dominating

THE BEAUTIFUL NAMES

16	الْوَهَّابُ	Al-Wahhāb	The Giver of Gifts
17	الرَّزَّاقُ	Ar-Razzāq	The Provider
18	الْفَتَّاحُ	Al-Fattāḥ	The Opener
19	الْعَلِيمُ	Al-'Alīm	The All-Knowing
20	الْقَابِضُ	Al-Qābiḍ	The Withholder
21	الْبَاسِطُ	Al-Bāsiṭ	The Extender
22	الْخَافِضُ	Al-Khāfiḍ	The Abaser
23	الرَّافِعُ	Ar-Rāfi'	The Exalter
24	الْمُعِزُّ	Al-Mu'izz	The Bestower of Honour
25	الْمُذِلُّ	Al-Mudhil	The Humiliator
26	السَّمِيعُ	As-Samī'	The Hearer of All (The All-Hearing)
27	الْبَصِيرُ	Al-Baṣīr	The Seer of All (The All-Seeing)
28	الْحَكَمُ	Al-Ḥakam	The Judge
29	الْعَدْلُ	Al-'Adl	The Just
30	اللَّطِيفُ	Al-Laṭīf	The Subtle One

THE BEAUTIFUL NAMES

31	الْخَبِيرُ	Al-Khabīr	The All-Aware
32	الْحَلِيمُ	Al-Ḥalīm	The Forbearing
33	الْعَظِيمُ	Al-'Aẓīm	The Magnificent
34	الْغَفُورُ	Al-Ghafūr	The Exceedingly Forgiving
35	الشَّكُورُ	Ash-Shakūr	The Most Appreciative
36	الْعَلِيُّ	Al-'Aliyy	The Highest
37	الْكَبِيرُ	Al-Kabīr	The Greatest
38	الْحَفِيظُ	Al-Ḥafīẓ	The Preserver
39	الْمُقِيتُ	Al-Muqīt	The Nourisher
40	الْحَسِيبُ	Al-Ḥasīb	The Reckoner
41	الْجَلِيلُ	Al-Jalīl	The Mighty
42	الْكَرِيمُ	Al-Karīm	The Most Generous
43	الرَّقِيبُ	Ar-Raqīb	The Watchful
44	الْمُجِيبُ	Al-Mujīb	The Responsive One
45	الْوَاسِعُ	Al-Wāsi'	The All-Comprehending

THE BEAUTIFUL NAMES

46	الْحَكِيمُ	Al-Ḥakīm	The All-Wise
47	الْوَدُودُ	Al-Wadūd	The Most Loving
48	الْمَجِيدُ	Al-Majīd	The Most Honourable
49	الْبَاعِثُ	Al-Bā'ith	The Resurrector
50	الشَّهِيدُ	Ash-Shahīd	The Witness
51	الْحَقُّ	Al-Ḥaqq	The Truth
52	الْوَكِيلُ	Al-Wakīl	The Trustee
53	الْقَوِيُّ	Al-Qawiyy	The All-Strong
54	الْمَتِينُ	Al-Matīn	The Most Firm
55	الْوَلِيُّ	Al-Waliyy	The Protecting Friend
56	الْحَمِيدُ	Al-Ḥamīd	The Praiseworthy
57	الْمُحْصِي	Al-Muḥṣī	The One Who Keeps Record
58	الْمُبْدِئُ	Al-Mubdī	The Initiator
59	الْمُعِيدُ	Al-Mu'īd	The Restorer
60	الْمُحْيِي	Al-Muḥyī	The Giver of Life

THE BEAUTIFUL NAMES

61	الْمُمِيتُ	Al-Mumīt	The Destroyer
62	الْحَيُّ	Al-Ḥayy	The Ever-Living
63	الْقَيُّومُ	Al-Qayyūm	The Sustainer
64	الْوَاجِدُ	Al-Wājid	The Finder
65	الْمَاجِدُ	Al-Mājid	The Illustrious
66	الْوَاحِدُ	Al-Wāḥid	The One
67	الْأَحَدُ	Al-Aḥad	The Only One
68	الصَّمَدُ	Aṣ-Ṣamad	The Eternal
69	الْقَادِرُ	Al-Qādir	The All Powerful
70	الْمُقْتَدِرُ	Al-Muqtadir	The Omnipotent
71	الْمُقَدِّمُ	Al-Muqaddim	The Expediter
72	الْمُؤَخِّرُ	Al-Mu'akhkhir	The Delayer
73	الْأَوَّلُ	Al-Awwal	The First
74	الْآخِرُ	Al-Ākhir	The Last
75	الظَّاهِرُ	Aẓ-Ẓāhir	The Manifest

THE BEAUTIFUL NAMES

76	الْبَاطِنُ	Al-Bāṭin	The Hidden One
77	الْوَالِي	Al-Wālī	The Governor
78	الْمُتَعَالِي	Al-Muta'ālī	The Self Exalted
79	الْبَرُّ	Al-Barr	The Source of Goodness
80	التَّوَّابُ	At-Tawwāb	The Relenting
81	الْمُنْتَقِمُ	Al-Muntaqim	The Avenger
82	الْعَفُوُّ	Al-'Afuww	The Pardoner
83	الرَّؤُفُ	Ar-Ra-ūf	The Most Kind
84	مَالِكُ الْمُلْكِ	Mālik-Ul-Mulk	Master of the Kingdom
85	ذُو الْجَلاَلِ وَالإِكْرَامِ	Dhul-Jalāli Wal-Ikrām	Lord of Majesty and Bounty
86	الْمُقْسِطُ	Al-Muqsiṭ	The Requiter
87	الْجَامِعُ	Al-Jāmi'	The Uniter
88	الْغَنِيُّ	Al-Ghaniyy	The Wealthy
89	الْمُغْنِيُّ	Al-Mughniyy	The Enricher

THE BEAUTIFUL NAMES

90	الْمَانِعُ	Al-Māni'	The Preventer
91	الضَّارُّ	Aḍ-Ḍārr	The Distresser
92	النَّافِعُ	An-Nāfi'	The Benefactor
93	النُّورُ	An-Nūr	The Light
94	الْهَادِي	Al-Hādī	The Guide
95	الْبَدِيعُ	Al-Badī'	The Originator
96	الْبَاقِي	Al-Bāqī	The Everlasting
97	الْوَارِثُ	Al-Wārith	The Inheritor
98	الرَّشِيدُ	Ar-Rashīd	The Director
99	الصَّبُورُ	Aṣ-Ṣabūr	The Patient

THE ABRAHAMIC INVOCATION OF PEACE

الصَّلَاةُ الإِبْرَاهِيمِيَّة

AṢ-ṢALĀH AL-IBRĀHĪMIYYAH

Virtues of sending ṣalawāt or invoking blessings upon the Prophet ﷺ

Allāh ﷻ says, "Indeed, Allāh showers His blessings upon the Prophet, and His angels pray for him. O believers! Invoke Allāh's blessings upon him, and salute him with worthy greetings of peace." [Al-Aḥzāb 33:56]

The Prophet ﷺ said:

- "Everyone who invokes a blessing on me will receive ten blessings from Allāh" [Ṣaḥīḥ Muslim 384]
- "The person closest to me on the Day of Judgement is the one who sent the most ṣalawāt upon me" [Jāmi' At-Tirmidhī 484]

اَللّٰهُمَّ صَلِّ عَلَى مُحَمَّدٍ وَعَلَى آلِ مُحَمَّدٍ كَمَا صَلَّيْتَ عَلَى إِبْرَاهِيمَ وَآلِ إِبْرَاهِيمَ إِنَّكَ حَمِيدٌ مَجِيدٌ وَبَارِكْ عَلَى مُحَمَّدٍ وَعَلَى آلِ مُحَمَّدٍ كَمَا بَارَكْتَ عَلَى إِبْرَاهِيمَ وَآلِ إِبْرَاهِيمَ إِنَّكَ حَمِيدٌ مَجِيدٌ

Allāhumma ṣalli 'alā Muḥammadin wa 'alā āli Muḥammadin kamā ṣallayta 'alā Ibrāhīm wa āli Ibrāhīm innaka ḥamīdum majīd, wa bārik 'alā Muḥammadin wa 'alā āli Muḥammadin kamā bārakta 'alā Ibrāhīm wa āli Ibrāhīm innaka ḥamīdum majīd

"O Allāh, send peace upon Muḥammad and upon the family of Muḥammad, as You sent peace upon Ibrāhīm and the family of Ibrāhīm, and send blessings upon Muḥammad and upon the family of Muḥammad as You sent blessings upon Ibrāhīm and the family of Ibrāhīm. You are indeed the praiseworthy, the most honourable".

[Sunan An-Nasaī 1290]

STEP 4: Make Du'ā'

1. Supplicate with du'ā's from the Qur'ān and Sunnah
Although it is permissible to choose your own words according to your needs, the du'ā's from the Qur'ān and Sunnah are unmatched in their style, prose and completeness. Indeed, they are blessed du'ā's that the Prophet ﷺ would teach to the Companions, which in turn were taught by the Companions to those after them, and eventually preserved in the books of Sunnah.

Imām Al-Qurṭubī ﵀ states, "It is incumbent upon mankind that they utilise the supplications from the book of Allāh and authentic Sunnah and abandon anything else. They should not say 'I choose this', for Allāh ﷻ has (already) chosen for his Prophet and friends and taught them how to supplicate." [At-Tafsīr Al-Qurṭubī v.4 p.231 under verse 3:147]

Imām Ibn Taymiyyah ﵀ wrote, "So people should supplicate via that which is found in the Qur'ān and Sunnah, for there is no doubt in their excellence and blessings. These (supplications) are of the Straight Path, the Path of those whom Allāh has favoured such as the prophets, the sincere, the martyrs, and the righteous, and what a great company they are!" [Majmū' Al-Fatāwā v.1 p.346]

2. Pray sincerely and seek forgiveness for one's self
Part of the etiquette of du'ā' is to ponder over one's relationship with Allāh ﷻ and acknowledge one's shortcomings and sins in front of Him. This can only be done if one has sincerity towards Allāh ﷻ, feeling guilty for the sins that he has performed, asking for Allāh's ﷻ forgiveness, and making a sincere determination not to return to that sin. Additionally, if the sin involved transgressing the rights of others, it is required to return those rights or an equivalent amount of good to the person from whom it was taken.

اَللّٰهُمَّ أَنْتَ رَبِّي، لاَ إِلَهَ إِلاَّ أَنْتَ، خَلَقْتَنِي وَأَنَا عَبْدُكَ، وَأَنَا عَلَى عَهْدِكَ وَوَعْدِكَ مَا اسْتَطَعْتُ، أَعُوذُ بِكَ مِنْ شَرِّ مَا صَنَعْتُ، أَبُوءُ لَكَ بِنِعْمَتِكَ عَلَيَّ وَأَبُوءُ لَكَ بِذَنْبِي، فَاغْفِرْ لِي، فَإِنَّهُ لاَ يَغْفِرُ الذُّنُوبَ إِلاَّ أَنْتَ

Allāhumma anta rabbī lā ilāha illā anta, khalaqtanī wa ana 'abduk, wa ana 'alā 'ahdika wa wa'dika mastaṭa'tu, a'ūdhu bika min sharri mā ṣana'tu, abū-u laka bi ni'matika 'alayya wa abū-u bi dhanbī, faghfirlī fa innahu lā yaghfirudh dhunūba illā anta

The Prophet ﷺ said, "The best supplication for seeking forgiveness is to say, 'O Allāh! You are my Lord. There is no true god except You. You have created me, and I am Your slave, and I hold to Your promise as far as I can. I seek refuge in You from the evil of what I have done. I acknowledge the favours that You have bestowed upon me, and I confess my sins. Pardon me, for none but You has the power to pardon.' He who supplicates in these terms during the day with firm belief in it and dies on the same day (before the evening), he will be one of the dwellers of Jannah; and if anyone supplicates in these terms during the night with firm belief in it and dies before the morning, he will be one of the dwellers of Jannah." [Ṣaḥīḥ Al-Bukhārī 6306]

Allāh ﷻ says:

رَبَّنَا ظَلَمْنَآ أَنفُسَنَا وَإِن لَّمْ تَغْفِرْ لَنَا وَتَرْحَمْنَا لَنَكُونَنَّ مِنَ الْخَٰسِرِينَ

Rabbanā ẓalamnā anfusanā wa in lam taghfirlanā wa tarḥamnā la nakūnanna minal khāsirīn

"Our Lord! We have wronged ourselves. If You do not forgive us and have mercy on us, we will certainly be losers." [Al-'Arāf 7:23]

Allāh ﷻ also says, "And seek your Lord's forgiveness and turn to Him in repentance. He will grant you a good provision for an appointed term and graciously reward the doers of good." [Hūd 11:3]

The Prophet ﷺ said, "If anyone continually seeks forgiveness, Allāh will appoint for him a way out of every distress, and a relief from every anxiety, and will provide for him from where he did not reckon." [Sunan Abī Dawūd 1518]

3. Pray for matters of this world and the next
The true Muslim asks Allāh ﷻ to bless him in this world and in the Hereafter. To ask Allāh ﷻ only with regard for matters of this world is a sign of weakness in one's īmān, as the blessings of the Hereafter are the true blessings.

Allāh ﷻ says:

رَبَّنَآ ءَاتِنَا فِى الدُّنْيَا حَسَنَةً وَفِى الْءَاخِرَةِ حَسَنَةً وَقِنَا عَذَابَ النَّارِ

Rabbanā Ātinā fid dunyā ḥasanataw wa fil Ākhirati ḥasanataw wa qinā 'adhāban nār

"Yet there are others who say, "Our Lord! Grant us the good of this world and the Hereafter, and protect us from the torment of the Fire." [Al-Baqarah 2:201-202]

It is they who will receive a (heavenly) reward for the good they have done. Surely Allāh ﷻ is swift in reckoning.

4. Pray for all Muslims
Part of the completeness of one's īmān is that a person loves for his brother what he loves for himself. Therefore, just as he desires that he be guided to the truth, and be forgiven for his sins, so too should he desire the same for his fellow Muslims. So it is encouraged for the Muslim to remember and pray for all of his brothers and sisters when he is making du'ā', including his own parents.

Allāh ﷻ says, "So, know (well, O Prophet,) that there is no god (worthy of worship) except Allāh. And seek forgiveness for your misjudgements and for (the sins of) the believing men and women." [Muḥammad 47:19]

Allāh ﷻ also says:

رَبِّ اغْفِرْ لِى وَلِوَٰلِدَىَّ وَلِمَن دَخَلَ بَيْتِىَ مُؤْمِنًا وَلِلْمُؤْمِنِينَ وَٱلْمُؤْمِنَٰتِ وَلَا تَزِدِ ٱلظَّٰلِمِينَ إِلَّا تَبَارًۢا

Rabbighfirlī wa li wālidayya wa li man dakhala baytiya mu-minan wa lil mu-minīna wal mu-mināt, wa lā tazidiẓ ẓālimīna illā tabārā

"My Lord! Forgive me, my parents, and whoever enters my house in faith, and (all) believing men and women. And increase the wrongdoers only in destruction." [Nūḥ 71:28]

The Prophet ﷺ said:

- "He who does not have wealth with which to give in charity then let him seek forgiveness for the believing men and believing women, for that is charity" [Al-Mu'jam Al-Awsaṭ Aṭ-Ṭabarānī 2693]
- "There is no believing servant who supplicates for his brother behind his back (in his absence) except that the Angels say: 'The same be for you too'" [Ṣaḥīḥ Muslim 2732]

5. End your du'ā' by sending ṣalawāt upon the Messenger of Allāh ﷺ

Umar ﷺ said, "Du'ā' is suspended between the heaven and the earth and none of it ascends until you send ṣalawāt upon your Prophet." [Jāmi' At-Tirmidhī 486]

Abū Sulaymān ad-Dārānī ﷺ said, "Whoever wants to ask Allāh for his needs, let him start by sending ṣalawāt upon the Prophet then ask for what he needs, and then end his du'ā' with ṣalawāt (again) upon the Prophet. For sending ṣalawāt upon the Prophet will be accepted, and Allāh is too generous to refuse (the du'ā' made) between the two ṣalawāt." [Al-Qawl Al-Badī' fi Aṣ-Ṣalāti 'alā Al-Ḥabīb As-Shafī' p.435]

It is like wings for the du'ā' with which it soars up to the clouds of the sky.

6. Say 'Āmīn'

Āmīn means 'O Allāh! Accept (or respond to) this du'ā'. The purpose of saying Āmīn is so that it might increase the chances that a person's du'ā will be answered.

The Prophet ﷺ said, "No group of people gathers of which a portion supplicate and the entirety say Āmīn except Allāh answers their supplication." [Al-Mu'jam Al-Kabīr Aṭ-Ṭabarānī 3536]

7. HOW DO WE ENSURE ACCEPTANCE?

Reminders After Du'ā'

Have a firm conviction that Allāh ﷻ will answer your du'ā'

The Messenger of Allāh ﷺ said, "No Muslim makes du'ā' which does not entail a sin or the severing of ties of kinship without Allāh giving him one of three:

1 - He fulfils his du'ā' immediately
2 - He stores it for him in the Hereafter
3 - He averts from him a similar evil"

The Companions said, "If that is so, we will make du'ā' even more." He replied, "Allāh will respond even more." [Musnad Aḥmad 11133]

The Prophet ﷺ said:

- "There is no Muslim on the face of the earth that asks Allāh for anything except that Allāh gives it to him, or averts from him a similar evil, as long as he does not ask for something evil or breaking the ties of kinship" [Jāmi` At-Tirmidhī 3381]
- "Make du'ā' to Allāh whilst you are certain of a response, because Allāh does not accept a du'ā' from a heedless, distracted heart" [Jāmi` At-Tirmidhī 3479]

Do not be impatient or hasty

The Prophet ﷺ said, "The supplication of the servant is granted as long as he does not supplicate for sin or for severing the ties of blood, or he does not become impatient." It was said, "Allāh's Messenger, what does: 'If he does not grow impatient' imply?" He said, "That he should say like this: 'I supplicated and I supplicated but I did not find it being responded to.' Then he becomes frustrated and abandons supplication." [Ṣaḥīḥ Muslim 2735]

Do not become despondent

Even after prolonged supplications and patience, you must not think that your du'ā' has been rejected. One should remain optimistic and ignore the demoralising whispers of Shaytān. It is part of one's īmān to expect the best from Allāh ﷻ, and to be sure that Allāh ﷻ will respond to your du'ā', as He is the Ever-Merciful, All-Knowing.

"Allāh ﷻ says, 'I am just as My slave thinks I am and I am with him when he remembers Me.'" [Ṣaḥīḥ Al-Bukhārī 7405]

One should not despair, thinking that there is nothing that can be done. Indeed this is all the more reason to turn to Allāh ﷻ, full of hope and sincerity because the One that decreed the situation in the first place is the only One that can change that decree, so it is essential to turn to Him.

Indeed, Allāh ﷻ responded to the du'ā' of the worst of the creation, Iblis, may Allāh ﷻ curse him, when he said, (Satan appealed) "My Lord! Then delay my end until the Day of their resurrection." Allāh ﷻ said, "You will be delayed." [Al-Ḥijr 15:36-37]

So if even Iblis' du'ā' can be accepted, then surely the du'ā' of a Muslim has more right than his!

Avoiding consuming ḥarām

Do not forget your consciousness of Allāh ﷻ (taqwā) for it is the essence of all matters. This taqwā makes a person realise that Allāh ﷻ is watching him at all times.

The Messenger of Allāh ﷺ made mention of a man beseeching Allāh ﷻ, one who raised his hands to the sky saying: "'O Lord! O Lord!' but his food was unlawful, his drink was unlawful, his clothing was unlawful, and he was nourished with unlawful; so how will his du'ā' be accepted?!" [Ṣaḥīḥ Muslim 1015]

The Prophet ﷺ also said, "O people, Allāh is Good and He therefore accepts only that which is good. And Allāh commanded the believers as He commanded the Messengers by saying: 'O messengers! Eat from what is good and lawful, and act righteously. Indeed, I fully know what you do.'" [Ṣaḥīḥ Muslim 1015]

In these two aḥādīth, we are informed about one of the greatest causes of one's du'ā' not being responded to. Not only that, but in the first of the two sayings, the Prophet ﷺ made a point of stressing how ridiculous it was that anyone could expect such a du'ā' to be answered.

So it is essential that one who wishes his du'ā' to be accepted should ensure that he eats from pure money, money that has been earned by permissible means, and that he eats pure food, food that he is allowed to eat.

Avoiding sinning

There is no doubt that a person's sins come between him and the response of his du'ā'. Therefore, when a person makes du'ā' for long periods of time, without receiving a response, this should cause him to turn towards himself, and examine his actions. Perhaps there is something that he is doing that is the cause of his du'ā' being unanswered, such as non-fulfilment of his obligations, forgoing the rights of others, or some such straightforward oversight.

The Prophet ﷺ said, "By the One in Whose Hand is my soul! Either you command good and forbid evil, or Allāh will soon send upon you a punishment from Him, then you will call upon Him, but He will not respond to you." [Jāmi` At-Tirmidhī 2169]

Imparting good advice

Part of one's īmān is that one loves for one's brother what one loves for oneself. This necessitates one's wanting good for one's brother, and averting evil from him. You should therefore enjoin what is good and forbid what is evil (in the most appropriate of ways), and believe in Allāh ﷻ.

The Prophet ﷺ said, "I swear by Him in whose Hands is my soul, you will of a surety command what is good, and forbid what is evil, or else it is very possible that Allāh will send upon you His punishment, so you will make du'ā' to Him, and you will not be responded to." [Jāmi` At-Tirmidhī 2169]

So leaving this obligation brings about Allāh's ﷻ anger and punishment, and part of this punishment is that our du'ā's are not answered.

Ultimately remember that Allāh ﷻ is Malik

Allāh ﷻ is the true King, the Owner of All Kingdoms. No one can interfere in His decisions, and no one can question His resolutions. So the Muslim does not question the will of Allāh ﷻ, rather he accepts it, and is pleased with it.

As Allāh ﷻ says in the Qur'ān, "He is not questioned regarding what He does, but rather they will be questioned (regarding what they do)." [Surah al-Anbiya 23]

Du'ā' is a manifestation of Allāh's ﷻ ultimate wisdom

Of Allāh's ﷻ many beautiful names is 'Al-Ḥakīm', often translated as 'The All-Wise'. So to Allāh ﷻ belongs the greatest wisdom; all of His decrees are wise. When He gives, He gives with wisdom, and when He prevents, He prevents with wisdom.

In His Qur'ān, Allāh ﷻ describes His own wisdom as: "Profound (or complete and all-encompassing) wisdom." [Al-Qamar 54:5]

The fact that a person's du'ā' is responded to or not is an indication and manifestation of many of Allāh's ﷻ names and attributes. So a person should keep the names and attributes of Allāh ﷻ in mind when his du'ā' is not responded to, for the very action or inaction with regard to granting the du'ā' (on Allāh's ﷻ part) is a great manifestation of His names and attributes.

Of these names are: **Al-Mu'ṭī** (the One that Gives), **Al-Māni'** (the Withholder), **Al-Ḥakam** (the Judge), **Al-'Adl** (the Just), **Al-Karīm** (the Most Generous), **Al-Ḥakīm** (the All-Wise), and many others.

None of these names should be considered 'minor' or an accompaniment; whether a person's du'ā' is answered or not, all of these names, and more, are manifested in Allāh's ﷻ Decrees. The Muslim who reflects on his situation with Allāh ﷻ, stretching his or her powers of contemplation with special regard to the things he has asked for, will come to realise that when Almighty Allāh ﷻ gives, He gives out of generosity, wisdom and justice, and when He withholds, He withholds out of power, wisdom, and justice.

Du'ā' is answered in one of three ways

The Messenger of Allāh ﷺ said, "There is not a man who calls upon Allāh with a supplication, except that he is answered. Either it shall be granted to him in the world, or reserved for him in the Hereafter, or his sins shall be expiated for it according to the extent that he supplicated, as long as he does not supplicate for some sin, or for the severing of the ties of kinship, and he does not become hasty."

[Jāmi' At-Tirmidhī 3604]

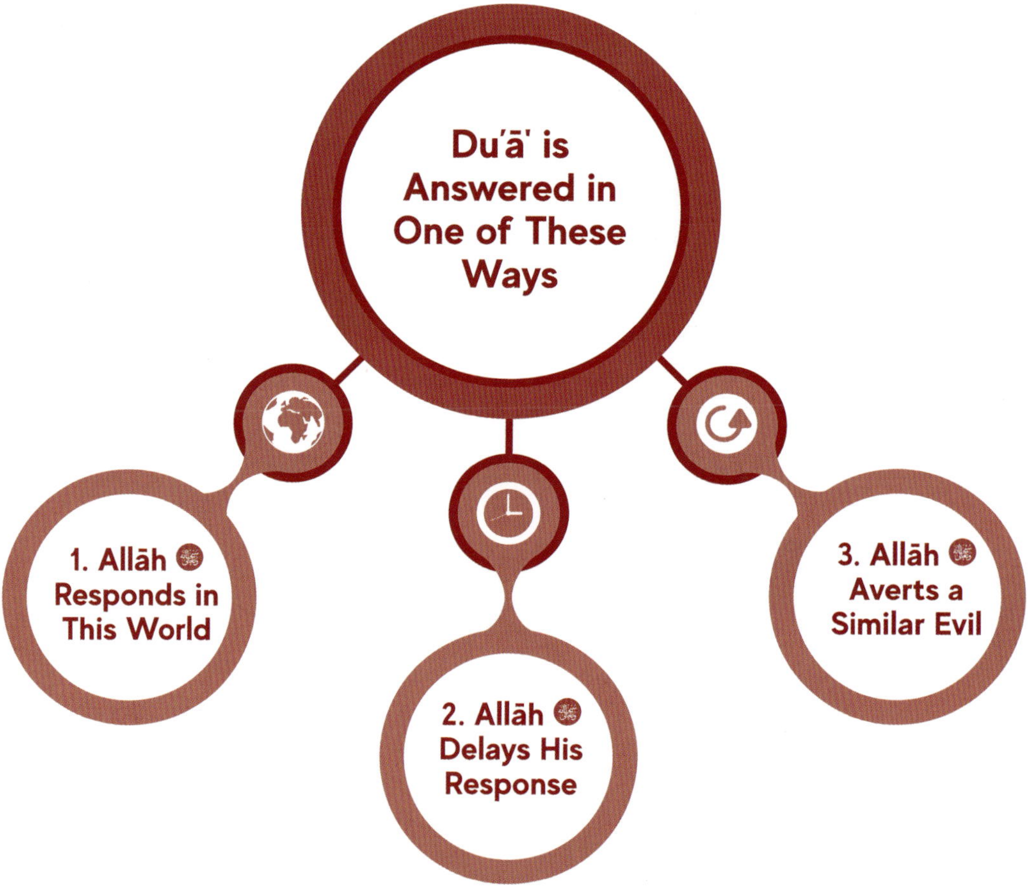
Du'ā' is Answered in One of These Ways
1. Allāh Responds in This World
2. Allāh Delays His Response
3. Allāh Averts a Similar Evil

1. Du'ā' might actually have been responded to
We have already mentioned the ḥadīth in which the Prophet ﷺ guaranteed that a person's du'ā' will be accepted in one of three ways. However, the 'acceptance' of a du'ā' might be in a manner that is not apparent.

2. Allāh ﷻ delays His response
As Allāh ﷻ says, "Every soul will taste death. And We test you (O humanity) with good and evil as a trial, then to Us you will ˹all˺ be returned." [Al-Anbiyā 21:35]

The Prophet ﷺ said, "Indeed greater reward comes with greater trial. And indeed, when Allāh loves a people He subjects them to trials, so whoever is content (with Allāh), then for him is pleasure, and whoever is discontent, then for him is wrath." [Jāmi' At-Tirmidhī 2396]

It is possible that Allāh ﷻ will give him the reward of his du'ā' on the Day of Judgement, and this reward will be more beloved to him on that Day than the response of his du'ā' in this life.

When the response of a du'ā' is delayed, this is a type of test and trial that is inflicted upon the servant. This necessitates him being patient during this trial. So a person should realise that, just like his entire life is a trial and test for him, so too is this delayed response. This is just one of the many trials that he has to face if he eventually wishes to enter Paradise at the pleasure of his Creator.

So the believer accepts the divine wisdom of Allāh ﷻ, and does not cause a delay in response to swerve him from the true īmān in Allāh ﷻ.

When a person's du'ā' is not responded to, then this is a trial from Allāh ﷻ, and this should make a person optimistic that he is from amongst those whom Allāh ﷻ loves. Such a test should make him increase in his patience and draw him closer to Allāh ﷻ.

Any delay should cause a believer to contemplate his life, the good and the bad, to examine his du'ā', and why he is making it and to examine his day-to-day: what he wants to achieve within it. Of his mundane affairs, he will choose to examine his wealth (how he earns it and how he spends it) and to ponder over his deeds, both good and bad. Ultimately, seeing that his good deeds are in deficit and his evil deeds profuse, he should prefer to turn to Allāh ﷻ in repentance, and change his lifestyle. And these are the affairs of the sincere believer.

Any delay in response is actually a regenerative experience and a purification for the Muslim, for it forces him to re-examine his relationship with Allāh ﷻ, and try to strengthen it. Had his du'ā' received an immediate response, then this examination would not have occurred, nor would any extra good come out of it, hence in brief, this delay is a great blessing from Allāh ﷻ.

3. Allāh ﷻ averts from you a similar evil

Allāh ﷻ chooses what is better for His servant. The Prophet ﷺ said, "There is no Muslim on the face of the earth that asks Allāh for anything except that Allāh gives it to him, or averts from him a similar evil, as long as he does not ask for something evil or breaking the ties of kinship." [Jāmi' At-Tirmidhī 3381]

It is possible that Allāh ﷻ knows that a certain matter will, in reality, lead to evil consequences. The human, the Muslim, might detect good in desiring money with a view to spending it for the sake of Allāh ﷻ. Yet Allāh ﷻ knows that if this person were to be given his desired money, he would instead find ruinous ways of spending in reprehensible ways, and his spirituality would suffer.

So beware, O Muslim, of succumbing to anger, or complaining, against Allāh's ﷻ Decree, for it is possible that the matter that you so desire might be the very cause of your destruction!

The very concise example used in the last few paragraphs shows just how possible it is that Allāh ﷻ, in His ultimate wisdom, knows the detrimental nature of that state or thing which His servant requests. Allāh's ﷻ Decree will, by His Nature, always be what is best for His servants in this world and the Hereafter. Each servant must come to realise that not all of his du'ā's are to his benefit; everything that Allāh ﷻ has decreed for him is good, even if he does not see the wisdom behind that decree. So, when an affliction befalls him, he will know and realise that hidden in it is great good and benefit for him.

The great sage and ascetic Sufyān Ath-Thawrī said, "Verily, when He withholds, He actually gives, because He did not withhold on account of miserliness or stinginess, but rather He looked at the benefit of the servant. So the fact that He withheld is actually His choice (for the servant) and His excellent decision". [Madārij As-Sālikīn 2/207]

A person's knowledge of good and evil is relative, whereas Allāh's knowledge is infinite. So a person should resign himself to the fact that His Lord's decision is better than his own.

As Allāh states, "you may hate something which Allāh turns into a great blessing." [An-Nisā 4:19]

الغَضَب

Anger

RELATED EMOTIONS

Frustrated | Wound Up | Agitated | Annoyed | Bitter
Argumentative | Aggressive | Enraged | Furious | Contemptuous
Harsh | Hostile | Offended | Wound up

INVOKING NAMES OF ALLĀH

- Al-'Adl - the Just
- Aṣ-Ṣabūr - the Patient
- Al-Ḥalīm - the Forbearing
- Ar-Raḥmān - The All Compassionate
- Ar-Raḥīm - the All Merciful
- Al-Ghaffār - Full of Forgiveness
- At-Tawwāb - The Relenting
- Al-Wadūd - the Most Loving
- Al-Ḥaqq - The Truth
- As-Salām - the Source of Peace

AṢ-ṢALĀH AL-IBRĀHĪMIYYAH

ACCEPTED PRAYERS

- Seeking Refuge from Satan in Times of Anger
- Seeking Truth in Times of Anger
- Seeking Truth in Speech in Times of Anger
- Seeking Protection from Allāh's Anger
- Removing Anger from One's Heart and Seeking Protection from Satan
- Removing Anger from One's Heart and Seeking Protection from Misleading Trials
- Removing Bitterness
- Hastening Towards Peace
- Praying for Peace

CHAPTER 1

Anger [Ghadab] الغَضَب

Anger can be compared to a chained, restless beast imprisoned in the heat of the midday sun: near-impossible to restrain once it breaks its chains, and doubtless of no benefit to its owner once unleashed. Intense anger or wrath is known as 'ghadab'.

A man asked the Prophet ﷺ "What will keep me away from the anger of Allāh?" The Prophet ﷺ said, "Do not become angry." [Musnad Aḥmad 6635]

The Messenger of Allāh ﷺ became angry at times. He ﷺ once said, "I am one of the sons of Ādam; I get angry as you get angry" [Sunan Abī Dawūd 4659]. The Prophet's ﷺ anger could be seen on his face. But his anger was always in response to a deviation from 'normal' human character and behaviour that would be offensive to Allāh ﷻ.

Scholars agree that anger is not prohibited per se. Indeed it is part of the wisdom behind the Qur'ānic commandment to enjoin what is right and forbid what is evil. However, as much as anger remains an essential quality of the human creation, if is not guided to something useful - if used recklessly and left untamed - it can possess, consume, and ultimately destroy a person.

Anger

Invoking Allāh's Names

الْعَدْلُ

Al-'Adl
The Just

الصَّبُورُ

Aṣ-Ṣabūr
The Patient

الْحَلِيمُ

Al-Ḥalīm
The Forbearing

الرَّحْمَانُ

Ar-Raḥmān
The All Compassionate

الرَّحِيمُ

Ar-Raḥīm
The All Merciful

الْغَفَّارُ

Al-Ghaffār
Full of Forgiveness

التَّوَّابُ

At-Tawwāb
The Relenting

الْوَدُودُ

Al-Wadūd
The Most Loving

الْحَقُّ

Al-Ḥaqq
The Truth

السَّلَامُ

As-Salām
The Source of Peace

Anger

Contemplation and Reflection on Allāh's ﷻ Blessed Names

- You put frustration, annoyance and/or bitterness under the guidance of patience, self-control, reason and religion.
- You do not take objection to Allāh ﷻ in His plan and in His decree, whether an outcome corresponds to your preferences or not.
- You show mercy to others by encouragement and counselling.
- You are quick to identify situations where others are seeking to enrage, bully or tease you; the resolute and unwavering reaction that you have developed involves something like averting your eyes to the ground and smiling.
- Your way is to choose gentleness and mildness rather than argumentation.
- You look upon others with the eye of mercy and speak with the voice of forgiveness, sparing no effort to ensure you are deriving Allāh's ﷻ pleasure and not exposing yourself to His wrath.
- You remember that mildness (rather than aggressiveness) is among the finest qualities of mankind. You are able to 'climb down' in social situations where constant quarrelling or rage has shown itself. Drinking water, sitting or lying on the floor: each of these, you appreciate, is a passive and non-confrontational action.
- You do not turn away from any needy people out of irritation or frustration, without meeting their needs to the extent of your ability. At the very least you offer the disadvantaged person assistance through (private) prayer or by showing empathy on account of their need, as though you are sharing in their misfortune and their destitution.
- You desire for Allāh's ﷻ creatures whatever you desire for yourself, for example, by overlooking their wrongdoings. If you prefer others to yourself, you are even higher than this.
- You tolerate any offence and hurt caused to you because you realise that Allāh ﷻ is sufficient to take offenders to task.
- You understand that every servant whose heart is free from his lower self (e.g. pride, argumentation, bitterness, evil intent) and whose limbs are unblemished by sins and forbidden actions, will be one who comes to Allāh ﷻ with a pure heart.

Anger

Aṣ-Ṣalāh Al-Ibrāhīmiyyah

اَللّٰهُمَّ صَلِّ عَلَى مُحَمَّدٍ وَعَلَى آلِ مُحَمَّدٍ كَمَا صَلَّيْتَ عَلَى
إِبْرَاهِيمَ وَآلِ إِبْرَاهِيمَ إِنَّكَ حَمِيدٌ مَجِيدٌ وَبَارِكْ عَلَى
مُحَمَّدٍ وَعَلَى آلِ مُحَمَّدٍ كَمَا بَارَكْتَ عَلَى إِبْرَاهِيمَ وَآلِ
إِبْرَاهِيمَ إِنَّكَ حَمِيدٌ مَجِيدٌ

Allāhumma ṣalli ʿalā Muḥammadin wa ʿalā āli Muḥammadin kamā ṣ allayta ʿalā Ibrāhīm wa āli Ibrāhīm innaka ḥamīdum majīd, wa bārik ʿalā Muḥammadin wa ʿalā āli Muḥammadin kamā bārakta ʿalā Ibrāhīm wa āli Ibrāhīm innaka ḥamīdum majīd

O Allāh, send peace upon Muḥammad and upon the family of Muḥammad, as You sent peace upon Ibrāhīm and the family of Ibrāhīm, and send blessings upon Muḥammad and upon the family of Muḥammad as You sent blessings upon Ibrāhīm and the family of Ibrāhīm. You are indeed the praiseworthy, the most honourable. [Sunan An-Nasaī 1290]

Anger

Seeking Refuge from Satan in Times of Anger

أَعُوذُ بِاللهِ مِنَ الشَّيْطَانِ الرَّجِيمِ

A'ūdhu billāhi minash shaytānir rajīm

I seek refuge in Allāh from the cursed Satan. [Saḥīḥ al-Bukhārī 5764, Saḥīḥ Muslim 2610]

Seeking Truth in Times of Anger

اَللّٰهُمَّ أَسْأَلُكَ خَشْيَتَكَ فِي الْغَيْبِ وَالشَّهَادَةِ وَكَلِمَةَ الْحَقِّ فِي الْغَضَبِ وَالرِّضَا

Allāhumma innī as-aluka khashyataka fil ghaybi wash shahādati wa kalimatal ḥaqqi fil ghaḍabi war riḍā

O Allāh, I ask You for Your fear in private and in public, and for the word of truth in times of joy and anger. [Musnad Aḥmad 18325]

Seeking Truth in Speech in Times of Anger

اَللّٰهُمَّ وَأَسْأَلُكَ خَشْيَتَكَ فِي الْغَيْبِ وَالشَّهَادَةِ وَأَسْأَلُكَ كَلِمَةَ الْحَقِّ فِي الرِّضَا وَالْغَضَبِ وَأَسْأَلُكَ الْقَصْدَ فِي الْفَقْرِ وَالْغِنَى

Allāhumma wa as-aluka khashyataka fil ghaybi wash shahādati wa as-aluka kalimatal haqqi fir riḍā wal ghaḍabi wa as-alukal qaṣda fil faqri wal ghinā

O Allāh, cause me to fear You in secret and in public. I ask You to make me true in speech in times of pleasure and of anger. I ask You to make me moderate in times of wealth and poverty. [Sunan An-Nasaī 1305]

Anger

Seeking Protection from Allāh's ﷻ Anger

اَللّٰهُمَّ إِنِّي أَعُوذُ بِرِضَاكَ مِنْ سَخَطِكَ وَأَعُوذُ بِمُعَافَاتِكَ مِنْ عُقُوبَتِكَ وَأَعُوذُ بِكَ مِنْكَ لاَ أُحْصِي ثَنَاءً عَلَيْكَ أَنْتَ كَمَا أَثْنَيْتَ عَلَى نَفْسِكَ

Allāhumma innī a'ūdhu bi riḍāka min sakhatik, wa a'ūdhu bi mu'āfātika min uqūbatik, wa a'ūdhu bika minka la uhṣī thanā-an 'alayka anta kamā athnayta 'alā nafsik

O Allāh, I seek protection in Your pleasure from Your anger, and in Your forgiveness from Your punishment. I seek protection in You from You. I cannot fully praise You. You are the way You have praised Yourself. [Jāmi` At-Tirmidhī 3566]

Removing Anger from One's Heart and Seeking Protection from Satan

اَللّٰهُمَّ اغْفِرْ لِي ذَنْبِي، وَأَذْهِبْ غَيْظَ قَلْبِي، وَأَجِرْنِي مِنَ الشَّيْطَانِ

Allāhummaghfirlī dhanbī wa adh-hib ghayẓa qalbī wa ajirnī minash shayṭān

O Allāh, forgive me my sin. Let the anger of my heart be gone. Protect me from Satan. [Ibn As-Sunnī in 'Amal Al-Yawm wa Al-Laylah 622]

Removing Anger from One's Heart and Seeking Protection from Deviating Trials

اَللّٰهُمَّ رَبَّ مُحَمَّدٍ، اغْفِرْ لِي ذَنْبِي، وَأَذْهِبْ غَيْظَ قَلْبِي، وَأَجِرْنِي مِنْ مُضِلَّاتِ الْفِتَنِ

Allāhumma rabba Muḥammadin ighfirlī dhanbī wa adh-hib ghayẓa qalbī wa ajirnī min muḍillātil fitan

O Allāh, the Lord of Muḥammad, forgive my sins, remove the anger of my heart and protect me from misleading trials. [Ibn As-Sunnī in 'Amal Al-Yawm wa Al-Laylah 455]

Anger

Removing Bitterness

رَبَّنَا اغْفِرْ لَنَا وَلِإِخْوَانِنَا الَّذِينَ سَبَقُونَا بِالْإِيمَانِ وَلَا تَجْعَلْ فِي قُلُوبِنَا غِلًّا لِّلَّذِينَ ءَامَنُوا رَبَّنَا إِنَّكَ رَءُوفٌ رَّحِيمٌ

Rabbanaghfir lanā wa li ikhwāninalladhīna sabaqūnā bil īmāni wa lā taj'al fī qulūbinā ghillal lilladhīna āmanu rabbāna innaka ra-ūfur rahīm

Our Lord! Forgive us and our fellow believers who preceded us in faith, and do not allow bitterness into our hearts towards those who believe. Our Lord! Indeed, You are Ever Gracious, Most Merciful. [Al-Ḥashr 59:10]

Hastening Towards Peace

اَللّٰهُمَّ إِنِّي أَسْأَلُكَ تَعْجِيلَ عَافِيَتِكَ، أَوْ صَبْرًا عَلَى بَلِيَّتِكَ أَوْ خُرُوجًا مِنَ الدُّنْيَا إِلَى رَحْمَتِكَ

Allāhumma innī as-aluka ta'jīl 'āfiyatik aw ṣabran 'alā baliyyatik aw khurūjam minad dunyā ilā raḥmatik

O Allāh, I ask for your haste in granting me peace, and taking me out of the trials of this world to your mercy. [Ibn ḥibbān 922]

Praying for Peace

اَللّٰهُمَّ أَنْتَ السَّلَامُ وَمِنْكَ السَّلَامُ تَبَارَكْتَ يَا ذَا الْجَلَالِ وَالْإِكْرَام

Allāhumma antas salām wa minkas salām tabārakta yā dhal jalāli wal ikrām

"O Allāh, You are peace and from You is peace. Blessed are You, the Majestic and Noble." [Saḥīḥ Muslim 592]

كَرَاهِيَةُ المَوْتِ

Antipathy Towards Death

RELATED EMOTIONS

Reluctant | Anxious | Insecure | Fearful | Annoyed | Threatened
Agitated | Apprehensive | Astray | Cynical | Depressed | Distressed
Doubtful | Frustrated | Grudging | Hostile | Ignorant | Lazy
Neglectful | Oblivious | Reluctant | Threatened | Cowardly

INVOKING NAMES OF ALLĀH

- **Al-Bā'ith - The Resurrector**
- **Al-Ḥasīb - The Reckoner**
- **Al-Mu'īd - The Restorer**
- **Al-Jāmi' - The Uniter**
- **Al-Muḥyī - The Giver of Life**
- **Al-Mumīt - the Slayer**
- **Al-Ḥakīm - the All-Wise**

AṢ-ṢALĀH AL-IBRĀHĪMIYYAH

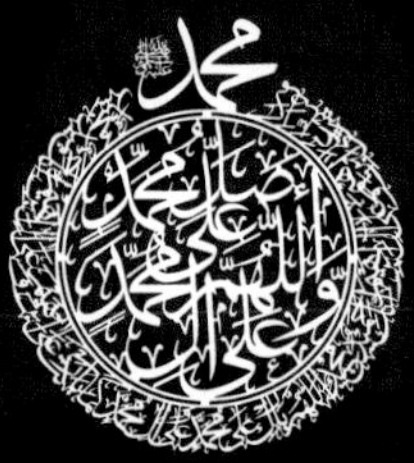

ACCEPTED PRAYERS

- **Seeking the Purpose of Creation**
- **Seeking the Reality of the Unseen and Life After Death**
- **Acknowledging that Everything is for Allāh**
- **Acknowledging the True Life of the Hereafter**
- **Pursuing Good Deeds and Acknowledging the Importance of the Hereafter**
- **Seeking Refuge from the Trials and Tribulations Before and After Death**
- **Acknowledging Our Origin and Inevitable Return to Allāh**

CHAPTER 2

Antipathy Towards Death

[Karāhiyat al-Mawt] كَرَاهِيَةُ الْمَوْت

Antipathy towards death is when one flees from the ending that befalls every creature, and becomes annoyed when it is even mentioned. It is as if one chooses to remain completely ignorant of Allāh's ﷻ abundant statements describing the temporary nature of this life. This may be due to an excessive love for dunyā (the world) and chasing after the temporary things of this world.

Allāh ﷻ states:

- "Every soul will taste death" [Āli 'Imrān 3:185]
- "Say, 'The death you are running away from will inevitably come to you. Then you will be returned to the Knower of the seen and unseen, and He will inform you of what you used to do'" [Al-Jumu'ah 62:8]

Fear of death is natural, so one naturally protects oneself from it. When the angels, in the form of human beings, visited the Prophet Ibrāhīm ﷺ, he offered them food. When he saw that they did not reach for the food, he grew fearful. Scholars say that Ibrāhīm ﷺ thought they had come to take his life.

Antipathy Towards Death

Invoking Allāh's ﷻ Names

الْبَاعِث
Al-Bā'ith
The Resurrector

الْحَسِيب
Al-Ḥasīb
The Reckoner

الْمُعِيد
Al-Mu'īd
The Restorer

الْجَامِع
Al-Jāmi'
The Uniter

الْمُحْيِي
Al-Muḥyī
The Giver of Life

الْمُمِيت
Al-Mumīt
The Slayer

الْحَكِيم
Al-Ḥakīm
The All-Wise

Antipathy Towards Death

Contemplation and Reflection on Allāh's ﷻ Blessed Names

- You remind yourself that feeling any dislike or reluctance to face death is at odds with the reality of this life. Death is close, you say to yourself, and what is more, it comes to us all. Knowing this, your insecurity becomes only temporary. You can also clearly see that your anxieties and insecurities leave you when you accept your mortality and the mortality of those whom you love.
- You realise that it is Allāh ﷻ who restores creatures' lives on the Day of Resurrection, raising up those in the grave, and revealing what is in the hearts of humankind.
- You remind yourself that the grave is either one of the pits of the fires of hell or one of the gardens of paradise, so you concern yourself with whatever will benefit you in the world to come.
- You understand that, for the believer there is comfort in death; that it takes you from an abode of difficulty and trial to one of peace and infinite freedom.
- You appreciate that a shrewd or wise person is one who accepts the inevitable (i.e. you are not annoyed or threatened by the concept), and one who is never reluctant to judge his soul, working for whatever comes after death. On the other hand, the incompetent one is he who places his soul under the authority of his passions and false hopes.

Antipathy Towards Death

Aṣ-Ṣalāh Al-Ibrāhīmiyyah

اَللّٰهُمَّ صَلِّ عَلَى مُحَمَّدٍ وَعَلَى آلِ مُحَمَّدٍ كَمَا صَلَّيْتَ عَلَى

إِبْرَاهِيمَ وَآلِ إِبْرَاهِيمَ إِنَّكَ حَمِيدٌ مَجِيدٌ وَبَارِكْ عَلَى

مُحَمَّدٍ وَعَلَى آلِ مُحَمَّدٍ كَمَا بَارَكْتَ عَلَى إِبْرَاهِيمَ وَآلِ

إِبْرَاهِيمَ إِنَّكَ حَمِيدٌ مَجِيدٌ

Allāhumma ṣalli ʿalā Muḥammadin wa ʿalā āli Muḥammadin kamā ṣ allayta ʿalā Ibrāhīm wa āli Ibrāhīm innaka ḥamīdum majīd, wa bārik ʿalā Muḥammadin wa ʿalā āli Muḥammadin kamā bārakta ʿalā Ibrāhīm wa āli Ibrāhīm innaka ḥamīdum majīd

O Allāh, send peace upon Muḥammad and upon the family of Muḥammad, as You sent peace upon Ibrāhīm and the family of Ibrāhīm, and send blessings upon Muḥammad and upon the family of Muḥammad as You sent blessings upon Ibrāhīm and the family of Ibrāhīm. You are indeed praiseworthy, the most honourable. [Sunan An-Nasaī 1290]

Antipathy Towards Death

Seeking a Reminder of the Purpose of Creation

رَبَّنَا مَا خَلَقْتَ هَٰذَا بَٰطِلًا سُبْحَٰنَكَ فَقِنَا عَذَابَ النَّارِ

Rabbanā mā khalaqta hādhā bāṭilā, subḥānaka faqinā adhāban nār

Our Lord! You have not created (all of) this without purpose. Glory be to You! Protect us from the torment of the Fire. [Āli 'Imrān 3:191]

Seeking the Reality of the Unseen and Life After Death

اَللّٰهُمَّ بِعِلْمِكَ الْغَيْبَ وَقُدْرَتِكَ عَلَى الْخَلْقِ أَحْيِنِي مَا عَلِمْتَ الْحَيَاةَ خَيْرًا لِي
وَتَوَفَّنِي إِذَا عَلِمْتَ الْوَفَاةَ خَيْرًا لِي وَأَسْأَلُكَ الرِّضَاءَ بَعْدَ الْقَضَاءِ وَأَسْأَلُكَ بَرْدَ
الْعَيْشِ بَعْدَ الْمَوْتِ وَأَسْأَلُكَ لَذَّةَ النَّظَرِ إِلَى وَجْهِكَ وَالشَّوْقَ إِلَى لِقَائِكَ فِي
غَيْرِ ضَرَّاءَ مُضِرَّةٍ وَلَا فِتْنَةٍ مُضِلَّةٍ

Allāhumma bi 'ilmikal ghayba wa qudratika 'alal khalqi aḥyinī mā 'alimtal ḥayāta khayran lī wa tawaffanī idhā 'alimtal wafāta khayran lī, wa as-alukar riḍā ba'dal qaḍ'ā, wa as'aluka bardal 'ayshi ba'dal mawti wa as-aluka ladhdhatan naẓari ilā wajhik wash shawqa ila liqā-ika fi ghayri ḍarrā-a muḍirratin wa la fitnatin muḍillatin

O Allāh, by Your knowledge of the unseen and Your power over creation, keep me alive so long as You know that living is good for me and cause me to die when You know that death is better for me. I ask You to make me pleased with that which You have decreed and for an easy life after death. I ask You for the sweetness of looking upon Your face and a longing to meet You in a manner that does not entail a calamity that will bring about harm or a trial that will cause deviation. [Sunan An-Nasaī 1305]

Antipathy Towards Death

Acknowledging that Everything is for Allāh ﷻ

اَللّٰهُمَّ لَكَ صَلاَتِي وَنُسُكِي وَمَحْيَاىَ وَمَمَاتِي وَإِلَيْكَ مَآبِي وَلَكَ رَبِّ تُرَاثِ

Allāhumma laka ṣalātī wa nusukī wa maḥyāya wa mamātī wa ilayka ma-ābī wa laka rabbī turāth

O Allāh, my ṣalāh, my sacrifice, my life, and my death are all for You. To You is my return and Yours, my Lord, is what I leave behind. [Jāmi` At-Tirmidhī 3520]

Acknowledging the True Life of the Hereafter

اَللّٰهُمَّ لاَ عَيْشَ إِلاَّ عَيْشُ الآخِرَة

Allāhumma lā 'aysha illā 'ayshal ākhirah

O Allāh! There is no life worth living except the life of the Hereafter [Ṣaḥīḥ Al-Bukhārī 6413]

Pursuing Good Deeds and Acknowledging the Importance of the Hereafter

رَبَّنَا آتِنَا فِي الدُّنْيَا حَسَنَةً وَفِي الْآخِرَةِ حَسَنَةً وَقِنَا عَذَابَ النَّارِ

Rabbanā ātinā fid dunyā ḥasanatan wa fil ākhirati ḥasanatan wa qinā adhāban nār

"Our Lord! Grant us the good of this world and the Hereafter, and protect us from the torment of the Fire." [Al-Baqarah 2:201]

Antipathy Towards Death

Seeking Refuge from the Trials and Tribulations Before and After Death

اَللّٰهُمَّ إِنِّي أَعُوذُ بِكَ مِنْ عَذَابِ الْقَبْرِ، وَمِنْ عَذَابِ النَّارِ
وَمِنْ فِتْنَةِ الْمَحْيَا وَالْمَمَاتِ، وَمِنْ فِتْنَةِ الْمَسِيحِ الدَّجَّالِ

Allāhumma innī a'ūdhu bika min 'adhābil qabr, wa-min 'adhābin nār, wa min fitnatil maḥyā wal mamāt, wa min fitnatil masīḥ ad-dajjāl

O Allāh, I seek refuge in You from the punishment of the grave, from the punishment of the Hellfire, from the trials of life and death, and from the evil of the trial of the False Messiah. [Ṣaḥīḥ Al-Bukhārī 1377]

Acknowledging Our Origin and Inevitable Return to Allāh ﷻ

إِنَّا لِلّٰهِ وَإِنَّا إِلَيْهِ رَاجِعُونَ اللَّهُمَّ أْجُرْنِي فِي مُصِيبَتِي وَأَخْلِفْ لِي خَيْرًا مِنْهَا

Innā lillāhi wa innā ilayhi rāji'ūn. Allāhumma ajurnī fī muṣībatī wakhluf lī khayran minhā

To Allāh we belong and to Him we will return! O Allāh! Reward me due to this calamity, and grant me something better than it in exchange. [Ṣaḥīḥ Muslim 918]

التَواضُعُ المَلُؤُوم

Blameworthy Modesty

RELATED EMOTIONS

Shy | Embarrassed | Apprehensive | Insecure | Vulnerable
Threatened | Uninterested | Ashamed | Ignorant | Reluctant | Shy
Uneasy | Cowardly

INVOKING NAMES OF ALLĀH

- **Al-Ḥakīm - The All-Wise**
- **Al-'Alīm - The All-Knowing**
- **Al-'Adl - The Just**
- **Al-Khāfiḍ - The Abaser**
- **Ar-Rāfi' - The Exalter**
- **Al-Qawiyy - The All-Strong**
- **Al-Matīn - The Most Firm**
- **Al-Fattāḥ - The Opener**

AṢ-ṢALĀH AL-IBRĀHĪMIYYAH

ACCEPTED PRAYERS

- **Making a Task Easy**
- **Rectifying Speech and Guiding the Heart**
- **Seeking Knowledge**
- **Seeking Wisdom**
- **Seeking Steadfastness and Determination**
- **Seeking Protection from the Wrongdoers**

CHAPTER 3

Blameworthy Modesty

[At-Tawāḍu' al-Malūm] التَواضُعُ المَلُوُوم

In general, modesty is something praised in Islām and is considered virtuous. The type of modesty that becomes blameworthy is that which prevents one from criticising clear brutality or corruption. This form of modesty results in shyness at an unsuitable time, when one instead needs to be direct and courageous. Something blameworthy (munkar) is wrong regardless of the status of the wrongdoer, whether he or she is a close relative or a person normally held in high regard.

Apart from preventing a person from avoiding munkar, unwarranted or blameworthy modesty is also the failure to seek sacred knowledge.

Blameworthy Modesty

Invoking Allāh's ﷻ Names

الْحَكِيمُ
Al-Ḥakīm
The All-Wise

الْعَلِيمُ
Al-'Alīm
The All-Knowing

الْعَدْلُ
Al-'Adl
The Just

الْخَافِضُ
Al-Khāfiḍ
The Abaser

الرَّافِعُ
Ar-Rāfi'
The Exalter

الْقَوِيُّ
Al-Qawiyy
The All-Strong

الْمَتِينُ
Al-Matīn
The Most Firm

الْفَتَّاحُ
Al-Fattāḥ
The Opener

Blameworthy Modesty

Contemplation and Reflection on Allāh's ﷻ Blessed Names

- Your insecurity or shyness, or indeed your ignorance, does not prevent you from making a sincere and conscientious effort to unlock and open the doors to divine knowledge (i.e. Allāh ﷻ is the All-Wise, our source and provider of all knowledge).
- Your hesitation does not prevent you from condemning any act of injustice or oppression, regardless of the status of or relationship with the other.
- You turn to Allāh ﷻ as the source of all power to strengthen and make firm your faith and spirit.
- Your loyalty should only be to the truth, and you are not to be swayed by any other consideration (such as vulnerability in the face of impending threat).
- You exalt the truth and abase falsehood, by taking an interest in and supporting those who are right and by reproaching those who are wrong.
- Considering that no harm will result, you offer your services in moments where you see that others would benefit from encouragement or action.

Blameworthy Modesty

Aṣ-Ṣalāh Al-Ibrāhīmiyyah

اَللّٰهُمَّ صَلِّ عَلَى مُحَمَّدٍ وَعَلَى آلِ مُحَمَّدٍ كَمَا صَلَّيْتَ عَلَى
إِبْرَاهِيمَ وَآلِ إِبْرَاهِيمَ إِنَّكَ حَمِيدٌ مَجِيدٌ وَبَارِكْ عَلَى
مُحَمَّدٍ وَعَلَى آلِ مُحَمَّدٍ كَمَا بَارَكْتَ عَلَى إِبْرَاهِيمَ وَآلِ
إِبْرَاهِيمَ إِنَّكَ حَمِيدٌ مَجِيدٌ

Allāhumma ṣalli 'alā Muḥammadin wa 'alā āli Muḥammadin kamā ṣ allayta 'alā Ibrāhīm wa āli Ibrāhīm innaka ḥamīdum majīd, wa bārik 'alā Muḥammadin wa 'alā āli Muḥammadin kamā bārakta 'alā Ibrāhīm wa āli Ibrāhīm innaka ḥamīdum majīd

O Allāh, send peace upon Muḥammad and upon the family of Muḥammad, as You sent peace upon Ibrāhīm and the family of Ibrāhīm, and send blessings upon Muḥammad and upon the family of Muḥammad as You sent blessings upon Ibrāhīm and the family of Ibrāhīm. You are indeed praiseworthy, the most honourable. [Sunan An-Nasaī 1290]

Blameworthy Modesty

Making a Task Easy

رَبِّ ٱشْرَحْ لِى صَدْرِى وَيَسِّرْ لِىٓ أَمْرِى وَٱحْلُلْ عُقْدَةً مِّن لِّسَانِى يَفْقَهُوا۟ قَوْلِى

Rabbish rahlī ṣadrī wa yassir lī amrī waḥlul 'uqdatam mil lisānī yafqahū qawlī

My Lord! Uplift my heart for me, and make my task easy, and remove the impediment from my tongue so people may understand my speech [Ṭāhā 20:25-28]

Rectifying Speech and Guiding the Heart

رَبِّ تَقَبَّلْ تَوْبَتِي ، وَاغْسِلْ حَوْبَتِي ، وَأَجِبْ دَعْوَتِي ، وَثَبِّتْ حُجَّتِي ، وَسَدِّدْ لِسَانِي ، وَاهْدِ قَلْبِي ، وَاسْلُلْ سَخِيمَةَ صَدْرِي

Rabbi taqabbal tawbatī, waghsil ḥawbatī, wa ajib da'watī, wa thabbit ḥujjatī, wa saddid lisānī, wahdi qalbī, waslul sakhīmata ṣadrī

My Lord, accept my repentance, wash away my sins, accept my supplications, strengthen my case, rectify my speech, guide my heart, and remove the malice from my heart. [Jāmi` At-Tirmidhī 3551]

Seeking Knowledge

رَّبِّ زِدْنِي عِلْمًا

Rabbī zidnī 'ilmā

My Lord! Increase me in knowledge. [Ṭāhā 20:114]

Blameworthy Modesty

Seeking Wisdom

رَبِّ هَبْ لِي حُكْمًا وَأَلْحِقْنِي بِالصَّالِحِينَ، وَاجْعَل لِّي لِسَانَ صِدْقٍ فِي الْآخِرِينَ، وَاجْعَلْنِي مِن وَرَثَةِ جَنَّةِ النَّعِيمِ

Rabbi hab lī ḥukman wa alhiqnī bisṣṣāliḥīn, waj'al lī lisāna ṣidqin fil ākhirīn, waj'alnī min warathati jannatin na'īm

My Lord! Grant me wisdom, and join me with the righteous. Bless me with honourable mention among later generations. Make me one of those awarded the Garden of Bliss. [Ash-Shu'arā 26: 83-85]

Seeking Steadfastness and Determination

اَللّٰهُمَّ إِنِّي أَسْأَلُكَ الثَّبَاتَ فِي الأَمْرِ وَأَسْأَلُكَ عَزِيمَةَ الرُّشْدِ وَأَسْأَلُكَ شُكْرَ نِعْمَتِكَ وَحُسْنَ عِبَادَتِكَ وَأَسْأَلُكَ لِسَانًا صَادِقًا وَقَلْبًا سَلِيمًا وَأَعُوذُ بِكَ مِنْ شَرِّ مَا تَعْلَمُ وَأَسْأَلُكَ مِنْ خَيْرِ مَا تَعْلَمُ وَأَسْتَغْفِرُكَ مِمَّا تَعْلَمُ إِنَّكَ أَنْتَ عَلاَّمُ الْغُيُوبِ

Allāhumma innī as-alukath thabāta fil amri wa as-aluka 'azīmatar rushdi wa as-aluka shukra ni'matika wa ḥusna 'ibādatik, wa as-aluka lisānan ṣādiqa, wa qalban salīma, wa a'ūdhu bika min sharri ma ta'lam, wa as-aluka min khayri ma ta'lam, wa astaghfiruka mimmā ta'lam, innaka anta 'allāmul ghuyūb

O Allāh, I beg You for steadfastness in religious affairs. I beg You for determination to follow the guidance. I beg You to enable me to show gratitude for Your bounties and to worship You with the best devotion. I beg You for a truthful tongue and a sound heart. I seek Your protection from the evil of all that only You are aware of. I beg You for the good that only You know. And I seek forgiveness from You for what You know (of my sins). Surely, You are the All-Knowing of the hidden. [Jāmi` At-Tirmidhī 3407]

Blameworthy Modesty

Seeking Protection from the Wrongdoers

عَلَى اللهِ تَوَكَّلْنَا رَبَّنَا لَا تَجْعَلْنَا فِتْنَةً لِلْقَوْمِ الظَّالِمِينَ وَنَجِّنَا بِرَحْمَتِكَ مِنَ الْقَوْمِ الْكَافِرِينَ

'AlAllāhi tawakkalnā rabbanā lā taj'alnā fitnatal lil qawmiẓ ẓālimīn wa najjinā bi raḥmatika minal qawmil kāfirīn

In Allāh we trust. Our Lord! Do not subject us to the persecution of the oppressive people, and deliver us by Your mercy from the disbelieving people. [Yūnus 10:85-86]

التَّفَاخُر الكِبر التَّكَبُّر

Boasting, Arrogance & Pride

RELATED EMOTIONS

Self-righteous | Egotistic | Arrogant | Harsh | Cruel | Callous | Careless | Contemptuous | Insincere | Judgemental | Obstinate | Pretentious | Self-absorbed | Self-righteous | Unkind | Vain | Vulgar

INVOKING NAMES OF ALLĀH سبحانه وتعالى

- **Al-Bāri' - The Originator**
- **Al-Jalīl - The Mighty**
- **Al-'Aẓīm - The Magnificent**
- **Al-Kabīr - The Greatest**
- **Al-Muṣawwir - The Fashioner**
- **Al-Mubdī - The Initiator**
- **Aṣ-Ṣamad - The Eternal**
- **Al-'Aliyy - The Highest**
- **Al-Jalīl - The Mighty**
- **Mālik-Ul-Mulk - Master of the Kingdom**
- **Dhul-Jalāli Wal-Ikrām - Lord of Majesty and Bounty**
- **Ar-Raqīb - The Watchful**
- **As-Samī' - The Hearer of All (The All-Hearing)**
- **Al-Baṣīr - The Seer of All (The All-Seeing)**
- **Al-Mudhil - The Humiliator**
- **Al-Laṭīf - the Benevolent**

AṢ-ṢALĀH AL-IBRĀHĪMIYYAH

ACCEPTED PRAYERS

- **Removing Arrogance**
- **Developing Humility**
- **Being Continually Mindful of Allāh** سبحانه وتعالى
- **Living and Dying Humbly**
- **Dependence on Allāh** سبحانه وتعالى **Alone**

CHAPTER 4

Boasting [Tafākhur]

Arrogance [Kibr] الكِبْرُ & Pride [Takabbur]

In a nutshell, tafākhur (boasting) and kibr (arrogance) are to willingly and consciously regard oneself superior to others in religious or worldly matters in a way which creates contempt in the heart for others. What is suggested here is unhealthy glorification of the self.

For the person practising Islām, this 'I am better than you' mentality is forbidden. Ironically - and perhaps fittingly - the person who allows arrogance into their heart usually finds that other people come to dislike him or her.

There are many forms of pride, most being subtle and creeping. It works its way into the heart and influences the character of a believer when he or she fails to adequately check their intentions.

Allāh ﷻ says, "So do not (falsely) elevate yourselves. He knows best who is (truly) righteous." [An-Najm 53:32]

The Prophet ﷺ said, "Arrogance is refusing to admit the truth and considering people inferior." [Ṣaḥīḥ Muslim 91:147, Al-Ḥākim 7367]

The Prophet ﷺ warned against arrogance: "No one will enter Paradise who has an atom's weight of arrogance in his heart" [Ṣaḥīḥ Muslim 91:147, 91:149]. Similar to this is pride (or takabbur), which is to think of oneself as being closer to perfection in attributes than others.

Boasting, Arrogance & Pride

Invoking Allāh's ﷻ Names

الْبَارِئُ	الْجَلِيلُ	الْعَظِيمُ	الْكَبِيرُ
Al-Bāri' **The Originator**	**Al-Jalīl** **The Mighty**	**Al-'Aẓīm** **The Magnificent**	**Al-Kabīr** **The Greatest**
الْمُصَوِّرُ	الْمُبْدِئُ	الصَّمَدُ	الْعَلِيُّ
Al-Muṣawwir **The Fashioner**	**Al-Mubdī** **The Initiator**	**Aṣ-Ṣamad** **The Eternal**	**Al-'Aliyy** **The Highest**
الْجَلِيلُ	مَالِكُ الْمُلْكِ	ذُو الْجَلَالِ وَالْإِكْرَام	الرَّقِيبُ
Al-Jalīl **The Mighty**	**Mālik-Ul-Mulk** **Master of the Kingdom**	**Dhul-Jalāli Wal-Ikrām** **Lord of Majesty and Bounty**	**Ar-Raqīb** **The Watchful**
السَّمِيعُ	الْبَصِيرُ	الْمُذِلُّ	اللَّطِيفُ
As-Samī' **The Hearer of All** **(The All-Hearing)**	**Al-Baṣīr** **The Seer of All** **(The All-Seeing)**	**Al-Mudhil** **The Humiliator**	**Al-Laṭīf** **The Benevolent**

Boasting, Arrogance & Pride

Contemplation and Reflection on Allāh's ﷻ Blessed Names

- You are reminded that it is Allāh ﷻ who incomparably originated, created and fashioned the inexhaustible variety in His creation of the heavens and the earth and what is between these, and it is He who enjoys all power and might, so you replace all feelings of self-righteousness, ego and arrogance with humility and gentleness.
- You understand that He is Eternal, and that this absolute uniqueness makes Him unequalled.
- You are reminded that 'might is His garment and pride is His cloak', and that whoever seeks to compete with Allāh ﷻ in might and pride, through perpetual displays of self-righteousness and egotism, Allāh Almighty ﷻ will humiliate him.
- You remember that Allāh ﷻ alone is the Truth and the Absolute Ruler and we, being His subjects, are obliged to abide by His commands. And so you stand before Him in utmost humility and devotion (in an attempt to gain true spiritual elevation).
- You remember your humble origins and the true source of all of your blessings, and that such blessings, such as wealth and status, can be diminished or suddenly removed at any time.
- You appreciate that He hears secrets as well as whispers, and witnesses and sees in such a way that nothing is remote from Him, so you do not use your senses except in His divine obedience.
- You replace arrogance, harshness and cruelty with tolerance, gentleness, and a sincere display of benevolence: kindness, grace, pleasing manners and exemplary actions.

Boasting, Arrogance & Pride

Aṣ-Ṣalāh Al-Ibrāhīmiyyah

اَللّٰهُمَّ صَلِّ عَلَى مُحَمَّدٍ وَعَلَى آلِ مُحَمَّدٍ كَمَا صَلَّيْتَ عَلَى
إِبْرَاهِيمَ وَآلِ إِبْرَاهِيمَ إِنَّكَ حَمِيدٌ مَجِيدٌ وَبَارِكْ عَلَى
مُحَمَّدٍ وَعَلَى آلِ مُحَمَّدٍ كَمَا بَارَكْتَ عَلَى إِبْرَاهِيمَ وَآلِ
إِبْرَاهِيمَ إِنَّكَ حَمِيدٌ مَجِيدٌ

Allāhumma ṣalli 'alā Muḥammadin wa 'alā āli Muḥammadin kamā ṣ allayta 'alā Ibrāhīm wa āli Ibrāhīm innaka ḥamīdum majīd, wa bārik 'alā Muḥammadin wa 'alā āli Muḥammadin kamā bārakta 'alā Ibrāhīm wa āli Ibrāhīm innaka ḥamīdum majīd

O Allāh, send peace upon Muḥammad and upon the family of Muḥammad, as You sent peace upon Ibrāhīm and the family of Ibrāhīm, and send blessings upon Muḥammad and upon the family of Muḥammad as You sent blessings upon Ibrāhīm and the family of Ibrāhīm. You are indeed praiseworthy, the most honourable. [Sunan An-Nasaī 1290]

Boasting, Arrogance & Pride

Removing Arrogance

اَللّٰهُمَّ اجْعَلْنِي شَكُورًا، وَاجْعَلْنِي صَبُورًا، وَاجْعَلْنِي فِي عَيْنَيَّ صَغِيرًا، وَفِي أَعْيُنِ النَّاسِ كَبِيرًا

Allāhummaj'alnī shakūrā, waj'alnī ṣabūrā, waj'alnī fī 'aynayya ṣaghīrā, wa fī -a'yunin nāsi kabīrā

O Allāh, make me one who is highly grateful. Make me one who is persevering. Make me small in my own eyes but great in the eyes of others. [Musnad Al-Bazzār 4439]

Developing Humility

اَللّٰهُمَّ إِنِّي أَعُوذُ بِكَ مِنْ قَلْبٍ لاَ يَخْشَعُ وَدُعَاءٍ لاَ يُسْمَعُ وَمِنْ نَفْسٍ لاَ تَشْبَعُ وَمِنْ عِلْمٍ لاَ يَنْفَعُ أَعُوذُ بِكَ مِنْ هَؤُلاَءِ الأَرْبَعِ

Allāhumma innī a'ūdhu bika min qalbin lā yakhsha', wa du'ā'in lā yusma', wa min nafsin lā tashba', wa min 'ilmin lā yanfa', a'ūdhu bika min hā'ulā-il-arba'

O Allāh, I seek refuge in You from a heart that does not humble itself, and from a supplication that is not heard, and from a soul that is never satisfied, and from knowledge that does not benefit, I seek refuge in You from these four" [Jāmi' At-Tirmidhī 3482]

Boasting, Arrogance & Pride

Being Continually Mindful of Allāh ﷻ

رَبِّ اجْعَلْنِي لَكَ شَكَّارًا لَكَ ذَكَّارًا لَكَ رَهَّابًا لَكَ مِطْوَاعًا
لَكَ مُخْبِتًا إِلَيْكَ أَوَّاهًا مُنِيبًا

Rabbij`alnī laka shakkārā, laka dhakkārā, laka rahhābā, laka miṭwā`ā, laka mukhbitan ilayka awwāham munībā

My Lord, make me ever-grateful to You, ever-remembering of You, ever-fearful of You, ever-obedient to You, ever-humble to You, oft-turning and returning to You. [Jāmi` At-Tirmidhī 3551]

Living and Dying Humbly

اَللّٰهُمَّ أَحْيِنِي مِسْكِينًا وَأَمِتْنِي مِسْكِينًا وَاحْشُرْنِي فِي
زُمْرَةِ الْمَسَاكِينِ يَوْمَ الْقِيَامَةِ

Allāhumma aḥyinī miskīnā wa amitnī miskīnā waḥshurnī fī zumratil masākīni yawmal qiyāmah

O Allāh, give me life of a humble person and death of a humble person, and raise me on the Day of Judgement among humble persons. [Jāmi` At-Tirmidhī 2352]

Boasting, Arrogance & Pride

Dependence on Allāh ﷻ Alone

اَللّٰهُمَّ لَكَ أَسْلَمْتُ، وَبِكَ آمَنْتُ، وَعَلَيْكَ تَوَكَّلْتُ، وَإِلَيْكَ أَنَبْتُ، وَبِكَ خَاصَمْتُ، وَإِلَيْكَ حَاكَمْتُ، فَاغْفِرْ لِي مَا قَدَّمْتُ وَمَا أَخَّرْتُ، وَأَسْرَرْتُ وَأَعْلَنْتُ، أَنْتَ إِلَهِي لاَ إِلَهَ لِي غَيْرُكَ

Allāhumma laka aslamtu wa bika āmantu wa 'alayka tawakkaltu wa ilayka anabtu wa bika khāṣamtu wa ilayka ḥākamtu faghfirlī mā qaddamtu wa mā akhkhartu wa asrartu wa a'lantu, anta ilāhī lā ilāha lī ghayruk

O Allāh! I surrender myself to You, and I believe in You and I depend upon You, and I repent to You and with You (and Your evidence) I stand against my opponents, and to you I leave the judgement (for those who refuse my message). O Allāh! Forgive me my sins that I did in the past or will do in the future, and also the sins I did in secret or in public. You are my only God (Whom I worship) and there is no other God for me (i.e. I worship none but You). [Ṣaḥīḥ Al-Bukhārī 7385]

كَرَاهِيَةُ الإِسْتِنْكَار

Displeasure with Blame or Disapproval

RELATED EMOTIONS

Uneasy | Resentful | Brooding | Frustrated | Offended | Annoyed
Agitated | Annoyed | Anxious | Argumentative | Deceitful
Depressed | Disappointed | Distressed | Grudging | Obstinate
Resentful | Reluctant | Uneasy | Wound up

INVOKING NAMES OF ALLĀH

- **Al-Ḥamīd - the Praiseworthy**
- **Al-Mu'izz - the Honourer**
- **Al-Khāfiḍ - the Abaser**
- **Ar-Rāfi' - the Exalter**
- **Al-Ḥakīm - the All-Wise**
- **Al-Ḥaqq - The Truth**

AṢ-ṢALĀH AL-IBRĀHĪMIYYAH

ACCEPTED PRAYERS

- **Avoiding Allāh's Displeasure**
- **Placing Your Trust in Allāh Alone**
- **Seeking Conviction in the Truth**
- **Seeking the Truth and Guidance to Avoid Falsehood**
- **Seeking Wisdom and Honour**
- **Seeking His Pleasure**

CHAPTER 5

Displeasure with Blame or Disapproval

[Karāhiyat al-Istinkār] كَرَاهِيَةُ الإِسْتِنْكَار

This particular undesirable behaviour is so extremely efficient in steering a person toward a love of this world that it can come to form a considerable barrier between a person and the station of iḥsān (excellence in worship).

Being uneasy at the thought of blame or criticism, and searching for praise from Allāh's ﷻ creation, one forgets that true praise is for the Creator and the most deserving, Allāh ﷻ, the 'Ḥamīd'. This crucial understanding slips away, and takes with it the integrity of the individual who so panders to his or her own whims and yearns for the approval of others.

Displeasure with Blame or Disapproval

Invoking Allāh's ﷻ Names

الْحَمِيدُ

Al-Ḥamīd
The Praiseworthy

الْمُعِزُّ

Al-Mu'izz
The Honourer

الْخَافِضُ

Al-Khāfiḍ
The Abaser

الرَّافِعُ

Ar-Rāfi'
The Exalter

الْحَكِيمُ

Al-Ḥakīm
The All-Wise

الْحَقُّ

Al-Ḥaqq
The Truth

Displeasure with Blame or Disapproval

Contemplation and Reflection on Allāh's ﷻ Blessed Names

- You realise that though you may hold praiseworthy attributes, you are not free from blame or deficiency, unlike Allāh ﷻ who is absolutely free from fault.
- You understand that if your actions are beloved in the eyes of Allāh ﷻ, then the criticism of people should not make you feel uneasy or frustrated.
- You remind yourself of the One who gives honour (exalts) to whomever He wills and removes it from whomever He wills (abases).
- You are willing to defend and uphold the truth no matter how unpopular it may be (causing annoyance or offence), realising that truth has the power to penetrate the hearts of people.
- Your wisdom drives you to place trust in Allāh ﷻ alone, being concerned with avoiding His displeasure by seeking refuge in His pleasure and approval.
- You remind yourself that deeds cannot be divorced from their intentions, and that the depth of wisdom that rests with Allāh ﷻ is found in the ḥadīth 'all actions are governed by the intention'. This leads you to think good of people in the first instance.
- You spend your time in the more profitable activities: pleasing people without directly seeking their favour.

Displeasure with Blame or Disapproval

Aṣ-Ṣalāh Al-Ibrāhīmiyyah

اَللّٰهُمَّ صَلِّ عَلَى مُحَمَّدٍ وَعَلَى آلِ مُحَمَّدٍ كَمَا صَلَّيْتَ عَلَى
إِبْرَاهِيمَ وَآلِ إِبْرَاهِيمَ إِنَّكَ حَمِيدٌ مَجِيدٌ وَبَارِكْ عَلَى
مُحَمَّدٍ وَعَلَى آلِ مُحَمَّدٍ كَمَا بَارَكْتَ عَلَى إِبْرَاهِيمَ وَآلِ
إِبْرَاهِيمَ إِنَّكَ حَمِيدٌ مَجِيدٌ

Allāhumma ṣalli 'alā Muḥammadin wa 'alā āli Muḥammadin kamā ṣ allayta 'alā Ibrāhīm wa āli Ibrāhīm innaka ḥamīdum majīd, wa bārik 'alā Muḥammadin wa 'alā āli Muḥammadin kamā bārakta 'alā Ibrāhīm wa āli Ibrāhīm innaka ḥamīdum majīd

O Allāh, send peace upon Muḥammad and upon the family of Muḥammad, as You sent peace upon Ibrāhīm and the family of Ibrāhīm, and send blessings upon Muḥammad and upon the family of Muḥammad as You sent blessings upon Ibrāhīm and the family of Ibrāhīm. You are indeed praiseworthy, the most honourable. [Sunan An-Nasaī 1290]

Displeasure with Blame or Disapproval

Avoiding Allāh's ﷻ Displeasure

اَللّٰهُمَّ إِنِّي أَعُوذُ بِكَ مِنْ زَوَالِ نِعْمَتِكَ وَتَحَوُّلِ
عَافِيَتِكَ وَفُجَاءَةِ نِقْمَتِكَ وَجَمِيعِ سَخَطِكَ

Allāhumma innī a'ūdhu bika min zawāl ni'matika wa taḥawwuli 'āfiyatika wa fujā-ati niqmatika wa jamī' sakhatik

O Allāh, I seek refuge in You from the withdrawal of Your blessing and the change of Your protection (of me) and from Your sudden wrath, and from every displeasure of Yours. [Ṣaḥīḥ Muslim 2739]

Placing Trust in Allāh ﷻ Alone

حَسْبِيَ اللّٰهُ لَآ إِلَٰهَ إِلَّا هُوَ، عَلَيْهِ تَوَكَّلْتُ، وَهُوَ رَبُّ الْعَرْشِ الْعَظِيمِ

Ḥasbiy Allāhu lā ilāha illā hū, 'alayhi tawakkaltu wa huwa rabbul 'arshil 'aẓīm

Allāh is sufficient for me. There is none worthy of worship but Him. I have placed my trust in Him, and He is the lord of the Majestic Throne. [Sunan Abī Dawūd 5081]

Displeasure with Blame or Disapproval

Seeking Conviction in the Truth

اَللّٰهُمَّ إِنِّي أَعُوذُ بِكَ مِنَ الشَّكِّ فِي الْحَقِّ بَعْدَ الْيَقِينِ ، وَأَعُوذُ بِكَ مِنَ الشَّيْطَانِ الرَّجِيمِ ، وَأَعُوذُ بِكَ مِنْ شَرِّ يَوْمِ الدِّينِ

Allāhumma innī a'ūdhu bika minash shakki fil ḥaqqi ba'dal yaqīn, wa a'ūdhu bika minash Shayṭānir rajīm, wa a'ūdhu bika min sharri yawmid dīn

O Allāh, I seek Your protection from harbouring any doubts about the Truth after attaining firm conviction. I seek Your protection against the cursed Shayṭān. I seek Your protection from the harm of the Day of Judgement. [Abū Nu'aym Al-Aṣbahānī in Tārīkh Aṣbahān v.2 pg.170/219/276]

Seeking the Truth and Guidance to Avoid Falsehood

اَللّٰهُمَّ أَرِنَا الْحَقَّ حَقًّا وَارْزُقْنَا اتِّبَاعَهُ، وَأَرِنَا الْبَاطِلَ بَاطِلًا وَوَفِّقْنَا لِاجْتِنَابِهِ

Allāhumma arinal ḥaqqa ḥaqqā warzuqnattibā'ah wa arinal bāṭila bāṭilā wa waffiqnā lijtinābih

O Allāh, show me the truth as truth and guide me to follow it. Show me the false as false and guide me to avoid it. [Tafsīr Ibn Kathīr 1:571 under verse 2:213]

Displeasure with Blame or Disapproval

Seeking Wisdom and Honour

رَبِّ هَبْ لِي حُكْمًا وَأَلْحِقْنِي بِالصَّالِحِينَ، وَاجْعَل لِّي لِسَانَ صِدْقٍ فِي الْآخِرِينَ، وَاجْعَلْنِي مِن وَرَثَةِ جَنَّةِ النَّعِيمِ

Rabbi hab lī ḥukman wa alhiqnī biṣṣāliḥīn, waj'al lī lisāna ṣidqin fil ākhirīn, waj'alnī min warathati jannatin na'īm

My Lord! Grant me wisdom, and join me with the righteous. Bless me with honourable mention among later generations. Make me one of those awarded the Garden of Bliss. [Ash-Shu'arā 26: 83-85]

Seeking His Pleasure

اَللّٰهُمَّ أَعُوذُ بِرِضَاكَ مِنْ سَخَطِكَ وَبِمُعَافَاتِكَ مِنْ عُقُوبَتِكَ وَأَعُوذُ بِكَ مِنْكَ لاَ أُحْصِي ثَنَاءً عَلَيْكَ أَنْتَ كَمَا أَثْنَيْتَ عَلَى نَفْسِكَ

Allāhumma innī a'ūdhu bika bi riḍāka min sakhatik wa bi mu'āfātika min 'uqūbatik wa a'ūdhu bika minka la uḥṣī thanā-an 'alayka anta kamā athnayta 'alā nafsik

O Allāh, I seek refuge in Your pleasure from Your anger and in Your forgiveness from Your punishment, and I seek refuge in You from You. I cannot fully praise You, for You are as You have praised Yourself. [Ṣaḥīḥ Muslim 486]

كَرَاهِيَةُ القَدَر

Displeasure with the Divine Decree

RELATED EMOTIONS

Disappointed | Frustrated | Impatient | Bitter | Annoyed | Hostile
Agitated | Anxious | Arrogant | Cynical | Depressed | Distressed
Doubtful | Fearful | Furious | Grudging | Ignorant | Insecure
Overwhelmed | Reluctant | Resentful | Uneasy | Cowardly

INVOKING NAMES OF ALLĀH ﷾

- **Al-Qahhār - The Ever-Dominating**
- **Al-Ḥakam - The Judge**
- **An-Nāfi' - The Benefactor**
- **Al-Qābiḍ - The Withholder**
- **Al-Bāsiṭ - The Extender**
- **Al-Ḥakīm - The All-Wise**
- **Al-Ḥaqq - The Truth**
- **Al-'Alīm - The All-Knowing**
- **Al-'Adl - The Just**
- **Aṣ-Ṣabūr - The Patient**

AṢ-ṢALĀH AL-IBRĀHĪMIYYAH

ACCEPTED PRAYERS

- **Seeking Trust in Allāh ﷾**
- **Seeking Increasing Love for Allāh ﷾**
- **Seeking Pleasure with Allāh's ﷾ Decree**
- **Achieving True Conviction**
- **Seeking Contentment with Fate**
- **Seeking Satisfaction of the Soul**

CHAPTER 6

Displeasure with the Divine Decree

[Karāhiyat al-Qadr] كَرَاهِيَةُ القَدر

It has been said that there is a quality in people of which most are unaware, yet it consumes good deeds: when one is displeased with what Allāh ﷻ has decreed (i.e. Allāh's ﷻ divine decree or qadr), resulting in plunging into heedlessness (ghaflah). This is usually because one holds an attitude that stems from a denial of His All-Powerful nature and that Allāh ﷻ alone decrees all things. Put simply, this can also be referred to as ingratitude.

Allāh ﷻ says, "Perhaps you dislike something which is good for you and like something which is bad for you. Allāh knows and you do not know." [Al-Baqarah 2:216]

There are four possible states in which the human being can live, according to revealed sources. A person is either receiving blessings (ni'mah) or tribulations (balā') from Allāh ﷻ, or is either living in obedience (ṭā'ah) to Allāh ﷻ or in disobedience (ma'ṣiyah). Each condition is purposefully exacted upon the individual, as part of the test of life from Allāh ﷻ, and is designed to elicit a response.

Displeasure with the Divine Decree

Invoking Allāh's ﷻ Names

الْقَهَّارُ
Al-Qahhār
The Ever-Dominating

الْحَكَمُ
Al-Ḥakam
The Judge

النَّافِعُ
An-Nāfi'
The Benefactor

الْقَابِضُ
Al-Qābiḍ
The Withholder

الْبَاسِطُ
Al-Bāsiṭ
The Extender

الْحَكِيمُ
Al-Ḥakīm
The All-Wise

الْحَقُّ
Al-Ḥaqq
The Truth

الْعَلِيمُ
Al-'Alīm
The All-Knowing

الْعَدْلُ
Al-'Adl
The Just

الصَّبُورُ
Aṣ-Ṣabūr
The Patient

Displeasure with the Divine Decree

Contemplation and Reflection on Allāh's ﷻ Blessed Names

- You realise that it is Allāh ﷻ that has all-encompassing knowledge, as well as absolute control over you and all that is around you, and that His mastery over the heavens and the earth and what is between these is an undeniable reality.
- You come to realise that Allāh ﷻ grants provisions to His creatures in a certain measure, withholding as well as extending sustenance out of His infinite wisdom and will.
- You learn to understand that neither regret nor bitterness will cancel what is decreed, and if it is not decreed, there is no sense worrying about it.
- You therefore appreciate that what is decreed comes to pass (is made manifest), and as a result you act well in seeking your livelihood, with a tranquil spirit, a calm soul, and a heart free from disruption.
- You understand that the perfection of faith consists in not taking objection to Him, but rather in knowing that all that occurs is via Allāh's ﷻ will. All things, you observe, are clearly guided by and subservient to Him, in the best order and direction, according to the highest standpoint of justice and compassion.
- You remind yourself that the best way for your soul and spirit is to accept His plan, His just decree, and all of His actions, whether they correspond to your will or not.
- You understand that were He not to do what He did, something else would have happened which would be much more harmful than what did happen.
- You understand that this is the way Allāh ﷻ is just, and faith in Him cuts short objections and resistance, both outward and inward.
- You develop an inherent trust in the Creator alone (called 'tawakkul'), which means that you 'act in accordance with' Allāh's ﷻ plan, i.e. you adopt the principles and commands of the sharī'ah, and place trust in Allāh ﷻ.
- You are content and at ease with the decree of Allāh ﷻ; you do not show frustration or annoyance.
- You remind yourself that Allāh's ﷻ decree is ultimately final and irrevocable, so you obey His commands in order to please Him.

Displeasure with the Divine Decree

Aṣ-Ṣalāh Al-Ibrāhīmiyyah

اَللّٰهُمَّ صَلِّ عَلَى مُحَمَّدٍ وَعَلَى آلِ مُحَمَّدٍ كَمَا صَلَّيْتَ عَلَى
إِبْرَاهِيمَ وَآلِ إِبْرَاهِيمَ إِنَّكَ حَمِيدٌ مَجِيدٌ وَبَارِكْ عَلَى
مُحَمَّدٍ وَعَلَى آلِ مُحَمَّدٍ كَمَا بَارَكْتَ عَلَى إِبْرَاهِيمَ وَآلِ
إِبْرَاهِيمَ إِنَّكَ حَمِيدٌ مَجِيدٌ

Allāhumma ṣalli 'alā Muḥammadin wa 'alā āli Muḥammadin kamā ṣ allayta 'alā Ibrāhīm wa āli Ibrāhīm innaka ḥamīdum majīd, wa bārik 'alā Muḥammadin wa 'alā āli Muḥammadin kamā bārakta 'alā Ibrāhīm wa āli Ibrāhīm innaka ḥamīdum majīd

O Allāh, send peace upon Muḥammad and upon the family of Muḥammad, as You sent peace upon Ibrāhīm and the family of Ibrāhīm, and send blessings upon Muḥammad and upon the family of Muḥammad as You sent blessings upon Ibrāhīm and the family of Ibrāhīm. You are indeed praiseworthy, the most honourable. [Sunan An-Nasaī 1290]

Displeasure with the Divine Decree

Seeking Trust in Allāh ﷻ

رَّبَّنَا عَلَيْكَ تَوَكَّلْنَا وَإِلَيْكَ أَنَبْنَا وَإِلَيْكَ ٱلْمَصِيرُ

Rabbanā 'alayka tawakkalnā wa ilayka anabnā wa ilaykal maṣīr

Our Lord! In You we trust. And to You we (always) turn. And to You is the final return. [Al-Mumtaḥinah 60:4]

Seeking Increasing Love for Allāh ﷻ

اَللّٰهُمَّ اجْعَلْ حُبَّكَ أَحَبَّ إِلَيَّ مِنْ نَفْسِي وَأَهْلِي وَمِنَ الْمَاءِ الْبَارِدِ

Allāhummaj'al ḥubbaka aḥabba ilayya min nafsī wa ahlī wa minal mā-il bārid

O Allāh, make Your love dearer to me than myself, my family, and cold water. [Jāmi' At-Tirmidhī 3490]

Seeking Pleasure with Allāh's ﷻ Decree

اَللّٰهُمَّ وَأَسْأَلُكَ نَعِيمًا لاَ يَنْفَدُ وَأَسْأَلُكَ قُرَّةَ عَيْنٍ لاَ تَنْقَطِعُ وَأَسْأَلُكَ الرِّضَاءَ
بَعْدَ الْقَضَاءِ وَأَسْأَلُكَ بَرْدَ الْعَيْشِ بَعْدَ الْمَوْتِ

Allāhumma wa as-aluka na'īman la yanfad wa as-aluka qurrata 'aynin la tanqaṭi' wa as-alukar riḍā ba'dal qaḍ'ā, wa as'aluka bardal 'ayshi ba'dal mawt

O Allāh I ask You for everlasting delight and joy that will never cease. I ask You to make me pleased with that which You have decreed and for an easy life after death. [Sunan An-Nasaī 1305]

Displeasure with the Divine Decree

Achieving True Conviction

اَللّٰهُمَّ إِنِّي أَسْأَلُكَ إِيمَانًا يُباشِرُ قَلْبِي، ويَقِينًا صادِقًا حَتّى أَعْلَمَ أَنَّهُ لا يُصِيبُنِي إِلّا ما كَتَبْتَ لِي، ورَضِّنِي بِما قَسَمْتَ لِي

Allāhumma innī as-aluka īmānan yubāshiru qalbī wa yaqīnan ṣādiqan ḥattā a'lama annahū lā yuṣībunī illā mā katabta lī wa raḍḍinī bimā qasamta lī

O Allāh, I beg You for the faith that settles deep in my heart, a true conviction so that I understand that nothing can afflict me beyond what You have decreed for me, and satisfaction with the provision which You have apportioned for me. [Aṭ-Ṭabarānī in Al-Mu'jam Al-Awṣaṭ 5974]

Seeking Contentment with Fate

اَللّٰهُمَّ رَضِّنِي بِقَضَائِكَ، وَبَارِكْ لِي فِي قَدَرِكَ، حَتَّى لَا أُحِبَّ تَعْجِيلَ مَا أَخَّرْتَ وَلَا تَأْخِيرَ مَا عَجَّلْتَ

Allāhumma raḍḍinī bi qaḍā-ika wa bārik lī fī qadarika ḥattā lā uḥibba ta'jīla ma akhkharta wa lā ta-khīra mā 'ajjalta

O Allāh, make me happy with Your Will, and bless me in your decree so that I do not want to hasten what you delayed or to delay what you hastened. [Aṭ-Ṭabarānī in Ad-Du'ā 410]

Displeasure with the Divine Decree

Seeking Satisfaction of the Soul

اَللّٰهُمَّ إِنِّي أَسْأَلُكَ نَفْسًا بِكَ مُطْمَئِنَّةً، تُؤْمِنُ بِلِقَائِكَ، وَتَرْضَى بِقَضَائِكَ، وَتَقْنَعُ بِعَطَائِكَ

Allāhumma innī as-aluka nafsan bika muṭma-innah, tu-minu biliqā-ik, wa tarḍā bi qaḍā-ik, wa taqna'u bi 'aṭā-ik

O Allāh, I beg of You a soul satisfied with You, one that believes in meeting with You, is pleased with Your decree, and is content with Your gifts. [Al-Mu'jam Al-Kabīr Aṭ-Ṭabarānī 7490]

الحَسَد

Envy

RELATED EMOTIONS

Frustrated | Bitter | Annoyed | Malicious | Covetous | Resentful
Depressed | Agitated | Distressed | Insecure | Judgemental
Obstinate | Resentful | Vindictive | Grudging | Hostile

INVOKING NAMES OF ALLĀH

- **Al-Barr - The Source of Good**
- **As-Salām - The Source of Peace**
- **Ar-Raqīb - The Watchful**
- **Al-Wāsi' - The All-Comprehending**
- **Al-Ḥafīẓ - The Preserver**
- **Al-Wadūd - The Most Loving**

AṢ-ṢALĀH AL-IBRĀHĪMIYYAH

ACCEPTED PRAYERS

- **Seeking Protection from every Devil & the Envious Eye**
- **Seeking Protection from the Temptations of Devils**
- **Seeking Protection from Cunning Friends**
- **Seeking Protection from Enemies**
- **Seeking Protection from Envy**
- **Seeking Protection from Evil Whisperings**
- **Avoiding Affliction from Calamities**
- **Seeking Protection as Morning Comes**
- **Seeking Reliance on Allāh Alone**
- **Seeking Refuge from Being Envious**

CHAPTER 7

Envy [Ḥasad] الحسد

Envy is when you identify a blessing (or perceived blessing) bestowed on someone else, and then desire, through some trick or deception, that the blessing be extinguished. It has 3 stages:

1. Envy as a human quality: in this degree of envy, man is excused and is not at fault
2. Acting according to the demands of envy: in this degree, man is a sinner
3. Opposing the demands of envy: in this degree, man deserves praise and will be rewarded

The Qur'ān therefore teaches us to seek refuge in Allāh ﷻ: "Say (O Prophet), 'I seek refuge in the Lord of the daybreak...and from the evil of an envier when they envy.'" [Al-Falaq 113: 1&5]

The Prophet ﷺ said, "Resort to secrecy for the fulfilment and success of your needs for, verily, everyone who has a blessing is envied" [Al-Mu'jam Aṣ-Ṣaghīr Aṭ-Ṭabrānī 1186, Al-Mu'jam Al-Kabīr Aṭ-Ṭabrānī 183, Al-Bayhaqī in Shu'ab Al-Īmān 6228]; that is to say that someone of means will invariably have someone who envies him for what he possesses.

Envy can be caused by a number of things: holding animosity towards others (enmity or 'adāwah, when someone is doing better than oneself), arrogance, pride (takabbur), deceit (gharūr), poor self-worth or low-esteem (ta'azzu), an inferiority complex, vanity, love for leadership and status, extreme greed for wealth, material gain, money or possessions.

Envy

Invoking Allāh's ﷻ Names

الْبَرُّ

Al-Barr
The Source of Good

السَّلَامُ

As-Salām
The Source of Peace

الرَّقِيبُ

Ar-Raqīb
The Watchful

الْوَاسِعُ

Al-Wāsiʿ
The All-Comprehending

الْحَفِيظُ

Al-Ḥafīẓ
The Preserver

الْوَدُودُ

Al-Wadūd
The Most Loving

Envy

Contemplation and Reflection on Allāh's ﷻ Blessed Names

- You understand that every servant whose heart is free from resentment, bitterness and evil intent, and whose limbs are unblemished by sins and forbidden actions (i.e. a doer of good), will be one who comes to Allāh ﷻ with a peaceful heart.
- You appreciate that the true prestige and superiority of man consists in his knowledge and character, and not in material wealth.
- You realise that Allāh ﷻ observes you and sees you in every situation, so your attention is directed to your Lord and your heart.
- You understand that Satan is your enemy and that he takes every opportunity to prompt you to deceptions and disobedience.
- You place trust in Allāh's ﷻ constant protection, that overpowers evil and wards off the evil thoughts prompted by Satan.
- Indeed, you act contrary to your impulse of envy by showing kindness to a person when it seems appealing to resent or harm him (there is no hypocrisy in this); this inclines that person towards you (when you show them good).

Envy

Aṣ-Ṣalāh Al-Ibrāhīmiyyah

اَللّٰهُمَّ صَلِّ عَلَى مُحَمَّدٍ وَعَلَى آلِ مُحَمَّدٍ كَمَا صَلَّيْتَ عَلَى
إِبْرَاهِيمَ وَآلِ إِبْرَاهِيمَ إِنَّكَ حَمِيدٌ مَجِيدٌ وَبَارِكْ عَلَى
مُحَمَّدٍ وَعَلَى آلِ مُحَمَّدٍ كَمَا بَارَكْتَ عَلَى إِبْرَاهِيمَ وَآلِ
إِبْرَاهِيمَ إِنَّكَ حَمِيدٌ مَجِيدٌ

Allāhumma ṣalli 'alā Muḥammadin wa 'alā āli Muḥammadin kamā ṣ allayta 'alā Ibrāhīm wa āli Ibrāhīm innaka ḥamīdum majīd, wa bārik 'alā Muḥammadin wa 'alā āli Muḥammadin kamā bārakta 'alā Ibrāhīm wa āli Ibrāhīm innaka ḥamīdum majīd

O Allāh, send peace upon Muḥammad and upon the family of Muḥammad, as You sent peace upon Ibrāhīm and the family of Ibrāhīm, and send blessings upon Muḥammad and upon the family of Muḥammad as You sent blessings upon Ibrāhīm and the family of Ibrāhīm. You are indeed praiseworthy, the most honourable. [Sunan An-Nasaī 1290]

Envy

Seeking Protection from every Devil and the Envious Eye

أَعُوذُ بِكَلِمَاتِ اللهِ التَّامَّةِ مِنْ كُلِّ شَيْطَانٍ وَهَامَّةٍ
وَمِنْ كُلِّ عَيْنٍ لَامَّةٍ

A'ūdhu bi kalimātillāhit tāmmati min kulli Shayṭāniw wa hāmmah wa min kulli 'aynil lāmmah

I seek protection in the perfect words of Allāh from every devil and beast and from every envious blameworthy eye. [Ṣaḥīḥ Al-Bukhārī 3371]

Seeking Protection from the Temptations of Devils

رَبِّ أَعُوذُ بِكَ مِنْ هَمَزَاتِ ٱلشَّيَٰطِينِ وَأَعُوذُ بِكَ رَبِّ أَن يَحْضُرُونِ

Rabbi a'ūdhu bika min hamazātish shayāṭini wa a'ūdhu bika rabbi ay yaḥḍurūn

My Lord! I seek refuge in You from the temptations of the devils. And I seek refuge in You, my Lord, that they (even) come near me. [Al-Mu'minūn 23: 97-98]

Seeking Protection from Cunning Friends

اَللّٰهُمَّ إِنِّي أَعُوذُ بِكَ مِنْ خَلِيلٍ مَاكِرٍ عَيْنُهُ تَرَانِي ، وَقَلْبُهُ تَرْعَانِي ، إِنْ رَأَى
حَسَنَةً دَفَنَهَا ، وَإِذَا رَأَى سَيِّئَةً أَذَاعَهَا

Allāhumma innī a'ūdhu bika khalīlim mākir, 'aynuhu tarānī, wa qalbuhū tar'ānī, in ra-ā ḥasanatan dafanahā wa idhā ra-ā sayyi-atan adhā'ahā.

O Allāh, I seek Your protection from a cunning friend whose eyes see me yet his heart keeps guard over me: if he sees any good, he conceals it and if he sees any bad, he announces it. [Aṭ-Ṭabarānī in Ad-Du'ā 1339]

Envy

Seeking Protection from Enemies

اَللّٰهُمَّ احْفَظْنِي بِالْإِسْلَامِ قَائِمًا، وَاحْفَظْنِي بِالْإِسْلَامِ قَاعِدًا، وَاحْفَظْنِي بِالْإِسْلَامِ رَاقِدًا، وَلَا تُشْمِتْ بِي عَدُوًّا حَاسِدًا، وَاللّٰهُمَّ إِنِّي أَسْأَلُكَ مِنْ كُلِّ خَيْرٍ خَزَائِنُهُ بِيَدِكَ، وَأَعُوذُ بِكَ مِنْ كُلِّ شَرٍّ خَزَائِنُهُ بِيَدِكَ

Allāhummahfaẓnī bil Islāmi qā-imā, wahfaẓnī bil Islāmi qā-'idā, wahfaẓnī bil Islāmi rāqidā, wa lā tushmit bī 'aduwwan ḥāsida, wa Allāhumma innī as-aluka min kulli khayrin khazā-inuhū biyadik, wa a'ūdhu bika min kulli sharrin khazā-inuhū biyadik

O Allāh, protect me with Islām standing, protect me with Islām sitting, protect me with Islām lying down. Let not my enemies gloat over me in envy. O Allāh, I ask you for every good that is stored in your hand, and I seek refuge in you from every evil that is stored in your hand. [Al-Ḥākim 1924]

Seeking Protection from Envy

قُلْ أَعُوذُ بِرَبِّ ٱلْفَلَقِ ۝ مِن شَرِّ مَا خَلَقَ ۝ وَمِن شَرِّ غَاسِقٍ إِذَا وَقَبَ ۝ وَمِن شَرِّ ٱلنَّفَّٰثَٰتِ فِى ٱلْعُقَدِ ۝ وَمِن شَرِّ حَاسِدٍ إِذَا حَسَدَ ۝

Qul a-'udhu bi rabbil falaq. Min sharri mā khalaq. Wa min sharri ghāsiqin idhā waqab. Wa min sharrin naffāthāti fil 'uqad. Wa min sharri ḥāsidin idhā ḥasad

Say, (O Prophet,) "I seek refuge in the Lord of the daybreak. from the evil of whatever He has created, and from the evil of the night when it grows dark, and from the evil of those (witches casting spells by) blowing onto knots, and from the evil of an envier when they envy." [Al-Falaq 113:1-5]

Envy

Seeking Protection from Evil Whisperings

قُلۡ أَعُوذُ بِرَبِّ ٱلنَّاسِ ۝ مَلِكِ ٱلنَّاسِ ۝ إِلَٰهِ ٱلنَّاسِ ۝ مِن شَرِّ ٱلۡوَسۡوَاسِ ٱلۡخَنَّاسِ ۝ ٱلَّذِى يُوَسۡوِسُ فِى صُدُورِ ٱلنَّاسِ ۝ مِنَ ٱلۡجِنَّةِ وَٱلنَّاسِ ۝

Qul a-'udhu bi rabbin nās. Malikin nās. Ilāhin nās. Min sharril waswāsil khannās. Alladhī yuwaswisu fī ṣudūrin nās. Minal jinnati wan nās

Say, (O Prophet,) "I seek refuge in the Lord of humankind, the Master of humankind, the God of humankind, from the evil of the lurking whisperer– who whispers into the hearts of humankind– from among jinn and humankind." [An-Nās 114:1-6]

Avoiding Affliction from Calamities

بِسْمِ اللهِ الَّذِي لَا يَضُرُّ مَعَ اسْمِهِ شَيْءٌ فِي الْأَرْضِ وَلَا فِي السَّمَاءِ وَهُوَ السَّمِيعُ الْعَلِيمُ

Bismillāhilladhī lā yaḍurru ma'asmihī shay-un fil arḍi wa lā fis samā-i wa huwas samī'-'ul 'alīm

In the Name of Allāh, with Whose name nothing on the earth or in the heaven can cause harm, and He is the All-Hearing, the All-Knowing. [Sunan Abī Dawūd 5088]

Envy

Seeking Protection as Morning Comes

اَللّٰهُمَّ إِنِّي أَصْبَحْتُ مِنْكَ فِي نِعْمَةٍ وَعَافِيَةٍ وَسِتْرٍ، فَأَتِمَّ عَلَيَّ نِعْمَتَكَ وَعَافِيَتَكَ وَسِتْرَكَ فِي الدُّنْيَا وَالْآخِرَةِ

Allāhumma innī aṣbaḥtu minka fī ni'matin wa 'āfiyatin wa sitr, fa atimma 'alayya ni'mataka wa 'āfiyataka wa sitraka fid dunyā wal ākhīrah

O Allāh! As morning comes upon me, I dwell in (your) favour, well-being, and protection; so complete Your favour upon me, Your well-being, and Your protection, in this world and the next. [Ibn As-Sunnī in 'Amal Al-Yawm wa Al-Laylah 55]

Seeking Reliance on Allāh ﷻ Alone

اَللّٰهُمَّ لَا يَأْتِي بِالْحَسَنَاتِ إِلَّا أَنْتَ، وَلَا يَدْفَعُ السَّيِّئَاتِ إِلَّا أَنْتَ، وَلَا حَوْلَ وَلَا قُوَّةَ إِلَّا بِكَ

Allāhumma lā ya-tī bil ḥasanāti illā anta wa lā yadfa'us sayyi-āti illa anta wa lā ḥawla wa lā quwwata illā bik

O Allāh, no one brings good things but You, and no one takes away evil things but You. there is no might and no power save You. [Al-Bayhaqī in Ad-Da'awāt Al-Kabīr 568]

Envy

Seeking Refuge from Being Envious

أَعُوذُ بِاللهِ مِنْ طَمَعٍ يَهْدِي إِلَى طَبْعٍ، وَمِنْ طَمَعٍ فِي غَيْرِ مَطْمَعٍ، وَمِنْ طَمَعٍ حَيْثُ لَا مَطْمَعَ

A'ūdhu billāhi min ṭama'in yahdī ilā ṭab'in, wa min ṭama'in fī ghayri maṭma'in, wa min ṭama'in ḥaythu lā maṭma'

I take refuge with Allāh from envy which leads to disgrace, and from coveting a thing which is not to be coveted, and from coveting a thing for which there is no hope (in attaining). [Musnad Aḥmad 22128]

الإسْرَاف

Extravagance

RELATED EMOTIONS

Addicted | Forgetful | Inadequate | Insecure | Immoderate
Depressed | Indifferent | Excessive | Oblivious

INVOKING NAMES OF ALLĀH

- **Al-Baṣīr - The Seer of All (The All-Seeing)**
- **Ar-Raqīb - The All Observant**
- **Al-Muhaymin - The Guardian**
- **Al-Khāfiḍ - The Abaser**
- **Al-Mu'izz - The Bestower of Honour**
- **Al-Karīm - The Most Generous**

AṢ-ṢALĀH AL-IBRĀHĪMIYYAH

ACCEPTED PRAYERS

- **Seeking Contentment with Provisions**
- **Seeking Forgiveness for Extravagance**
- **Seeking Protection from Affluence that Leads to Extravagance**
- **Seeking Protection from Wealth that leads to Punishment**
- **Seeking Moderation in Times of Wealth**
- **Placing Trust in Allāh Alone**

CHAPTER 8
Extravagance [Isrāf] الإسْرَاف

Extravagance is demonstrated through a lack of restraint in spending money or using resources, and is also referred to as wastefulness (tabdhir) or lavishness. It is when one, for instance, oversteps the mark by spending or consuming more than is necessary or reasonable.

Allāh ﷻ has created a natural balance and harmony. He ﷻ says, "As for the sky, He raised it (high), and set the balance (of justice) so that you do not defraud the scales." [Ar-Raḥmān 55 :7-8]

The Prophet ﷺ said, "By Allāh, it is not poverty that I fear for you, rather what I fear for you is that worldly riches may be given to you as they were given to those who came before you, and you will compete for them with one another as they competed with one another, and it will destroy you as it destroyed them." [Ṣaḥīḥ Al-Bukhārī 3158]

'Āishah ﵂ is reported to have said, "The first calamity for this nation after the Prophet's ﷺ death is fullness of their stomachs; when their stomachs became full, they became obese: their hearts weakened and their desires became wild." [Al-Jū'u Ibn Abī Dunyā: 22]

Extravagance

Invoking Allāh's ﷻ Names

الْبَصِيرُ

Al-Baṣīr The Seer of All (The All-Seeing)

الرَّقِيبُ

Ar-Raqīb
The All Observant

الْمُهَيْمِنُ

Al-Muhaymin
The Guardian

الْخَافِضُ

Al-Khāfiḍ
The Abaser

الْمُعِزُّ

Al-Mu'izz
The Bestower of Honour

الْكَرِيمُ

Al-Karīm
The Most Generous

Extravagance

Contemplation and Reflection on Allāh's ﷻ Blessed Names

- You do not underestimate His total surveillance of you or His being informed about you.
- You know that Allāh ﷻ observes you in every situation and you are determined to use this knowledge to foster a cleaner heart and to keep temptation at bay.
- You know that the lower elements of your soul are your enemy, and that Satan has a long-term goal to destroy all godly purposes within you; if you take prompts from either Satan or your base desires, you are well aware that you will become indifferent, forgetful and disobedient toward Allāh ﷻ.
- You take steps to renounce worldly gains and pleasures, reminding yourself of the negative consequences of seeking out the excesses and delights of this world. In the back of your mind, you are conscious of the physical and mental detriment that can arise quite easily from addictions (repeated excesses when self-control is lost).
- You come to realise that you exist, survive and indeed grow because of Allāh's ﷻ care, protection and generosity, and hence the temptation to compete with others seems needless, even evil to you.
- You realise that any feelings of vulnerability or inadequacy are stimulated by your leaning towards this temporal life, which is mere play and amusement.
- You remind yourself that it is the garment of **taqwā** that will help you adorn your heart, your inner self with praiseworthy traits, such as humility and modesty. In donning this garment you will ultimately beautify your character, at the same time lowering your insecurity and increasing your self-esteem.

Extravagance

Aṣ-Ṣalāh Al-Ibrāhīmiyyah

اَللّٰهُمَّ صَلِّ عَلَى مُحَمَّدٍ وَعَلَى آلِ مُحَمَّدٍ كَمَا صَلَّيْتَ عَلَى
إِبْرَاهِيمَ وَآلِ إِبْرَاهِيمَ إِنَّكَ حَمِيدٌ مَجِيدٌ وَبَارِكْ عَلَى
مُحَمَّدٍ وَعَلَى آلِ مُحَمَّدٍ كَمَا بَارَكْتَ عَلَى إِبْرَاهِيمَ وَآلِ
إِبْرَاهِيمَ إِنَّكَ حَمِيدٌ مَجِيدٌ

Allāhumma ṣalli ʿalā Muḥammadin wa ʿalā āli Muḥammadin kamā ṣallayta ʿalā Ibrāhīm wa āli Ibrāhīm innaka ḥamīdum majīd, wa bārik ʿalā Muḥammadin wa ʿalā āli Muḥammadin kamā bārakta ʿalā Ibrāhīm wa āli Ibrāhīm innaka ḥamīdum majīd

O Allāh, send peace upon Muḥammad and upon the family of Muḥammad, as You sent peace upon Ibrāhīm and the family of Ibrāhīm, and send blessings upon Muḥammad and upon the family of Muḥammad as You sent blessings upon Ibrāhīm and the family of Ibrāhīm. You are indeed praiseworthy, the most honourable. [Sunan An-Nasaī 1290]

Extravagance

Seeking Contentment with Provisions

اَللّٰهُمَّ قَنِّعْنِي بِمَا رَزَقْتَنِي، وَبَارِكْ لِي فِيهِ، وَاخْلُفْ عَلَيَّ كُلَّ غَائِبَةٍ بِخَيْرٍ

Allāhumma qanna'nī bimā razaqtanī wa bārik lī fīh wakhluf 'alayya kulla ghā-ibatin bi khayr

O Allāh, make me content with the provision You have given me and bless me in it and appoint good for me in every thing which I do not have. [Al-Adab Al-Mufrad 681]

Seeking Forgiveness for Extravagance

اَللّٰهُمَّ اغْفِرْ لِي خَطِيئَتِي وَجَهْلِي وَإِسْرَافِي فِي أَمْرِي، وَمَا أَنْتَ أَعْلَمُ بِهِ مِنِّي، اَللّٰهُمَّ اغْفِرْ لِي هَزْلِي وَجِدِّي وَخَطَايَ وَعَمْدِي، وَكُلُّ ذَلِكَ عِنْدِي

Allāhummaghfirlī khatī-atī wa jahlī wa isrāfī fī amrī, wa mā anta a'lamu bihī minnī, Allāhummaghfirlī hazlī wa jiddī wa khatāya wa 'amdī wa kullu dhālika 'indī

O Allāh, forgive my errors, my ignorance and my extravagance in my affairs and what You know better than I do. O Allāh, forgive me what I do both in jest and seriousness, my errors and what I do intentionally and all that I do. [Ṣaḥīḥ Al-Bukhārī 6399]

Extravagance

Seeking Protection from Affluence that Leads to Extravagance

اَللّٰهُمَّ إِنِّي أَعُوذُ بِكَ مِنْ كُلِّ عَمَلٍ يُخْزِينِي، وَأَعُوذُ بِكَ مِنْ كُلِّ صَاحِبٍ يُرْدِينِي، وَأَعُوذُ بِكَ مِنْ كُلِّ أَمَلٍ يُلْهِينِي، وَأَعُوذُ بِكَ مِنْ كُلِّ فَقْرٍ يُنْسِينِي، وَأَعُوذُ بِكَ مِنْ كُلِّ غِنًى يُطْغِينِي

Allāhumma innī a'ūdhu bika min kulli 'amalin yukhzīnī, wa a'ūdhu bika min kulli ṣāḥibin yurdīnī, wa a'ūdhu bika min kulli amalin yulhīnī, wa a'ūdhu bika min kulli faqrin yunsīnī, wa a'ūdhu bika min kulli ginan yuṭghīnī

O Allāh, I seek Your protection from actions that would humiliate me, companions who would ruin me, wishes that would distract me, poverty that would make me forget everything, and affluence that would lead me to exorbitance. [Ibn As-Sunnī in 'Amal Al-Yawm wa Al-Laylah 120]

Seeking Protection from Wealth that Leads to Punishment

اَللّٰهُمَّ إِنِّي أَعُوذُ بِكَ مِنْ مَالٍ يَكُونُ عَلَيَّ عَذَابًا

Allāhumma innī a'ūdhu bika min mālin yakūnu 'alayya 'adhābā

O Allāh, I seek Your protection from the wealth that will turn into punishment for me. [Aṭ-Ṭabarānī in Ad-Du'ā 1339]

Extravagance

Seeking Moderation in Times of Wealth

اَللّٰهُمَّ وَأَسْأَلُكَ خَشْيَتَكَ فِي الْغَيْبِ وَالشَّهَادَةِ وَأَسْأَلُكَ كَلِمَةَ الْحَقِّ فِي الرِّضَا وَالْغَضَبِ وَأَسْأَلُكَ الْقَصْدَ فِي الْفَقْرِ وَالْغِنَى

Allāhumma wa as-aluka khashyataka fil ghaybi wash shahādati wa as-aluka kalimatal haqqi fir riḍā wal ghaḍabi wa as-alukal qaṣda fil faqri wal ghinā

O Allāh, cause me to fear You in secret and in public. I ask You to make me true in speech in times of pleasure and of anger. I ask You to make me moderate in times of wealth and poverty. [Sunan An-Nasaī 1305]

Placing Trust in Allāh ﷻ Alone

حَسْبِيَ اللّٰهُ لآ إِلَهَ إِلَّا هُوَ، عَلَيْهِ تَوَكَّلْتُ، وَهُوَ رَبُّ الْعَرْشِ الْعَظِيمِ

ḤasbiyAllāhu lā ilāha illā hū, 'alayhi tawakkaltu wa huwa rabbul 'arshil 'aẓīm

Allāh is sufficient for me. There is none worthy of worship but Him. I have placed my trust in Him, and He is the lord of the Majestic Throne. [Sunan Abī Dawūd 5081]

الأمَل

False Hope

RELATED EMOTIONS

Indifferent | Lazy | Neglectful | Superstitious | Apathetic | Doubtful
Ignorant | Irrational | Uncertain

INVOKING NAMES OF ALLĀH

- **Al-Malik - the Absolute Ruler**
- **Al-Mumīt - the Slayer**
- **Al-Bā'ith - The Resurrector**
- **Al-Ḥakīm- the All-Wise**
- **Al-Mu'min - The Inspirer of Faith**
- **Al-Mu'akhkhir - The Delayer**

AṢ-ṢALĀH AL-IBRĀHĪMIYYAH

ACCEPTED PRAYERS

- **Prioritising Allāh's Pleasure**
- **Prioritising the Importance of Doing Good Deeds**
- **Seeking Truth and Avoiding Falsehood**
- **Seeking Good in the Hereafter and Protection from the Fire**
- **Seeking Hope and Trust in Allāh's Plan**
- **Putting One's Trust in Allāh**
- **Avoiding Superstition**

CHAPTER 9

False Hope [Amal] الأَمَل

Extended false hope (tatwīl al-amal) is a peculiar phenomenon. For many people it is an ever-present part of their psyche, a kind of everyday assurance that death for them is a long way away. At the same time however, in a heartbeat, it can act on an individual like a quick-acting poison to inspire immoral behaviour, or - at the very least - an inclination toward material possessions over and above any spiritual concerns. It is a mental environment that leads people to live their lives as if a long life is guaranteed. This delusion can generate hard-heartedness and inaction due to the heedlessness of the Hereafter.

Another kind of hope (umniyya) is having hope but neglecting the means to achieve what one hopes for, which is often referred to as an 'empty wish'. One hopes to become healthier, for example, but remains idle and is altogether careless about diet.

The cause of (extended) false hope may be due to:

- A heedlessness of the reality of death
- A lack of certainty (disbelief) in the Hereafter
- A negative understanding of the reality of Allāh ﷻ and His authority and presence
- Ignorance of the fact that the entire affair (of this life) is Allāh's ﷻ alone: that everything belongs to Allāh ﷻ

An enduring characteristic of the teachings of every Prophet and thus every revealed religion, is the idea that entry into Paradise is a matter of Allāh's ﷻ mercy. The reward of this eternal abode comes by combining faith with sincere deeds that confirm one's profession of faith. It is a misguided extension of false hope, however, that will exclude many from Paradise: many a soul that vouches for Islām will find itself cast into Hell on the Day of Judgement.

False Hope

Invoking Allāh's ﷻ Names

الْمَلِكُ

Al-Malik
The Absolute Ruler

الْمُمِيتُ

Al-Mumīt
The Slayer

الْبَاعِثُ

Al-Bā'ith
The Resurrector

الْحَكِيمُ

Al-Ḥakīm
The All-Wise

الْمُؤْمِنُ

Al-Mu'min
The Inspirer of Faith

الْمُؤَخِّرُ

Al-Mu'akhkhir
The Delayer

False Hope

Contemplation and Reflection on Allāh's ﷻ Blessed Names

- You begin to recognise Allāh's ﷻ power and authority in the world.
- You meditate on the reality of (sudden and unexpected) death, its agonies and the various states after it, reminding yourself that people die at all ages and that you may never get the chance to repent and make amends.
- You realise that out of His ultimate wisdom Allāh ﷻ most often defers punishing the guilty as part of His broader scheme, which should never be misinterpreted in the sense that you get away.
- You realise that death is the terminus after which you can not improve your record of deeds.
- You realise that 'Lā ilāha illAllāh' has a deep meaning that goes far beyond its short wording. Yours is (or should be) an energetic declaration of faith, a true 'seize the moment' testimony that stands in contrast to your deeds, especially your indifference, laziness or neglectfulness regarding the obligatory rites of worship. To set this right and work to make your religion complete, you begin to couple your faith with good works.
- You understand that a shrewd person and one with renewed wisdom is one who turns away from temporary advantage, judging his soul and working for whatever will benefit in the world to come, while the incompetent person subordinates his soul to its whims, passions, superstitions and false hopes.
- You are saved from stumbling into the darkness of superstition and unbelief because Allāh ﷻ has inspired you by bestowing faith upon you and showing you the way leading to Him.

False Hope

Aṣ-Ṣalāh Al-Ibrāhīmiyyah

اَللّٰهُمَّ صَلِّ عَلَى مُحَمَّدٍ وَعَلَى آلِ مُحَمَّدٍ كَمَا صَلَّيْتَ عَلَى
إِبْرَاهِيمَ وَآلِ إِبْرَاهِيمَ إِنَّكَ حَمِيدٌ مَجِيدٌ وَبَارِكْ عَلَى
مُحَمَّدٍ وَعَلَى آلِ مُحَمَّدٍ كَمَا بَارَكْتَ عَلَى إِبْرَاهِيمَ وَآلِ
إِبْرَاهِيمَ إِنَّكَ حَمِيدٌ مَجِيدٌ

Allāhumma ṣalli 'alā Muḥammadin wa 'alā āli Muḥammadin kamā ṣ allayta 'alā Ibrāhīm wa āli Ibrāhīm innaka ḥamīdum majīd, wa bārik 'alā Muḥammadin wa 'alā āli Muḥammadin kamā bārakta 'alā Ibrāhīm wa āli Ibrāhīm innaka ḥamīdum majīd

O Allāh, send peace upon Muḥammad and upon the family of Muḥammad, as You sent peace upon Ibrāhīm and the family of Ibrāhīm, and send blessings upon Muḥammad and upon the family of Muḥammad as You sent blessings upon Ibrāhīm and the family of Ibrāhīm. You are indeed praiseworthy, the most honourable. [Sunan An-Nasaī 1290]

False Hope

Prioritising Allāh's ﷻ Pleasure

اَللّٰهُمَّ اجْعَلْ خَيْرَ عُمُرِي آخِرَهُ، اللّٰهُمَّ اجْعَلْ خَوَاتِيمَ عَمَلِي رِضْوَانَكَ، اللّٰهُمَّ اجْعَلْ خَيْرَ أَيَّامِي يَوْمَ أَلْقَاكَ

Allāhummaj'al khayra 'umurī ākhirah, Allāhummaj'al khawātima 'amalī riḍwānak, Allāhummaj'al khayra ayyāmī yawma alqāk

O Allāh, make the last part of my life its best, my final deed (gaining) Your pleasure, and the day I meet You my best day. [Aṭ-Ṭabarānī in Al-Mu'jam Al-Awsaṭ 9411]

Prioritising the Importance of Doing Good Deeds

اَللّٰهُمَّ أَصْلِحْ لِي دِينِي الَّذِي هُوَ عِصْمَةُ أَمْرِي ، وَأَصْلِحْ لِي دُنْيَايَ الَّتِي فِيهَا مَعَاشِي ، وَأَصْلِحْ لِي آخِرَتِي الَّتِي فِيهَا مَعَادِي وَاجْعَلِ الْحَيَاةَ زِيَادَةً لِي فِي كُلِّ خَيْرٍ وَاجْعَلِ الْمَوْتَ رَاحَةً لِي مِنْ كُلِّ شَرٍّ

Allāhumma aṣliḥ lī dīnillathī huwa 'iṣmatu amrī, wa aṣliḥ lī dunyā-ya allatī fīhā ma'āshī, wa aṣlih lī ākhiratī allatī fīhā ma'ādī, waj'alil ḥayāta ziyādatan lī fī kulli khayr, waj'alil mawta rāḥatan lī min kulli sharr

O Allāh, set right my religion, which is the safeguard of my affairs; and set right my world, wherein is my living; and set right my next life, to which is my return, And make life for me an increase in all good and make death a relief for me from every evil. [Ṣaḥīḥ Muslim 2720]

False Hope

Seeking Truth and Avoiding Falsehood

اَللّٰهُمَّ أَرِنَا الْحَقَّ حَقًّا وَارْزُقْنَا اتِّبَاعَهُ، وَأَرِنَا الْبَاطِلَ بَاطِلًا وَوَفِّقْنَا لِاجْتِنَابِهِ

Allāhumma arinal ḥaqqa ḥaqqā warzuqnattibā'ah wa arinal bāṭila bāṭilā wa waffiqnā lijtinābih

O Allāh, show me the truth as truth and guide me to follow it. Show me the false as false and guide me to avoid it. [Tafsīr Ibn Kathīr 1:571 under verse 2:213]

Seeking Good in the Hereafter and Protection from the Fire

رَبَّنَا آتِنَا فِي الدُّنْيَا حَسَنَةً وَفِي الْآخِرَةِ حَسَنَةً وَقِنَا عَذَابَ النَّارِ

Rabbanā ātinā fid dunyā ḥasanatan wa fil ākhirati ḥasanatan wa qinā adhāban nār

"Our Lord! Grant us the good of this world and the Hereafter, and protect us from the torment of the Fire." [Al-Baqarah 2:201]

Seeking Hope and Trust in Allāh's ﷻ Plan

اَللّٰهُمَّ رَحْمَتَكَ أَرْجُو فَلَا تَكِلْنِي إِلَى نَفْسِي طَرْفَةَ عَيْنٍ وَأَصْلِحْ
لِي شَأْنِي كُلَّهُ لَا إِلٰهَ إِلَّا أَنْتَ

Allāhumma raḥmataka arjū, falā takilnī ilā nafsī ṭarfata 'aynin, wa aṣliḥ lī sha-nī kullah, lā ilāha illā anta

O Allāh! Your mercy is what I hope for. Do not abandon me to myself for an instant, but put all my affairs in good order for me. There is no god but You. [Sunan Abī Dawūd 5090]

False Hope

Putting One's Trust in Allāh ﷻ

اَللّٰهُمَّ لَا طَيْرَ إِلاَّ طَيْرُك، وَلا خَيْرَ إِلاَّ خَيْرُك، وَلَا إِلٰهَ غَيْرُك

Allāhumma lā ṭayra illā ṭayruk, wa lā khayra illā khayruk, wa lā ilāha ghayruk

O Allāh there is no portent other than Your portent, no goodness other than Your goodness, and none worthy of worship other than You. [Musnad Aḥmad 7045]

Avoiding Superstition

بِسْمِ اللهِ الَّذِي لَا يَضُرُّ مَعَ اسْمِهِ شَيْءٌ فِي الْأَرْضِ وَلَا فِي السَّمَاءِ وَهُوَ السَّمِيعُ الْعَلِيمُ

Bismillāhilladhī lā yaḍurru ma'asmihī shay-un fil arḍi wa lā fis samā-i wa huwas samī'-'ul 'alīm

In the Name of Allāh, with Whose name nothing on the earth or in the heaven can cause harm, and He is the All-Hearing, the All-Knowing. [Sunan Abī Dawūd 5088]

التَخَيُّل

Fantasizing

RELATED EMOTIONS

Lustful | Excessive | Addicted | Irrational | Deluded | Immature
Vulgar

INVOKING NAMES OF ALLĀH

- **Al-Baṣīr - The Seer of All (The All-Seeing)**
- **Al-Khabīr - the All-Aware**
- **Al-'Alīm - The All-Knowing**
- **Ar-Raqīb - The Watchful**
- **Ash-Shahīd - The Witness**
- **Al-Muḥṣī - The One Who Keeps Record**
- **Al-Bāṭin - The Hidden One**
- **Al-Māni' - The Preventer**

AṢ-ṢALĀH AL-IBRĀHĪMIYYAH

ACCEPTED PRAYERS

- **Admitting Wrong and Seeking Forgiveness**
- **Seeking Refuge from Mischief of Our Senses**
- **Seeking Refuge from Evil Actions and Desires**
- **Seeking Protection from Unlawful Desires**
- **Seeking Refuge from the Temptations of the Devils**
- **Purification from Wrongful Glances**
- **Covering Shame**
- **Seeking Forgiveness of Sins Committed in Public and in Private**
- **Seeking Pious Spouses and Children**
- **Allāh Taking Charge**

CHAPTER 10

Fantasizing [Takhayyul] التَخَيُّل

Extensive reflection, and working a prohibited action through one's mind, perhaps picturing the fantasy or describing it in detail to others is reaching the brink of active engagement: be it robbing a bank, winning at roulette or committing adultery. 'Fantasizing' is when the heart dwells on forbidden or prohibited matters and those inspirations that do not concern it. Included in this is thinking about the weaknesses or faults of others, whether they are present or not.

Fantasizing

Invoking Allāh's ﷻ Names

الْبَصِيرُ

Al-Baṣīr - The Seer of All (The All-Seeing)

الْخَبِيرُ

Al-Khabīr
The All-Aware

الْعَلِيمُ

Al-'Alīm
The All-Knowing

الرَّقِيبُ

Ar-Raqīb
The Watchful

الشَّهِيدُ

Ash-Shahīd
The Witness

الْمُحْصِي

Al-Muḥṣī
The One Who Keeps Record

الْبَاطِنُ

Al-Bāṭin
The Hidden One

الْمَانِعُ

Al-Māni'
The Preventer

Fantasizing

Contemplation and Reflection on Allāh's ﷻ Blessed Names

- You appreciate that Allāh ﷻ witnesses and sees in such a way that nothing is remote from Him, for nothing goes on in the realms of heaven or earth, no atom moves, and no soul is stirred or calmed, without His being aware of it, so you do not use your senses except for the benefit of divine guidance and obedience.
- You understand that every servant whose heart is free from evil intent and whose limbs are unblemished by sins and forbidden actions and self-induced addictions will be one who comes to Allāh ﷻ with a flawless heart.
- You remind yourself that being ever-conscious of Allāh ﷻ, fully attentive to the fact that He is watching over us, is an effective way to keep Satan and base desires at bay.
- You are aware that Allāh ﷻ is unseen in this world, yet He knows all inner circumstances!
- You take special care to base your actions in reality in order to avoid embarrassment and loss in the Afterlife.
- You realise that Satan is your enemy and that he takes every opportunity to prompt you to deceptions and disobedience.
- You become aware of your lower self and experienced in it, aware of its propensity to call you to lustful deception, delusions and excesses. You refuse to be tricked by it, you guard against it and you work to oppose it.

Fantasizing

Aṣ-Ṣalāh Al-Ibrāhīmiyyah

اَللّٰهُمَّ صَلِّ عَلَى مُحَمَّدٍ وَعَلَى آلِ مُحَمَّدٍ كَمَا صَلَّيْتَ عَلَى
إِبْرَاهِيمَ وَآلِ إِبْرَاهِيمَ إِنَّكَ حَمِيدٌ مَجِيدٌ وَبَارِكْ عَلَى
مُحَمَّدٍ وَعَلَى آلِ مُحَمَّدٍ كَمَا بَارَكْتَ عَلَى إِبْرَاهِيمَ وَآلِ
إِبْرَاهِيمَ إِنَّكَ حَمِيدٌ مَجِيدٌ

Allāhumma ṣalli 'alā Muḥammadin wa 'alā āli Muḥammadin kamā ṣ allayta 'alā Ibrāhīm wa āli Ibrāhīm innaka ḥamīdum majīd, wa bārik 'alā Muḥammadin wa 'alā āli Muḥammadin kamā bārakta 'alā Ibrāhīm wa āli Ibrāhīm innaka ḥamīdum majīd

O Allāh, send peace upon Muḥammad and upon the family of Muḥammad, as You sent peace upon Ibrāhīm and the family of Ibrāhīm, and send blessings upon Muḥammad and upon the family of Muḥammad as You sent blessings upon Ibrāhīm and the family of Ibrāhīm. You are indeed praiseworthy, the most honourable. [Sunan An-Nasaī 1290]

Fantasizing

Admitting Wrong and Seeking Forgiveness

رَبِّ إِنِّي ظَلَمْتُ نَفْسِي فَاغْفِرْ لِي

Rabbi innī ẓalamtu nafsī faghfirlī

My Lord! I have definitely wronged my soul, so forgive me. [Al-Qaṣaṣ 28:16]

Seeking Refuge from the Mischief of Our Senses

اَللّٰهُمَّ إِنِّي أَعُوذُ بِكَ مِنْ شَرِّ سَمْعِي وَمِنْ شَرِّ بَصَرِي وَمِنْ شَرِّ لِسَانِي وَمِنْ شَرِّ قَلْبِي وَمِنْ شَرِّ مَنِيِّي

Allāhumma innī a'ūdhu bika min sharri sam'ī wa min sharri baṣarī wa min sharri lisānī wa min sharri qalbī wa min sharri maniyyī

O Allāh, I seek refuge in You from the mischief of my hearing, sight, speech, heart and seed (sexual passion). [Sunan Abī Dawūd 1551]

Seeking Refuge from Evil Actions and Desires

اَللّٰهُمَّ إِنِّي أَعُوذُ بِكَ مِنْ مُنْكَرَاتِ الأَخْلاَقِ وَالأَعْمَالِ وَالأَهْوَاءِ

Allāhumma innī a'ūdhu bika min munkarātil akhlāqi wal a'māli wal ahwā

O Allāh, I seek refuge in You from evil character, evil actions, and evil desires. [Jāmi` At-Tirmidhī 3591]

Fantasizing

Seeking Protection from Unlawful Desires

اَللّٰهُمَّ اغْفِرْ ذَنْبِي وَطَهِّرْ قَلْبِي، وَحَصِّنْ فَرْجِي

Allāhummaghfir dhanbī wa ṭahhir qalbī, wa ḥaṣṣin farjī

O Allāh forgive my sin, cleanse my heart and guard my chastity. [Musnad Aḥmad 22211]

Seeking Refuge from the Temptations of the Devils

رَبِّ أَعُوذُ بِكَ مِنْ هَمَزَٰتِ ٱلشَّيَٰطِينِ وَأَعُوذُ بِكَ رَبِّ أَن يَحْضُرُونِ

Rabbi a'ūdhu bika min hamazātish shayāṭini wa a'ūdhu bika rabbi ay yaḥḍurūn

My Lord! I seek refuge in You from the temptations of the devils. And I seek refuge in You, my Lord, that they (even) come near me. [Al-Mu'minūn 23: 97-98]

FANTASIZING

Purification from Wrongful Glances

اَللّٰهُمَّ طَهِّرْ قَلْبِي مِنَ النِّفَاقِ وَعَمَلِي مِنَ الرِّيَاءِ وَلِسَانِي مِنَ الْكَذِبِ وَعَيْنِي مِنَ الْخِيَانَةِ، فَإِنَّكَ تَعْلَمُ خَائِنَةَ الأَعْيُنِ وَمَا تُخْفِي الصُّدُورُ

Allāhumma ṭahhir qalbī minan nifāq wa 'amalī minar riyā- wa lisānī minal kadhib wa 'aynī minal khiyānah, fa innaka ta'lamu khā-inatal a'yuni wa mā tukhfiṣ ṣudūr

O Allāh, purify my heart from hypocrisy, my deeds from ostentation and pretension, my tongue from lies, and my eyes from wrongful glances. For, indeed, You know what the eyes deceptively glance at and what the hearts conceal. [Al-Bayhaqī in Ad-Da'awāt Al-Kabīr 258]

Fantasizing

Covering Shame

اَللّٰهُمَّ اسْتُرْ عَوْرَاتِي وَآمِنْ رَوْعَاتِي

Allāhummastur 'awrātī wa āmin raw'ātī.

O Allāh! Cover my shame and calm my fears. [Sunan Abī Dawūd 5074]

Seeking Forgiveness of Sins Committed in Public and in Private

اَللّٰهُمَّ اغْفِرْ لِي مَا قَدَّمْتُ وَمَا أَخَّرْتُ وَمَا أَسْرَرْتُ وَمَا أَعْلَنْتُ وَمَا أَنْتَ أَعْلَمُ بِهِ مِنِّي أَنْتَ الْمُقَدِّمُ وَأَنْتَ الْمُؤَخِّرُ وَأَنْتَ عَلَى كُلِّ شَيْءٍ قَدِيرٌ

Allāhummaghfir lī mā qaddamtu wa mā akhkhartu wa mā asrartu wa mā a'lantu wa mā anta a'lamu bihī minnī, antal muqaddim wa antal mu-akhkhir wa anta 'alā kulli shay-in qadīr

O Allāh, grant me forgiveness from the fault which I did in haste or deferred, which I committed in privacy or in public and You are more aware of (them) than myself. You are the First and the Last and over all things You are Omnipotent. [Ṣaḥīḥ Muslim 2719a]

Fantasizing

Seeking Pious Spouses and Children

رَبَّنَا هَبْ لَنَا مِنْ أَزْوَٰجِنَا وَذُرِّيَّٰتِنَا قُرَّةَ أَعْيُنٍ وَٱجْعَلْنَا لِلْمُتَّقِينَ إِمَامًا

Rabbanā hab lanā min azwājina wa dhurriyyātinā qurrata a'yun waj'alnā lil muttaqīna imāmā

Our Lord! Bless us with (pious) spouses and offspring who will be the joy of our hearts, and make us models for the righteous. [Al-Furqān 25:74]

Allāh ﷻ Taking Charge

اَللّٰهُمَّ رَحْمَتَكَ أَرْجُو فَلاَ تَكِلْنِي إِلَى نَفْسِي طَرْفَةَ عَيْنٍ وَأَصْلِحْ لِي شَأْنِي كُلَّهُ لاَ إِلَهَ إِلاَّ أَنْتَ

Allāhumma raḥmataka arjū, falā takilnī ilā nafsī ṭarfata 'aynin, wa aṣliḥ lī sha-nī kullah, lā ilāha illā anta

O Allāh! Your mercy is what I hope for. Do not abandon me to myself for an instant, but put all my affairs in good order for me. There is no god but You. [Sunan Abī Dawūd 5090]

خَوْفُ الفَقْر

Fear of Poverty

RELATED EMOTIONS

Uncertain | Doubtful | Insecure | Helpless | Anxious | Overwhelmed-Distressed | Depressed | Apprehensive | Ashamed | Uneasy
Vulnerable | Worthless | Pessimistic

INVOKING NAMES OF ALLĀH

- **Al-Qādir - The All Powerful**
- **Al-Muqtadir - The Omnipotent**
- **Al-Qābiḍ - The Withholder**
- **Al-Bāsiṭ - The Extender**
- **Al-Ghaniyy - The Wealthy**
- **Ar-Razzāq - the Provider**
- **Al-Mughniyy - The Enricher**
- **Al-Qayyūm - The Sustainer**
- **Al-Wakīl - The Trustee**
- **Al-Muqīt - the Nourisher**
- **Al-Mujīb - The Responsive One**
- **Al-Wājid - The Finder**
- **Al-Wālī - The Governor**

AṢ-ṢALĀH AL-IBRĀHĪMIYYAH

ACCEPTED PRAYERS

- **Seeking Refuge from Disbelief and Poverty**
- **Seeking Ample Sustenance and Safety From All Trials**
- **Seeking Increase, Honour, Favour and Pleasure of Allāh**
- **Seeking Provision**
- **Seeking Provision of Sustenance**
- **Seeking Refuge from Debt, and Affliction of Wealth and Poverty**
- **Seeking Refuge from the Burden of Debts and Being Overpowered**
- **Seeking Independence from the Created**
- **Making Sustenance Plentiful in the Last Days**
- **Seeking Blessed Sustenance**
- **Seeking Easy Access to Your Provisions**
- **Relying on Allāh**
- **Rectification of Affairs**
- **Seeking Protection of Wealth**

CHAPTER 11

Fear of Poverty

[Khawf al-Faqr] خَوْفُ الفَقْر

When the heart is not correctly aligned to the decree of the Almighty, then dissatisfaction will always arise. Dislike of poverty can sit with a person when they are poor, but by far the more widespread disease is the fear of poverty when wealth is in place.

The general characteristic of this fear is that one's cash, capital, estates or resources will be destroyed or diminished, thus impacting on lifestyle and esteem. When this fear is placed in the heart of a person, the clinging greed intensifies, and they redouble their efforts to accumulate more wealth.

Without doubt, dissatisfaction with one's allotted portion goes hand in hand with spending little or no time in worshipping Allāh ﷻ or performing genuine acts of charity. The pursuit of worldly riches and comforts becomes the sufferer's goal in life.

The Prophet ﷺ said, "Whoever makes the Hereafter his goal, Allāh ﷻ makes his heart rich, and organizes his affairs, and the world comes to him whether it wants to or not. And whoever makes the world his goal, Allāh ﷻ puts his poverty right before his eyes, and disorganises his affairs, and the world does not come to him, except what has been decreed for him." [At-Tirmidhī 2465]

Fear of Poverty

Invoking Allāh's ﷻ Names

الْقَادِرُ Al-Qādir The All Powerful	الْمُقْتَدِرُ Al-Muqtadir The Omnipotent	الْقَابِضُ Al-Qābiḍ The Withholder	الْبَاسِطُ Al-Bāsiṭ The Extender
الْغَنِيُّ Al-Ghaniyy The Wealthy	الرَّزَّاقُ Ar-Razzāq The Provider	الْمُغْنِيُّ Al-Mughniyy The Enricher	الْقَيُّومُ Al-Qayyūm The Sustainer
الْوَكِيلُ Al-Wakīl The Trustee	الْمُقِيتُ Al-Muqīt The Nourisher	الْمُجِيبُ Al-Mujīb The Responsive One	الْوَاجِدُ Al-Wājid The Finder

الْوَالِي
Al-Wālī
The Governor

Fear of Poverty

Contemplation and Reflection on Allāh's ﷻ Blessed Names

- You appreciate that Allāh ﷻ is the One who created the means of sustenance as well as those who are sustained, that He ﷻ is the nourisher of all things, and that He is All-Knowing and All Powerful.
- You understand that out of His ultimate wisdom, Allāh ﷻ grants provisions to His creatures in a certain measure, withholding as well as extending sustenance out of His infinite wisdom and will.
- You understand that He is the One who protects, guards, and supports the believer in this world and the next!
- Because of this assurance, you replace your insecurity, anxiety and distress with patience, wisdom and religion.
- You know that Allāh ﷻ guides when someone is found astray, that He helps when someone is in need of assistance, that He provides relief to someone He finds in distress.
- You realise that external sustenance consists of nourishment and food, the fruit of which is bodily strength for a short period of time.
- However, you also appreciate the importance of increasing sustenance with respect to the inward, that which is directed to our hearts and innermost parts. You put your faith in this as the higher of the two modes of sustenance, for its fruit is eternal life.
- You remind yourself that you should expect sustenance only from Him, and should not rely on anyone but Him for it.
- You develop an inherent trust in the Creator alone (called 'tawakkul'), which means that you 'act in accordance with' Allāh's ﷻ plan, i.e. you adopt the principles and commands of the sharī'ah, and place trust in Allāh ﷻ, not allowing Satan's whisperings to overwhelm you.

Fear of Poverty

Aṣ-Ṣalāh Al-Ibrāhīmiyyah

اَللّٰهُمَّ صَلِّ عَلَى مُحَمَّدٍ وَعَلَى آلِ مُحَمَّدٍ كَمَا صَلَّيْتَ عَلَى
إِبْرَاهِيمَ وَآلِ إِبْرَاهِيمَ إِنَّكَ حَمِيدٌ مَجِيدٌ وَبَارِكْ عَلَى
مُحَمَّدٍ وَعَلَى آلِ مُحَمَّدٍ كَمَا بَارَكْتَ عَلَى إِبْرَاهِيمَ وَآلِ
إِبْرَاهِيمَ إِنَّكَ حَمِيدٌ مَجِيدٌ

Allāhumma ṣalli 'alā Muḥammadin wa 'alā āli Muḥammadin kamā ṣ allayta 'alā Ibrāhīm wa āli Ibrāhīm innaka ḥamīdum majīd, wa bārik 'alā Muḥammadin wa 'alā āli Muḥammadin kamā bārakta 'alā Ibrāhīm wa āli Ibrāhīm innaka ḥamīdum majīd

O Allāh, send peace upon Muḥammad and upon the family of Muḥammad, as You sent peace upon Ibrāhīm and the family of Ibrāhīm, and send blessings upon Muḥammad and upon the family of Muḥammad as You sent blessings upon Ibrāhīm and the family of Ibrāhīm. You are indeed praiseworthy, the most honourable. [Sunan An-Nasaī 1290]

Fear of Poverty

Seeking Refuge from Disbelief and Poverty

اَللّٰهُمَّ إِنِّي أَعُوْذُبِكَ مِنَ الْكُفْرِ، وَالْفَقْرِ، وَأَعُوْذُ بِكَ مِنْ عَذَابِ الْقَبْرِ، لَا إِلٰهَ إِلَّا أَنْتَ

Allāhumma innī a'ūdhu bika minal kufri, wal faqr, wa a'ūdhu bika min 'adhābil qabr, lā ilāha illā ant

O Allāh! I seek refuge in You from disbelief and poverty. O Allāh! I seek refuge in You from the torment of the grave. There is no God except You. [Sunan Abī Dawūd 5090]

Seeking Ample Sustenance and Safety From All Trials

اَللّٰهُمَّ أَسْأَلُكَ فَرَجًا قَرِيبًا، وَصَبَرًا جَمِيلًا، وَرِزْقًا وَاسِعًا، وَالْعَافِيَةَ مِنْ جَمِيعِ الْبَلَاءِ

Allāhumma as-aluka farajan qarība wa ṣabaran jamīla wa rizqan wāsi'ā wal 'āfiyata min jamī'il balā

O Allāh, I beg You for quick relief, noble patience, ample sustenance, and safety from all trials. [Al-Farj ba'd As-Shiddah Ibn Abī Dunyā 70]

Fear of Poverty

Seeking Increase, Honour, Favour and Pleasure of Allāh ﷻ

اَللّٰهُمَّ زِدْنَا وَلاَ تَنْقُصْنَا وَأَكْرِمْنَا وَلاَ تُهِنَّا وَأَعْطِنَا وَلاَ تَحْرِمْنَا وَآثِرْنَا وَلاَ تُؤْثِرْ عَلَيْنَا وَأَرْضِنَا وَارْضَ عَنَّا

Allāhumma zidnā wa lā tanquṣnā wa akrimnā wa lā tuhinnā wa a'tinā wa lā taḥrimnā wa āthirnā wa lā tu-thir 'alaynā wa arḍinā warḍa 'annā

O Allāh, increase (Your grace) for us and do not curtail it; give us honour and do not humiliate us; give us and do not deprive us; favour us and do not favour others over us; make us be pleased with You and be pleased with us. [Jāmi` At-Tirmidhī 3173]

Seeking Provision

رَبِّ إِنِّي لِمَآ أَنزَلْتَ إِلَيَّ مِنْ خَيْرٍ فَقِيرٌ

Rabbi innī limā anzalta ilayya min khayrin faqīr

My Lord! I am truly in (desperate) need of whatever provision You may have in store for me. [Al-Qaṣaṣ 28:24]

Seeking Provision of Sustenance

اَللّٰهُمَّ اغْفِرْ لِي وَارْحَمْنِي وَاهْدِنِي وَعَافِنِي وَارْزُقْنِي

Allāhummaghfirlī warḥamnī wahdinī wa 'āfinī warzuqnī

O Allāh, forgive my sins, have mercy on me, give me health and safety, and provide me with sustenance. [Ṣaḥīḥ Muslim 2697]

Fear of Poverty

Seeking Refuge from Debt, and Affliction of Wealth and Poverty

اَللّٰهُمَّ إِنِّي أَعُوذُ بِكَ مِنَ الْكَسَلِ وَالْهَرَمِ، وَالْمَأْثَمِ وَالْمَغْرَمِ، وَمِنْ شَرِّ فِتْنَةِ الْغِنَى، وَأَعُوذُ بِكَ مِنْ فِتْنَةِ الْفَقْرِ، وَأَعُوذُ بِكَ مِنْ فِتْنَةِ الْمَسِيحِ الدَّجَّالِ

Allāhumma innī a'ūdhu bika minal kasli wal haram, wal ma-thami wal maghram, wa min sharri fitnatil ghinā, wa a'ūdhu bika min fitnatil faqr, wa a'ūdhu bika min fitnatil masīḥid dajjāl

O Allāh! I seek refuge with You from laziness and geriatric old age, from all kinds of sins and from being in debt; and from the evil of the affliction of wealth; and I seek refuge with You from the affliction of poverty, and I seek refuge with You from the affliction of Al-Masīḥ Ad-Dajjāl. [Ṣaḥīḥ Al-Bukhārī 6368]

Seeking Refuge from the Burden of Debts and Being Overpowered

اَللّٰهُمَّ إِنِّي أَعُوذُ بِكَ مِنَ الْهَمِّ وَالْحَزَنِ وَالْعَجزِ وَالْكَسَلِ وَالْجُبْنِ وَالْبُخْلِ وَضَلَعِ الدَّيْنِ وَغَلَبَةِ الرِّجَالِ

Allāhumma innī a'ūdhu bika minal hammi wal ḥazani wal 'ajzi wal kasali wal jubni wal bukhli wa ḍala'id dayni wa ghalabatir rijāl

"O Allāh, I seek refuge in you from anxiety and sadness, weakness and laziness, miserliness and cowardice, the burden of debts and from being overpowered by men." [Ṣaḥīḥ Al-Bukhārī 6369]

Fear of Poverty

Seeking Independence from the Created

اَللّٰهُمَّ اكْفِنِي بِحَلَالِكَ عَنْ حَرَامِكَ وَأَغْنِنِي بِفَضْلِكَ عَمَّنْ سِوَاكَ

Allāhummakfinī bi ḥalālika `an ḥarāmika, wa aghninī bi faḍlika `amman siwāka

O Allāh, suffice me with Your lawful against Your prohibited, and make me independent of all those besides You. [Jāmi` At-Tirmidhī 3563]

Making Sustenance Plentiful in the Last Days

اَللّٰهُمَّ اجْعَلْ أَوْسَعَ رِزْقِكَ عَلَيَّ عِنْدَ كِبَرِ سِنِّي ، وَانْقِطَاعِ عُمُرِي

Allāhummaj'al awsa'a rizqika 'alayya 'inda kibari sinnī wa inqiṭā'i 'umurī

O Allāh, make my sustenance the most plentiful in my old age and during the last days of my life. [Al-Ḥākim 1987]

Seeking Blessed Sustenance

اَللّٰهُمَّ اغْفِرْلِي ذَنْبِي ، وَوَسِّعْ لِي فِي دَارِي ، وَبَارِكْ لِي فِيمَا رَزَقْتَنِي

Allāhummaghfirlī dhanbī wa wassi' lī fī dārī wa bārik lī fīmā razaqtanī

O Allāh, forgive my sin, make my home ample for me, and bless me in what you have sustained me with. [Musnad Aḥmad 16599]

Fear of Poverty

Seeking Easy Access to Your Provisions

اَللّٰهُمَّ افْتَحْ لَنَا أَبْوَابَ رَحْمَتِكَ وَسَهِّلْ لَنَا أَبْوَابَ رِزْقِكَ

Allāhummaftaḥ lanā abwāba raḥmatika wa sahhil lanā abwāba rizqik

O Allāh, open for us the doors to Your mercy and give us easy access to the doors to Your provisions. [Abū 'Awānah in Mustakhraj 1236]

Relying on Allāh ﷻ

اَللّٰهُمَّ أَنْتَ رَبِّي لَا إِلَهَ إِلَّا أَنْتَ، عَلَيْكَ تَوَكَّلْتُ، وَأَنْتَ رَبُّ الْعَرْشِ الْعَظِيمِ

Allāhumma anta rabbī lā ilāha illā anta, 'alayka tawakkaltu wa anta rabbul 'arshil 'aẓīm

O Allāh! You are my Lord, there is no god but You. Upon You I rely, and You are the Lord of the Glorious Throne. [Ibn As-Sunnī in 'Amal Al-Yawm wa Al-Laylah 57]

Rectification of Affairs

يَا حَيُّ يَا قَيُّومُ بِرَحْمَتِكَ أَسْتَغِيثُ، أَصْلِحْ لِي شَأْنِي كُلَّهُ، وَلَا تَكِلْنِي إِلَى نَفْسِي طَرْفَةَ عَيْنٍ

Yā ḥayyu yā Qayyūm, bi raḥmatika astaghīth, aṣliḥ lī sha-nī kullah, wa lā takilnī ilā nafsī ṭarafata 'ayn

O Ever-Living One, O Eternal One, by Your mercy I call on You to set right all my affairs. Do not place me in charge of my soul even for the blinking of an eye (i.e. a moment). [Al-Ḥākim 2000]

Fear of Poverty

Seeking Protection of Wealth

اَللّٰهُمَّ إِنِّي أَسْأَلُكَ العَفْوَ وَالعَافِيَةَ فِيْ دِيْنِيْ وَدُنْيَايَ وَأَهْلِي وَمَالِيْ

Allāhumma innī as-alukal `afwa wal `āfiyah fī dīnī wa dunyāya, wa ahlī, wa mālī

O Allāh, I seek Your forgiveness and Your protection in my religion, in my worldly affairs, in my family and in my wealth. [Sunan Abī Dawūd 5074]

الغِشّ

Fraud

RELATED EMOTIONS

Guilty | Ashamed | Anxious | Manipulative | Deceitful | Cruel
Insincere

INVOKING NAMES OF ALLĀH ﷻ

- Al-'Alīm - The All-Knowing
- Al-'Adl - the Just
- Al-Muqsiṭ - the Requiter
- Al-Baṣīr - The Seer of All (The All-Seeing)
- Al-Ḥasīb - The Reckoner
- As-Samī' - The Hearer of All (The All-Hearing)
- Ar-Raqīb - the Watchful
- Al-Khabīr - the All-Aware
- Ash-Shahīd - the Witness
- Al-Bāṭin - The Hidden One
- Al-Muḥṣī - The One Who Keeps Record
- Al-Ḥaqq - The Truth
- Al-Mu'akhkhir - The Delayer
- Al-Māni' - The Preventer
- Ar-Rashīd - The Director

AṢ-ṢALĀH AL-IBRĀHĪMIYYAH

ACCEPTED PRAYERS

- Admitting Wrongful Doing
- Admitting Wrong and Seeking Forgiveness
- Seeking Truth and Refraining from Falsehood
- Seeking Guidance and Integrity
- Seeking Protection from Wealth that Turns into Punishment
- Seeking Help Against Corrupt People
- Seeking Refuge from Slipping Unintentionally
- Seeking Protection from the Evil of One's Soul
- Seeking Forgiveness of Sins
- Seeking Protection from Treachery
- Praying for a Truthful Tongue, a Sound Heart and Uprightness
- Dying as One of the Virtuous

CHAPTER 12

Fraud [Ghish] الغِشّ

The next disease is fraud or 'ghish'. It isn't wholly confined to deceiving customers or the tax man: it might involve concealment of any worldly or religious fault, blemish, or harm, possibly due to greed or love of wealth.

For some people, the definition of fraud (whether related to a product or a service) is the act of deceit in making something useless or defective seem useful and beneficial.

The Prophet ﷺ happened to pass by a heap of eatables (corn). He thrust his hand in that (heap) and his fingers were moistened. He said to the owner of that heap of eatables (corn): "What is this?" He replied: "O Messenger of Allāh, these have been drenched by rainfall." He (the Prophet ﷺ) remarked: "Why did you not place this (the drenched part of the heap) over other eatables so that the people could see it? He who deceives is not of me (is not my follower)." [Ṣaḥīḥ Muslim 102:164]

Falsehood or lying (kidhb) is similar to fraud, in that it is when one speaks contrary to fact.

The Prophet ﷺ said:

- "Every ummah has a fitnah (means of testing). The fitnah of my ummah is wealth" [At-Tirmidhī 2336]
- "A time will come when one will not care how he gains his money: legally or illegally" [Ṣaḥīḥ Al-Bukhārī 2059]

Fraud

Invoking Allāh's ﷻ Names

الْعَلِيمُ Al-'Alīm The All-Knowing	الْعَدْلُ Al-'Adl The Just	الْمُقْسِطُ Al-Muqsiṭ The Requiter	الْبَصِيرُ Al-Baṣīr The Seer of All (The All-Seeing)
الْحَسِيبُ Al-Ḥasīb The Reckoner	السَّمِيعُ As-Samī' The Hearer of All (The All-Hearing)	الرَّقِيبُ Ar-Raqīb The Watchful	الْخَبِيرُ Al-Khabīr The All-Aware
الشَّهِيدُ Ash-Shahīd The Witness	الْبَاطِنُ Al-Bāṭin The Hidden One	الْمُحْصِي Al-Muḥṣī The One Who Keeps Record	الْحَقُّ Al-Ḥaqq The Truth
الْمُؤَخِّرُ Al-Mu'akhkhir The Delayer	الْمَانِعُ Al-Māni' The Preventer	الرَّشِيدُ Ar-Rashīd The Director	

Fraud

Contemplation and Reflection on Allāh's ﷻ Blessed Names

- You realise that Satan is your enemy and that he takes every opportunity to prompt you to the deceptions of manipulation and the disobedient act of betrayal.
- You remind yourself that Allāh ﷻ is the source of truth and calls you to demonstrate honesty and good character, avoiding falsehood and deceit.
- You remind yourself that Allāh ﷻ witnesses and sees in such a way that nothing is remote from Him: there is no such thing as 'secret information' with Allāh ﷻ. Allāh's ﷻ All-Awareness makes you especially careful about your answerability to Him and you are therefore very careful about your actions.
- You take special care to behave with honesty in all actions in order to avoid the intense embarrassment and loss that comes with the perfect justice and honesty of Judgement Day.
- You pledge to follow a path of obedience, freeing your heart from evil intent and your hands from sinful action.
- You remind yourself that if you speak or trade with honesty and integrity, you will be honoured with the company of the Prophets ﷺ, the truthful followers, the martyrs and the righteous on the Day of Resurrection.
- You remind yourself that each lie, each untruth, each moment of dishonesty marks your heart with a black dot and, if this does not cease, you will move steadily toward the point of no return, when the heart is irreversibly blackened: at this juncture your name joins the list of habitual liars.
- You realise that you will be held to account by Allāh ﷻ, who is the All-Enumerator, the Just, the Equitable, the Delayer and the One who takes to account, who demands justice for the wronged from the wrongdoer.
- You realise that out of His ultimate wisdom Allāh ﷻ most often defers punishing the guilty as part of His broader scheme, which should never be misinterpreted in the sense that you get away.
- You realise that death is the terminus after which you can not improve your record of deeds.
- You become one who is aware of his lower self and experienced in it, who knows its deceit, its delusions, and its tricks, so that you are on your guard against it and have gone to work to oppose it, adopting a watchfulness over it.

Fraud

Aṣ-Ṣalāh Al-Ibrāhīmiyyah

اَللّٰهُمَّ صَلِّ عَلَى مُحَمَّدٍ وَعَلَى آلِ مُحَمَّدٍ كَمَا صَلَّيْتَ عَلَى إِبْرَاهِيمَ وَآلِ إِبْرَاهِيمَ إِنَّكَ حَمِيدٌ مَجِيدٌ وَبَارِكْ عَلَى مُحَمَّدٍ وَعَلَى آلِ مُحَمَّدٍ كَمَا بَارَكْتَ عَلَى إِبْرَاهِيمَ وَآلِ إِبْرَاهِيمَ إِنَّكَ حَمِيدٌ مَجِيدٌ

Allāhumma ṣalli 'alā Muḥammadin wa 'alā āli Muḥammadin kamā ṣ allayta 'alā Ibrāhīm wa āli Ibrāhīm innaka ḥamīdum majīd, wa bārik 'alā Muḥammadin wa 'alā āli Muḥammadin kamā bārakta 'alā Ibrāhīm wa āli Ibrāhīm innaka ḥamīdum majīd

O Allāh, send peace upon Muḥammad and upon the family of Muḥammad, as You sent peace upon Ibrāhīm and the family of Ibrāhīm, and send blessings upon Muḥammad and upon the family of Muḥammad as You sent blessings upon Ibrāhīm and the family of Ibrāhīm. You are indeed praiseworthy, the most honourable. [Sunan An-Nasaī 1290]

Fraud

Admitting Wrongful Doing

لَآ إِلَٰهَ إِلَّآ أَنتَ سُبۡحَٰنَكَ إِنِّي كُنتُ مِنَ ٱلظَّٰلِمِينَ

Lā ilāha illā anta subḥānaka innī kuntu minaẓ ẓālimīn

There is no god (worthy of worship) except You. Glory be to You! I have certainly done wrong. [Al-Anbiyā 21:87]

Admitting Wrong and Seeking Forgiveness

رَبِّ إِنِّي ظَلَمۡتُ نَفۡسِي فَٱغۡفِرۡ لِي

Rabbi innī ẓalamtu nafsī fa-ghfirlī

My Lord! I have definitely wronged my soul, so forgive me. [Al-Qaṣaṣ 28:16]

Seeking Truth and Refraining from Falsehood

اَللّٰهُمَّ أَرِنَا الْحَقَّ حَقًّا وَارْزُقْنَا اتِّبَاعَهُ، وَأَرِنَا الْبَاطِلَ بَاطِلًا وَوَفِّقْنَا لِاجْتِنَابِهِ

Allāhumma arinal ḥaqqa ḥaqqā warzuqnattibā'ah wa arinal bāṭila bāṭilā wa waffiqnā lijtinābih

O Allāh, show me the truth as truth and guide me to follow it. Show me the false as false and guide me to avoid it. [Tafsīr Ibn Kathīr 1:571 under verse 2:213]

Fraud

Seeking Guidance and Integrity

اَللّٰهُمَّ اهْدِنِي وَسَدِّدْنِي

Allāhummahdinī wa saddidnī

O Allāh, guide me and keep me upright. [Ṣaḥīḥ Muslim 2725]

Seeking Protection from Wealth that Turns into Punishment

اَللّٰهُمَّ إِنِّي أَعُوذُ بِكَ مِنْ مَالٍ يَكُونُ عَلَيَّ عَذَابًا

Allāhumma innī a'ūdhu bika min mālin yakūnu 'alayya 'adhābā

O Allāh, I seek Your protection from the wealth that will turn into punishment for me. [Aṭ-Ṭabarānī in Ad-Du'ā 1339]

Seeking Help Against Corrupt People

رَبِّ ٱنصُرْنِى عَلَى ٱلْقَوْمِ ٱلْمُفْسِدِينَ

Rabbinṣurnī 'alal qawmil mufsidīn

My Lord! Help me against the people of corruption. [Al-'Ankabūt 29:30]

Fraud

Seeking Refuge from Slipping Unintentionally

بِسْمِ اللَّهِ تَوَكَّلْتُ عَلَى اللَّهِ اللَّهُمَّ إِنَّا نَعُوذُ بِكَ مِنْ أَنْ نَزِلَّ أَوْ نَضِلَّ أَوْ نَظْلِمَ أَوْ نُظْلَمَ أَوْ نَجْهَلَ أَوْ يُجْهَلَ عَلَيْنَا

Bismillāhi tawakkaltu 'alAllāhi Allāhumma innī a'ūdhu bika min an nazilla aw naḍilla aw naẓlima aw nuẓlama aw najhala aw yujhala 'alaynā

O Allāh! We seek refuge in You from slipping unintentionally or becoming misguided, or committing oppression or being oppressed, or acting ignorantly or being treated ignorantly. [Jāmi` At-Tirmidhī 3427]

Seeking Protection from the Evil of One's Soul

اَللّٰهُمَّ أَلْهِمْنِي رُشْدِي وَأَعِذْنِي مِنْ شَرِّ نَفْسِي

Allāhumma alhimnī rushdī, wa a-`idhnī min sharri nafsī

O Allāh, inspire me with my guidance, and protect me from the evil of my soul. [Jāmi` At-Tirmidhī 3483]

Fraud

Seeking Forgiveness of Sins

اَللّٰهُمَّ إِنِّي ظَلَمْتُ نَفْسِي ظُلْمًا كَثِيرًا، وَلاَ يَغْفِرُ الذُّنُوبَ إِلاَّ أَنْتَ، فَاغْفِرْ لِي مِنْ عِنْدِكَ مَغْفِرَةً، إِنَّكَ أَنْتَ الْغَفُورُ الرَّحِيمُ

Allāhumma innī ẓalamtu nafsī ẓulman kathīran, wa lā yaghfirudh dhunūba illa anta, fagh-firlī min 'indika maghfiratan, innaka antal ghafūrur raḥīm

O Allāh! I have wronged my soul very much (oppressed myself), and none forgives the sins but You; so please bestow Your forgiveness upon me. No doubt, You are the Exceedingly Forgiving, the All Forgiving. [Ṣaḥīḥ Al-Bukhārī 7387]

Seeking Protection from Treachery

اَللّٰهُمَّ إِنِّيْ أَعُوْذُ بِكَ مِنَ الْجُوْعِ ، فَإِنَّهُ بِئْسَ الضَّجِيْعُ ، وَأَعُوْذُ بِكَ مِنَ الْخِيَانَةِ ، فَإِنَّهَا بِئْسَتِ الْبِطَانَةُ

Allāhumma innī a'ūdhu bika minal jū', fa innahū bi-saḍ ḍajī', wa a'ūdhu bika minal khiyānah, fa innahā bi-satil biṭānah

O Allāh, I seek Your protection from hunger, as it is indeed an evil companion and I seek Your protection from treachery, as it is an evil confidante. [Sunan Abī Dawūd 1547]

Fraud

Praying for a Truthful Tongue, a Sound Heart and Uprightness

اَللّٰهُمَّ إِنِّي أَسْأَلُكَ الثَّبَاتَ فِي الأَمْرِ وَأَسْأَلُكَ عَزِيمَةَ الرُّشْدِ وَأَسْأَلُكَ شُكْرَ نِعْمَتِكَ وَحُسْنَ عِبَادَتِكَ وَأَسْأَلُكَ لِسَانًا صَادِقًا وَقَلْبًا سَلِيمًا وَأَعُوذُ بِكَ مِنْ شَرِّ مَا تَعْلَمُ وَأَسْأَلُكَ مِنْ خَيْرِ مَا تَعْلَمُ وَأَسْتَغْفِرُكَ مِمَّا تَعْلَمُ إِنَّكَ أَنْتَ عَلاَّمُ الْغُيُوبِ

Allāhumma innī as-alukath thabāta fil amri wa as-aluka 'azīmatar rushdi wa as-aluka shukra ni'matika wa ḥusna 'ibādatik, wa as-aluka lisānan ṣādiqa, wa qalban salīma, wa a'ūdhu bika min sharri ma ta'lam, wa as-aluka min khayri ma ta'lam, wa astaghfiruka mimmā ta'lam, innaka anta 'allāmul ghuyūb

O Allāh, I beg You for steadfastness in religious affairs. I beg You for determination to follow the guidance. I beg You to enable me to show gratitude for Your bounties and to worship You with the best devotion. I beg You for a truthful tongue, a sound heart, and an upright character. I seek Your protection from the evil of all that only You are aware of. I beg You for the good that only You know. And I seek forgiveness from You for what You know (of my sins). Surely, You are the All-Knowing of the hidden. [Jāmi` At-Tirmidhī 3407]

Dying as One of the Virtuous

رَبَّنَا فَٱغْفِرْ لَنَا ذُنُوبَنَا وَكَفِّرْ عَنَّا سَيِّـَٔاتِنَا وَتَوَفَّنَا مَعَ ٱلْأَبْرَارِ

Rabbanā faghfirlanā dhunūbanā wa kaffir 'annā sayyi-ātina wa tawaffanā ma'al abrār

Our Lord! Forgive our sins, absolve us of our misdeeds, and allow us (each) to die as one of the virtuous. [Āli 'Imrān 3:193]

قَسْوَةُ القَلْب

Hard-Heartedness

RELATED EMOTIONS

Indifferent | Apathetic | Insensitive | Uncharitable | Unkind | Harsh
Aggressive | Argumentative | Arrogant | Cruel | Cynical
Manipulative | Neglectful | Offended | Reckless | Vindictive

INVOKING NAMES OF ALLĀH

- **Al-Laṭīf - the Benevolent**
- **Al-Ḥalīm - the Most Forbearing**
- **Al-Wadūd - the Most Loving**
- **Al-Bā'ith - The Resurrector**
- **Ar-Raḥīm - the All Merciful**
- **Al-Muqaddim - The Expediter**
- **Al-Mughniyy - The Enricher**

AṢ-ṢALĀH AL-IBRĀHĪMIYYAH

ACCEPTED PRAYERS

- **Seeking Refuge from Bad Conduct and Deeds**
- **Seeking Tearful Prayers**
- **Seeking a Changed Heart**
- **Seeking a Guided Heart**
- **Remembrance of the Hereafter**
- **Seeking Righteousness**
- **Seeking a Righteous Companion**
- **Seeking Closeness to the Qur'ān**

CHAPTER 13

Hard-Heartedness

[Qaswat al-Qalb] قَسْوَةُ القَلْب

The hard heart is that which contains a mixture of harshness and toughness, a heart that is continually void of submission and a sense of turning to Allāh ﷻ in repentance. Possessing a hard heart is in fact the severest of punishments because one is oblivious to the consequences of committing sins, and therefore neither repents nor experiences an ounce of guilt. His immune system, so to speak, shuts down to all other diseases of the heart. This is why the disbelievers are punished with having a hard and harsh heart.

The Prophet ﷺ said, "When a slave (a person) commits a sin (an evil deed) a black dot appears on his heart. Then if that person gives up that evil deed (sin), begs Allāh to forgive him, and repents, then his heart is cleared (from that heart-covering dot); but if he repeats the evil deed (sin), then that covering is increased till his heart is completely covered with it. And this is ar-rān that Allāh mentioned (in the Qur'ān), 'But no! In fact, their hearts have been stained by all (the evil) they used to commit!' [Al-Muṭaffifīn 83:14]" [At-Tirmidhī 3334]

Hard-Heartedness

Invoking Allāh's ﷻ Names

اللَّطِيفُ

Al-Laṭīf
The Benevolent

الْحَلِيمُ

Al-Ḥalīm
The Most Forbearing

الْوَدُودُ

Al-Wadūd
The Most Loving

الْبَاعِثُ

Al-Bā'ith
The Resurrector

الرَّحِيمُ

Ar-Raḥīm
The All Merciful

الْمُقَدِّمُ

Al-Muqaddim
The Expediter

الْمُغْنِيُّ

Al-Mughniyy
The Enricher

Hard-Heartedness

Contemplation and Reflection on Allāh's ﷻ Blessed Names

- You remind yourself of the importance of showing preference and offering compassion towards the servants of Allāh ﷻ.
- On the occasions when you are capable of sharing experience and guidance, you put your best foot forward in a manner free from rebuke or harshness, fanaticism or disputation. The proof that you are doing this with a clean heart is that people come back to you for help and support.
- For you, dignified manner and conduct are the cornerstones of your benign strategy to attract others to the truth of Islām. You understand that the benevolent person works to maintain inward goodness. Emerging from this goodness, in your social interactions, are the noticeably positive qualities, pleasing manner, and praiseworthy actions that exemplify the Prophetic Sunnah. These are more effective than eloquent speech.
- You appreciate that 'mildness' is among the fine qualities of humankind.
- You remind yourself that the signs of a hard heart are speech or actions that display a love of this world, and anything that shows you have a dislike of or indifference to death.
- When you attend a burial, you focus on the large sticky clods of earth that have been removed from the ground to accommodate the coffin. You see how hard they are and - no matter how gently they are tossed into the grave - how they make a resounding thud upon the coffin top. Your prayer is that Allāh ﷻ grants you soft-heartedness, forgives the sins of the deceased and those who are witness to His Oneness, and affords you a grave that is like a garden of paradise, free from the crushing and pulverising that afflicts the souls of the hard-hearted.
- You make a firm commitment that when a sin is committed, you will quickly turn to Allāh ﷻ seeking His forgiveness because He is the most Lovingly Kind and entirely Merciful.
- You are not apathetic towards (you do not turn away from) any needy people, indeed you attempt to meet their needs to the extent of your ability. You will commit time or money or both to the poor in your neighbourhood, finding the means for them to be rid of their poverty.
- You remind yourself that if you cannot alleviate their poverty, you should assist the needy by prayer or by showing grief on account of their need, in sympathy and love towards them, as though you were thereby sharing in their misfortune and their destitution.
- You remind yourself of your true purpose in life, your accountability to your Creator, the Resurrection, the Ultimate Standing, and Judgement in the Hereafter.
- You learn that enrichment is not confined to material resources; that it also covers spiritual and emotional reinforcement, and hence you pray to Allāh ﷻ for spiritual wealth.

Hard-Heartedness

Aṣ-Ṣalāh Al-Ibrāhīmiyyah

اَللّٰهُمَّ صَلِّ عَلَى مُحَمَّدٍ وَعَلَى آلِ مُحَمَّدٍ كَمَا صَلَّيْتَ عَلَى
إِبْرَاهِيمَ وَآلِ إِبْرَاهِيمَ إِنَّكَ حَمِيدٌ مَجِيدٌ وَبَارِكْ عَلَى
مُحَمَّدٍ وَعَلَى آلِ مُحَمَّدٍ كَمَا بَارَكْتَ عَلَى إِبْرَاهِيمَ وَآلِ
إِبْرَاهِيمَ إِنَّكَ حَمِيدٌ مَجِيدٌ

Allāhumma ṣalli ʿalā Muḥammadin wa ʿalā āli Muḥammadin kamā ṣ allayta ʿalā Ibrāhīm wa āli Ibrāhīm innaka ḥamīdum majīd, wa bārik ʿalā Muḥammadin wa ʿalā āli Muḥammadin kamā bārakta ʿalā Ibrāhīm wa āli Ibrāhīm innaka ḥamīdum majīd

O Allāh, send peace upon Muḥammad and upon the family of Muḥammad, as You sent peace upon Ibrāhīm and the family of Ibrāhīm, and send blessings upon Muḥammad and upon the family of Muḥammad as You sent blessings upon Ibrāhīm and the family of Ibrāhīm. You are indeed praiseworthy, the most honourable. [Sunan An-Nasaī 1290]

Hard-Heartedness

Seeking Refuge from Bad Conduct and Deeds

اَللّٰهُمَّ إِنِّي أَعُوذُ بِكَ مِن مُنكَرَاتِ الأَخلاقِ، والأَعْمَالِ، والأَهْواءِ

Allāhumma innī a'ūdhu bika min munkarātil akhlāqi wal a'māli wal ahwā'

O Allāh! I seek refuge in You from reprehensible conduct, deeds and desires. [Jāmi' At-Tirmidhī 3591]

Seeking Tearful Prayers

اَللّٰهُمَّ ارْزُقْنِي عَيْنَيْنِ هَطَّالَتَيْنِ ، تَشْفِيَانِ الْقَلْبَ بِذُرُوفِ الدَّمْعِ مِنْ خَشْيَتِكَ ، قَبْلَ أَنْ يَكُونَ الدَّمْعُ دَمًا ، وَالأَضْرَاسُ جَمْرًا

Allāhummarzuqnī 'aynayni haṭṭālatayn, tashfiyānil qalba bi dhurūfid dam'i min khashyatik qabla ay yakūnad dam'u daman wal aḍrāsu jamrā

O Allāh, grant me profusely weeping eyes that comfort the heart with tears that flow out of Your fear, before the time comes when eyes will be shedding blood and teeth will become embers. [At-Ṭabarānī in Ad-Du'ā 1457]

Seeking a Changed Heart

يَا مُقَلِّبَ الْقُلُوبِ ثَبِّتْ قَلْبِي عَلَى دِينِكَ

Yā muqallibal qulūbi thabbit qalbī 'alā dīnik

O Turner of hearts, keep my heart steadfast on Your religion. [Jāmi' At-Tirmidhī 3522]

Hard-Heartedness

Seeking a Guided Heart

رَبَّنَا لَا تُزِغْ قُلُوبَنَا بَعْدَ إِذْ هَدَيْتَنَا وَهَبْ لَنَا
مِن لَّدُنكَ رَحْمَةً ۚ إِنَّكَ أَنتَ ٱلْوَهَّابُ

Rabbanā lā tuzig qulūbanā ba'da idh hadaytanā wa hab lanā min ladunka raḥmah, innaka antal wahhāb

Our Lord! Do not let our hearts deviate after you have guided us. Grant us Your mercy. You are indeed the Giver (of all bounties). [Āli 'Imrān 3:8]

Remembrance of the Hereafter

رَبَّنَا آتِنَا فِي الدُّنْيَا حَسَنَةً وَفِي الْآخِرَةِ حَسَنَةً وَقِنَا عَذَابَ النَّارِ

Rabbanā ātinā fid dunyā ḥasanatan wa fil ākhirati ḥasanatan wa qinā adhāban nār

"Our Lord! Grant us the good of this world and the Hereafter, and protect us from the torment of the Fire." [Al-Baqarah 2:201]

Hard-Heartedness

Seeking Righteousness

رَبِّ أَوْزِعْنِيٓ أَنْ أَشْكُرَ نِعْمَتَكَ ٱلَّتِيٓ أَنْعَمْتَ عَلَيَّ وَعَلَىٰ وَٰلِدَيَّ وَأَنْ أَعْمَلَ صَٰلِحًا تَرْضَىٰهُ وَأَدْخِلْنِي بِرَحْمَتِكَ فِي عِبَادِكَ ٱلصَّٰلِحِينَ

Rabbi awzi'nī an ashkura ni'matikallatī an'amta 'alayya wa 'alā wālidayya wa an -a'mala ṣāliḥan tarḍāhu wa adkhilnī bi raḥmatika fī 'ibādikaṣ ṣāliḥīn

My Lord! Inspire me to (always) be thankful for Your favours which You have blessed me and my parents with, and to do good deeds that please you. Admit me, by Your mercy, into (the company of) Your righteous servants. [An-Naml 27:19]

Seeking a Righteous Companion

اَللّٰهُمَّ يَسِّرْ لِي جَلِيسًا صَالِحًا

Allāhumma yassir lī jalīsan ṣāliḥā

O Allāh ! Bless me with a pious companion. [Ṣaḥīḥ Al-Bukhārī 3743]

Hard-Heartedness

Seeking Closeness to the Qur'ān

اَللّٰهُمَّ إِنِّي عَبْدُكَ، ابْنُ عَبْدِكَ، ابْنُ أَمَتِكَ نَاصِيَتِي بِيَدِكَ، مَاضٍ فِيَّ حُكْمُكَ، عَدْلٌ فِيَّ قَضَاؤُكَ، أَسْأَلُكَ بِكُلِّ اسْمٍ هُوَ لَكَ سَمَّيْتَ بِهِ نَفْسَكَ، أَوْ عَلَّمْتَهُ أَحَدًا مِنْ خَلْقِكَ، أَوْ أَنْزَلْتَهُ فِي كِتَابِكَ، أَوِ اسْتَأْثَرْتَ بِهِ فِي عِلْمِ الْغَيْبِ عِنْدَكَ، أَنْ تَجْعَلَ الْقُرْآنَ رَبِيعَ قَلْبِي، وَنُورَ صَدْرِي، وَجِلَاءَ حُزْنِي، وَذَهَابَ هَمِّي

Allāhumma innī 'abduk, ibnu 'abdik, ibnu amatik, nāṣiyatī bi yadik, māḍin fiyya ḥukmuk, 'adlun fiyya qaḍā-uk, as-aluka bi kullismin huwa lak, sammayta bihī nafsak, aw anzaltahū fī kitābik, aw 'allamtahū aḥadan min khalqik, awis-ta-tharta bihī fī 'ilmil ghaybi 'indak, an taj'alal qur-āna rabī'a qalbī, wa nūra ṣadrī, wa jalā-a ḥuznī, wa dhahāba hammī

O Allāh, I am Your slave, son of Your slave, son of Your handmaid, my forelock is in Your hand (i.e. You have total mastery over me), Your command over me is forever executed and Your decree over me is just. I ask You by every name belonging to You which You named Yourself with, or revealed in Your Book, or You taught to any of Your creation, or You have preserved in the knowledge of the unseen with You, that You make the Qur'ān the life of my heart and the light of my bosom, and a departure for my sorrow and a release for my anxiety. [Musnad Aḥmad 3712]

البُغْض

Hatred

RELATED EMOTIONS

Grudging | Bitter | Resentful | Vindictive | Hostile | Aggressive
Argumentative | Enraged | Furious

INVOKING NAMES OF ALLĀH

- Ar-Raḥmān - the All Compassionate
- Al-Ghafūr - The Exceedingly Forgiving
- Al-Ḥalīm - the Most Forbearing
- Al-Wadūd - The Most Loving
- At-Tawwāb - The Relenting
- Al-Barr - the Source of Good
- As-Salām - the Giver of Peace
- Ar-Raḥīm - the All Merciful
- Al-Ghaffār - The Forgiving

AṢ-ṢALĀH AL-IBRĀHĪMIYYAH

ACCEPTED PRAYERS

- Praying for Peace
- Removing Hatred from Your Chest
- Preventing Bitterness in Our Heart
- Joining Hearts and Mending Relationships
- Seeking Good for Another Believer Whom You Have Harmed
- Seeking Allāh's Protection from Another
- Seeking Victory Over the One Who Displays Enmity

CHAPTER 14

Hatred [Bughd] البُغض

Allāh ﷻ permits certain types of hatred: indeed, through revelation and the actions of the Noble Prophet ﷺ, we see that there are certain conditions whereby hatred can be deserving of merit. However, the hatred that is misguided and falls outside of the bounds of religion has no justification. Here, we are concerned with the hatred for other than that which Allāh ﷻ has decreed despicable.

Something similar to hatred is malice (ḥiqd), which asserts itself as repressed and frustrated anger when one lacks the power to take revenge or retribution. A more extreme form of anger is rancour (ghill), a despicable emotion that is rooted in being extremely angry at a person to the point that one wishes harm upon him.

The Prophet ﷺ once said to his Companions, "Do you want to see a man of Paradise?" A man then passed by and the Prophet ﷺ said, "That man is one of the people of Paradise." One Companion of the Prophet ﷺ took it upon himself to learn what it was about this man that earned him such a commendation from the Messenger of Allāh ﷺ. He spent time with this man and observed him closely: He noticed that he did not perform the night prayer vigil (tahajjud) or anything extraordinary; he appeared to be an average man of Madinah. The Companion finally confronted the man and told him what the Prophet ﷺ had said about him and asked if he did anything special. The man gave it some thought, and eventually replied, "The only thing that I can think of, other than what you have seen, is that I make sure that I never sleep with any rancour in my heart towards any believer, nor do I envy anyone for any goodness that Allāh has given them." That was his secret. [Musnad Aḥmad 12697]

Hatred

Invoking Allāh's ﷻ Names

الْرَّحْمَانُ
Ar-Raḥmān
The All Compassionate

الْغَفُورُ
Al-Ghafūr
The Exceedingly Forgiving

الْحَلِيمُ
Al-Ḥalīm
The Most Forbearing

الْوَدُودُ
Al-Wadūd
The Most Loving

الْتَّوَّابُ
At-Tawwāb
The Relenting

الْبَرُّ
Al-Barr
The Source of Good

الْسَّلَامُ
As-Salām
The Giver of Peace

الْرَّحِيمُ
Ar-Raḥīm
The All Merciful

الْغَفَّارُ
Al-Ghaffār
The Forgiving

Hatred

Contemplation and Reflection on Allāh's ﷻ Blessed Names

- You understand that love is an attribute of Allāh ﷻ while hatred is not, that hatred is the absence of love, and only through love can bitterness and hostility be removed from the heart.
- You show mercy to others by way of gentleness not argumentation, with eyes of mercy not mockery, sparing no effort to ensure you are not exposed to Allāh's ﷻ wrath.
- You remember that mildness (not aggressiveness and hostility) is among the finest qualities of mankind.
- You become generous and forbearing towards others, and strict with yourself. Foremost, you stop yourself from exposing the faults, sins or coarse habits of others, since you are sure that you would hate for someone else to do the same to you.
- You desire for Allāh's ﷻ creatures whatever you desire for yourself, and if you prefer others to yourself, you are even higher than this.
- You understand that every servant whose heart is free has become unburdened by his lower self. That same person, whose limbs are unblemished by sins and forbidden actions, will be one who comes to God the most High with a flawless heart.
- You put up with any offence and hurt caused to you because you realise that Allāh ﷻ is sufficient to take offenders to task.
- You know that the one who is loving and kind among Allāh's ﷻ servants is he who desires for Allāh's ﷻ creatures whatever he desires for himself. The perfection of this virtue occurs when not even thoroughly negative experiences keep him from selfless concern for the well-being of others.

Hatred

Aṣ-Ṣalāh Al-Ibrāhīmiyyah

اَللّٰهُمَّ صَلِّ عَلَى مُحَمَّدٍ وَعَلَى آلِ مُحَمَّدٍ كَمَا صَلَّيْتَ عَلَى
إِبْرَاهِيمَ وَآلِ إِبْرَاهِيمَ إِنَّكَ حَمِيدٌ مَجِيدٌ وَبَارِكْ عَلَى
مُحَمَّدٍ وَعَلَى آلِ مُحَمَّدٍ كَمَا بَارَكْتَ عَلَى إِبْرَاهِيمَ وَآلِ
إِبْرَاهِيمَ إِنَّكَ حَمِيدٌ مَجِيدٌ

Allāhumma ṣalli ʿalā Muḥammadin wa ʿalā āli Muḥammadin kamā ṣ allayta ʿalā Ibrāhīm wa āli Ibrāhīm innaka ḥamīdum majīd, wa bārik ʿalā Muḥammadin wa ʿalā āli Muḥammadin kamā bārakta ʿalā Ibrāhīm wa āli Ibrāhīm innaka ḥamīdum majīd

O Allāh, send peace upon Muḥammad and upon the family of Muḥammad, as You sent peace upon Ibrāhīm and the family of Ibrāhīm, and send blessings upon Muḥammad and upon the family of Muḥammad as You sent blessings upon Ibrāhīm and the family of Ibrāhīm. You are indeed praiseworthy, the most honourable. [Sunan An-Nasaī 1290]

Hatred

Praying for Peace

اَللّٰهُمَّ أَنْتَ السَّلامُ وَمِنْكَ السَّلام تَبارَكْتَ يا ذا الجَلالِ وَالإِكْرام

Allāhumma antas salām wa minkas salām tabārakta yā dhal jalāli wal ikrām

"O Allāh, You are peace and from You is peace. Blessed are You, the Majestic and Noble." [Ṣaḥīḥ Muslim 592]

Removing Hatred from Your Chest

رَبِّ تَقَبَّلْ تَوْبَتِي وَاغْسِلْ حَوْبَتِي وَأَجِبْ دَعْوَتِي وَثَبِّتْ حُجَّتِي وَاهْدِ قَلْبِي
وَسَدِّدْ لِسَانِي وَاسْلُلْ سَخِيمَةَ قَلْبِي

Rabbi taqabbal tawbatī waghsil ḥawbatī wa ajib da'watī wa thabbit ḥujjatī wahdi qalbī wa saddi lisānī waslul sakhīmata qalbī

O Lord, accept my repentance, wash away my sin, answer my supplication, establish my proof, direct my tongue, guide my heart, and remove the rancour from my chest. [Sunan Abī Dawūd 1510]

Hatred

Preventing Bitterness in Our Heart

رَبَّنَا ٱغْفِرْ لَنَا وَلِإِخْوَٰنِنَا ٱلَّذِينَ سَبَقُونَا بِٱلْإِيمَٰنِ وَلَا تَجْعَلْ فِى قُلُوبِنَا غِلًّا لِّلَّذِينَ
ءَامَنُوا۟ رَبَّنَآ إِنَّكَ رَءُوفٌ رَّحِيمٌ

Rabbānaghfir lanā wa li ikhwāninalladhīna sabaqūnā bil īmāni wa lā taj'al fī qulūbinā ghillal lilladhīna āmanu rabbāna innaka ra-ūfur raḥīm

Our Lord! Forgive us and our fellow believers who preceded us in faith, and do not allow bitterness into our hearts towards those who believe. Our Lord! Indeed, You are Ever Gracious, Most Merciful. [Al-Ḥashr 59:10]

Seeking Good for Another Believer Whom You Have Harmed

اَللّٰهُمَّ إِنِّي أَتَّخِذُ عِنْدَكَ عَهْدًا لَنْ تُخْلِفَنِيهِ فَإِنَّمَا أَنَا بَشَرٌ فَأَىُّ الْمُؤْمِنِينَ آذَيْتُهُ
شَتَمْتُهُ لَعَنْتُهُ جَلَدْتُهُ فَاجْعَلْهَا لَهُ صَلاَةً وَزَكَاةً وَقُرْبَةً تُقَرِّبُهُ بِهَا إِلَيْكَ يَوْمَ
الْقِيَامَةِ

Allāhumma innī attakhidhu 'indaka 'ahdan lan tukhlifanīhi fa innamā ana basharun fa ayyul mu-minīna ādhaytuhū shatamtuhū la'antuhū jaladtuhū faj'alhā lahū alātan wa zakātan wa qurbatan tuqarribuhū bihā ilayka yawmal qiyāmah

O Allāh, I seek from you an unbreakable promise. I am just a human being. So whichever believer I hurt or rebuke or hit or curse then change that for him into mercy, purification, and a means of closeness to You on the Day of Judgement. [Ṣaḥīḥ Muslim 2601b]

Hatred

Joining Hearts and Mending Relationships

اَللّٰهُمَّ أَلِّفْ بَيْنَ قُلُوبِنَا وَأَصْلِحْ ذَاتَ بَيْنِنَا وَاهْدِنَا سُبُلَ السَّلَامِ وَنَجِّنَا مِنَ
الظُّلُمَاتِ إِلَى النُّورِ وَجَنِّبْنَا الْفَوَاحِشَ مَا ظَهَرَ مِنْهَا وَمَا بَطَنَ وَبَارِكْ لَنَا فِي
أَسْمَاعِنَا وَأَبْصَارِنَا وَقُلُوبِنَا وَأَزْوَاجِنَا وَذُرِّيَّاتِنَا وَتُبْ عَلَيْنَا إِنَّكَ أَنْتَ التَّوَّابُ
الرَّحِيمُ وَاجْعَلْنَا شَاكِرِينَ لِنِعْمَتِكَ مُثْنِينَ بِهَا قَابِلِيهَا وَأَتِمَّهَا عَلَيْنَا

Allāhumma allif bayna qulūbina wa aṣliḥ dhāt bayninā wahdinā subulas salāmi wa najjinā minaẓ ẓulumāti ilan nūr, wa jannibnal fawāḥisha ma ẓahara minhā wa ma baṭan, wa bārik lanā fī asmā'inā wa abṣārinā wa qulūbinā wa azwājinā wa dhurriyyātinā wa tub 'alaynā innaka antat tawwābur raḥīm, waj'alnā shākirīna li ni'matika muthnīna bihā qābilīhā wa atimmahā 'alaynā

O Allāh, join our hearts, mend our relationships, and guide us to the paths of peace. Bring us out of darkness into light and keep us away from manifest and concealed obscenities. Bless us in our ears, our eyes, our hearts, our spouses, and our offspring. Accept our repentance. Indeed, You are the Most Forgiving, the Most Merciful. Make us grateful for Your blessings, so we receive them with due praise. And perfect them for us. [Sunan Abī Dawūd 969]

Hatred

Seeking Allāh's ﷻ Protection from Another

رَبِّ أَعِنِّي وَلاَ تُعِنْ عَلَيَّ وَانْصُرْنِي وَلاَ تَنْصُرْ عَلَيَّ وَامْكُرْ لِي وَلاَ تَمْكُرْ عَلَيَّ
وَاهْدِنِي وَيَسِّرْ هُدَايَ إِلَيَّ وَانْصُرْنِي عَلَى مَنْ بَغَى عَلَيَّ

Rabbi a-'innī wa la tu'in 'alyya wanṣurnī wa lā tanṣur 'alayya wamkur lī wa lā tamkur 'alayya wahdinī wa yassir hudāya ilayya wanṣurnī 'alā man baghā 'alayya

My Lord, help me and do not help anyone against me, support me and do not support anyone against me, plan for me and do not plan against me. Guide me and make guidance easy for me. Support me against those who transgress against me. [Sunan Abī Dawūd 1510]

Seeking Victory Over the One Who Displays Enmity

اَللّٰهُمَّ انْصُرْنَا عَلَى مَنْ عَادَانَا وَلاَ تَجْعَلْ مُصِيبَتَنَا فِي دِينِنَا وَلاَ تَجْعَلِ الدُّنْيَا
أَكْبَرَ هَمِّنَا وَلاَ مَبْلَغَ عِلْمِنَا وَلاَ تُسَلِّطْ عَلَيْنَا مَنْ لاَ يَرْحَمُنَا

Allāhummanṣurnā 'alā man 'ādānā wa lā taj'al muṣīybatanā fī dīninā wa lā taj'alid dunyā akbara hamminā wa lā mablagha 'ilminā wa lā tusalliṭ 'alaynā man lā yarḥamunā

O Allāh, help us to victory over the one who displays enmity to us. Do not let our misfortunes hit our religion. Do not make this world our greatest concern and the sum total of our knowledge. And do not impose over us one who shows no mercy to us. [Jāmi` At-Tirmidhī 3502]

HATRED

البُغْض

الغَفلَة

Heedlessness

RELATED EMOTIONS

Indifferent | Forgetful | Lazy | Careless | Reckless | Ignorant
Apathetic | Astray | Insensitive | Neglectful | Thoughtless
Obstinate | Oblivious

INVOKING NAMES OF ALLĀH ﷻ

- **An-Nūr - The Light**
- **Al-Hādī - The Guide**
- **Ar-Rashīd - The Director**
- **Al-Quddus - the Pure One**
- **Ar-Raqīb - the Watchful**
- **Al-Khabīr - the All-Aware**
- **Al-Bā'ith - The Resurrector**
- **Al-Muqaddim - The Expediter**
- **Al-'Afuww - The Pardoner**

AṢ-ṢALĀH AL-IBRĀHĪMIYYAH

ACCEPTED PRAYERS

- **Establishing Prayer and Acceptance**
- **Seeking Refuge from Laziness**
- **Seeking Forgiveness for Forgetfulness and Error**
- **Seeking Forgiveness for Ignorance and Carelessness**
- **Seeking Forgiveness for Faults in Private and Public**
- **Seeking God Consciousness and Obedience**
- **Achieving Mindfulness in Deeds**
- **Seeking Faithfulness and Mercy**
- **Seeking Steadfastness in Religion**
- **Seeking Steadfastness and Determination**
- **Seeking Steadfastness until the End**
- **Seeking Ease in Following Guidance**

CHAPTER 15

Heedlessness

[Ghaflah] الغَفْلَة

Heedlessness or ghaflah is being careless (paying a lack of attention) to what is infinitely more important in one's life (than material goods), i.e. what Allāh ﷻ has commanded us to do and what has been prohibited. The heedlessness referenced here is the most menacing form: being heedless of divine purpose, accountability, the resurrection, the ultimate standing, and judgement in the Hereafter.

Scholars have said that heedlessness is the one pathogen that breeds all the diseases of the heart. A mughaffal (a simpleton) is a person who is easily fooled, i.e. one who is diverted away from what is essential and consequential, yet inclined toward what is temporary and ultimately pointless.

Heedlessness

Invoking Allāh's ﷻ Names

النُّورُ

An-Nūr
The Light

الْهَادِي

Al-Hādī
The Guide

الرَّشِيدُ

Ar-Rashīd
The Director

الْقُدُّوسُ

Al-Quddus
The Pure One

الرَّقِيبُ

Ar-Raqīb
The Watchful

الْخَبِيرُ

Al-Khabīr
The All-Aware

الْبَاعِثُ

Al-Bā'ith
The Resurrector

الْمُقَدِّمُ

Al-Muqaddim
The Expediter

الْعَفُوُّ

Al-'Afuww
The Pardoner

Heedlessness

Contemplation and Reflection on Allāh's ﷻ Blessed Names

- You realise that Allāh ﷻ guides with His divine guidance whomsoever He wills by showing him the truth and inspiring him to follow it.
- You try your best to purify yourself by working towards righteousness, by respecting the Qur'ānic injunction to enjoin good and keep away from evil.
- You understand the importance of watchfulness, that it is praiseworthy if your heart and deeds are directed to your Allāh ﷻ.
- You realise that Allāh ﷻ observes you and sees you in every situation.
- You remind yourself that your own soul is an enemy to you, and that Satan is an enemy who misleads you into hasty, rash deeds; listening to Satan and your lower self will prompt you to forgetfulness, disobedience and ultimately heedlessness.
- You know that a 'mughaffal' (a simpleton) is a person who is easily fooled, i.e. one who is diverted away from what is essential and consequential, yet inclined toward what is temporary and ultimately pointless.
- You adopt a watchfulness over both your soul and Satan, by noticing the occasions when they work their deceptions, so that you can block both of them from using the entrances and the exits to your heart.
- You keep a journal, reflecting on the amount of active worship that you complete. You regularly review it, trying to improve on the small acts performed regularly: you know that these deeds are the best in keeping you from forgetting your purpose and becoming embroiled in triviality.
- You remind yourself of your true purpose in life, your accountability to your Creator, the resurrection, the ultimate standing, and judgement in the Hereafter.

Heedlessness

Aṣ-Ṣalāh Al-Ibrāhīmiyyah

اَللّٰهُمَّ صَلِّ عَلَى مُحَمَّدٍ وَعَلَى آلِ مُحَمَّدٍ كَمَا صَلَّيْتَ عَلَى
إِبْرَاهِيمَ وَآلِ إِبْرَاهِيمَ إِنَّكَ حَمِيدٌ مَجِيدٌ وَبَارِكْ عَلَى
مُحَمَّدٍ وَعَلَى آلِ مُحَمَّدٍ كَمَا بَارَكْتَ عَلَى إِبْرَاهِيمَ وَآلِ
إِبْرَاهِيمَ إِنَّكَ حَمِيدٌ مَجِيدٌ

Allāhumma ṣalli ʿalā Muḥammadin wa ʿalā āli Muḥammadin kamā ṣ allayta ʿalā Ibrāhīm wa āli Ibrāhīm innaka ḥamīdum majīd, wa bārik ʿalā Muḥammadin wa ʿalā āli Muḥammadin kamā bārakta ʿalā Ibrāhīm wa āli Ibrāhīm innaka ḥamīdum majīd

O Allāh, send peace upon Muḥammad and upon the family of Muḥammad, as You sent peace upon Ibrāhīm and the family of Ibrāhīm, and send blessings upon Muḥammad and upon the family of Muḥammad as You sent blessings upon Ibrāhīm and the family of Ibrāhīm. You are indeed praiseworthy, the most honourable. [Sunan An-Nasaī 1290]

Heedlessness

Establishing Prayer and Acceptance

رَبِّ ٱجْعَلْنِى مُقِيمَ ٱلصَّلَوٰةِ وَمِن ذُرِّيَّتِى ۚ رَبَّنَا وَتَقَبَّلْ دُعَآءِ

Rabbij'alnī muqīmaṣ ṣalāti wa min dhurriyyatī rabbanā wa taqabbal du'ā'

My Lord! Make me and those (believers) of my descendants keep up prayer. Our Lord! Accept my prayers. [Ibrāhīm 14:40]

Seeking Refuge from Laziness

اَللّٰهُمَّ إِنِّي أَعُوذُ بِكَ مِنَ الْهَمِّ وَالْحَزَنِ وَالْعَجزِ وَالْكَسَلِ وَالْجُبْنِ وَالْبُخْلِ وَضَلَعِ الدَّيْنِ وَغَلَبَةِ الرِّجَالِ

Allāhumma innī a'ūdhu bika minal hammi wal ḥazani wal 'ajzi wal kasali wal jubni wal bukhli wa ḍala'id dayni wa ghalabatir rijāl

"O Allāh, I seek refuge in you from anxiety and sadness, weakness and laziness, miserliness and cowardice, the burden of debts and from being overpowered by men." [Ṣaḥīḥ Al-Bukhārī 6369]

Heedlessness

Seeking Forgiveness for Forgetfulness and Error

رَبَّنَا لَا تُؤَاخِذْنَآ إِن نَّسِينَآ أَوْ أَخْطَأْنَا ۚ رَبَّنَا وَلَا تَحْمِلْ عَلَيْنَآ إِصْرًا كَمَا حَمَلْتَهُۥ
عَلَى ٱلَّذِينَ مِن قَبْلِنَا ۚ رَبَّنَا وَلَا تُحَمِّلْنَا مَا لَا طَاقَةَ لَنَا بِهِۦ وَٱعْفُ عَنَّا وَٱغْفِرْ لَنَا
وَٱرْحَمْنَآ ۚ أَنتَ مَوْلَىٰنَا فَٱنصُرْنَا عَلَى ٱلْقَوْمِ ٱلْكَٰفِرِينَ

Rabbānā lā tu-ākhidhnā in nasīna aw akhta-nā, rabbanā wa lā taḥmil ʿalaynā iṣrān kamā ḥamaltahu ʿalalladhīna min qablina, rabbanā wa lā tuḥammilnā mā lā ṭāqata la nā bih, waʿfu ʿannā waghfir lanā warḥamnā anta mawlānā fanṣurnā ʿalal qawmil kāfirīn

Our Lord! Do not punish us if we forget or make a mistake. Our Lord! Do not place a burden on us like the one you placed on those before us. Our Lord! Do not burden us with what we cannot bear. Pardon us, forgive us, and have mercy on us. You are our (only) Guardian. So grant us victory over the disbelieving people. [Al-Baqarah 2:286]

Seeking Forgiveness for Ignorance and Carelessness

اَللّٰهُمَّ اغْفِرْ لِي خَطِيئَتِي وَجَهْلِي وَإِسْرَافِي فِي أَمْرِي، وَمَا أَنْتَ أَعْلَمُ بِهِ مِنِّي، اَللّٰهُمَّ
اغْفِرْ لِي هَزْلِي وَجِدِّي وَخَطَايَ وَعَمْدِي، وَكُلُّ ذَلِكَ عِنْدِي

Allāhummaghfirlī khatī-atī wa jahlī wa isrāfī fī amrī, wa mā anta aʿlamu bihī minnī, Allāhummaghfirlī hazlī wa jiddī wa khatāya wa ʿamdī wa kullu dhālika ʿindī

O Allāh, forgive my errors, my ignorance and my extravagance in my affairs and what You know better than I do. O Allāh, forgive me what I do both in jest and seriousness, my errors and what I do intentionally and all that I do. [Ṣaḥīḥ Al-Bukhārī 6399]

Heedlessness

Seeking Forgiveness for Faults in Private and Public

اَللّٰهُمَّ اغْفِرْ لِي مَا قَدَّمْتُ وَمَا أَخَّرْتُ وَمَا أَسْرَرْتُ وَمَا أَعْلَنْتُ وَمَا أَنْتَ أَعْلَمُ
بِهِ مِنِّي أَنْتَ الْمُقَدِّمُ وَأَنْتَ الْمُؤَخِّرُ وَأَنْتَ عَلَى كُلِّ شَيْءٍ قَدِيرٌ

Allāhummaghfir lī mā qaddamtu wa mā akhkhartu wa mā asrartu wa mā a'lantu wa mā anta a'lamu bihī minnī, antal muqaddim wa antal mu-akhkhir wa anta 'alā kulli shay-in qadīr

O Allāh, grant me forgiveness from the fault which I did in haste or deferred, which I committed in privacy or in public and You are more aware of (them) than myself. You are the First and the Last and over all things You are Omnipotent. [Ṣaḥīḥ Muslim 2719a]

Seeking God Consciousness and Obedience

اَللّٰهُمَّ اجْعَلْنِي أَخْشَاكَ حَتَّى كَأَنِّي أَرَاكَ أَبَدًا حَتَّى أَلْقَاكَ ، وَأَسْعِدْنِي بِتَقْوَاكَ ،
وَلَا تُشْقِنِي بِمَعْصِيَتِكَ

Allāhummaj'alnī akhsāka ḥattā ka-annī arāka abadan ḥattā alqāk, wa as'idnī bi taqwāka wa lā tushqinī bi ma'ṣiyatik

O Allāh, make me fear You as if I see You all the time until I meet You. Make me blissful as a result of Your taqwa (Your fear and piety); do not make me wretched as a result of Your disobedience. [5982 Aṭ-Ṭabarānī in Al-Mu'jam Al-Awṣaṭ]

Heedlessness

Achieving Mindfulness in Deeds

اَللّٰهُمَّ اجْعَلْنِي مِنَ الَّذِينَ إِذَا أَحْسَنُوا اسْتَبْشَرُوا وَإِذَا أَسَاءُوا اسْتَغْفَرُوا

Allāhummaj'alnī minalladhīna idhā aḥsanū istabsharū wa idhā asā-ū istaghfarū

O Allāh, make me among those who, when they commit an act of virtue, rejoice, and when they commit a mistake, seek forgiveness.
[Sunan Ibn Mājah 3820]

Seeking Faithfulness and Mercy

اَللّٰهُمَّ أَقْبِلْ بِقَلْبِي إِلَى دِينِكَ، وَاحْفَظْ مَنْ وَرَاءَنَا بِرَحْمَتِكَ

Allāhumma aqbil bi qalbī ilā dīnik waḥfaẓ man warā-anā bi raḥmatik

O Allāh, turn my heart to Your religion and protect us from all around with Your mercy. [Musnad Abī Ya'lā 3485]

Seeking Steadfastness in Religion

يَا مُقَلِّبَ الْقُلُوبِ ثَبِّتْ قَلْبِي عَلَى دِينِكَ

Yā muqallibal qulūbi thabbit qalbī 'alā dīnik

O Turner of hearts, keep my heart steadfast on Your religion. [Jāmi` At-Tirmidhī 3522]

Heedlessness

Seeking Steadfastness and Determination

اَللّٰهُمَّ إِنِّي أَسْأَلُكَ الثَّبَاتَ فِي الأَمْرِ وَالْعَزِيمَةَ عَلَى الرُّشْدِ

Allāhumma innī as-alukath thabāta fil amri wal 'azīmati 'alar rushd

O Allāh, I ask You for steadfastness in the matter (of religion) and I ask You for determination upon guidance. [Sunan An-Nasaī 1304]

Seeking Steadfastness until the End

يَا وَلِيَّ الْإِسْلَامِ وَأَهْلِهِ ، ثَبِّتْنِي بِهِ حَتَّى أَلْقَاكَ

Yā Waliyyal Islāmi wa ahlih, thabbitnī bihī ḥattā alqāk

O Guardian of Islām and its followers, keep me firm on it (Islām) until I meet You. [Aṭ-Ṭabarānī in Al-Mu'jam Al-Awṣaṭ 661]

Seeking Ease in Following Guidance

رَبِّ أَعِنِّي وَلاَ تُعِنْ عَلَيَّ وَانْصُرْنِي وَلاَ تَنْصُرْ عَلَيَّ وَامْكُرْ لِي وَلاَ تَمْكُرْ عَلَيَّ
وَاهْدِنِي وَيَسِّرِ الْهُدَى لِي

Rabbi a-'innī wa lā tu'in 'alayya wanṣurnī wa lā tanṣur 'alayya wamkur lī wa lā tamkur 'alayya wahdinī wa yassiril hudā lī

My Lord, aid me and do not aid against me, and grant me victory and do not grant victory over me, plot for me and do not plot again. [Jāmi` At-Tirmidhī 3551]

البَغيُ

Iniquity

RELATED EMOTIONS

Anxious | Vulnerable | Helpless | Insecure | Threatened | Distresse
Hostile | Malicious | Agitated | Frustrated | Arrogant | Callous
Contemptuous | Cruel | Deceitful | Depressed | Disappointed
Egotistic | Fearful | Frustrated | Furious | Manipulative | Neglectful
Reckless | Thoughtless | Cowardly

INVOKING NAMES OF ALLĀH ﷻ

- **Al-Malik - The Absolute Ruler**
- **Ar-Raḥmān - The All Compassionate**
- **Ar-Raḥīm - The All Merciful**
- **Al-Mumin - the One Who Gives Security**
- **Al-Muhaymin - The Guardian**
- **Ar-Raqīb - The Watchful**
- **Al-Waliyy - The Protecting Friend**
- **Al-ʿAdl - The Just**
- **Al-Baṣīr - The Seer of All (The All-Seeing)**
- **Al-Khabīr - the All-Aware**
- **Al-Muqsiṭ - The Requiter**
- **Al-Muntaqim - The Avenger**
- **Al-Mujīb - The Responsive One**
- **Al-Qawiyy - The All-Strong**
- **Al-Matīn - The Most Firm**
- **Al-Wālī - The Governor**

AṢ-ṢALĀH AL-IBRĀHĪMIYYAH

ACCEPTED PRAYERS

- **Seeking Help**
- **Placing Trust in Allāh ﷻ Alone**
- **Seeking Strength in the Pursuit of Allāh's ﷻ Pleasure**
- **Seeking the Removal of Worry and Distress**
- **Seeking Refuge from Committing Oppression or Being Oppressed**
- **Seeking Refuge from Being Overpowered**
- **Seeking Refuge from the Evil of Others**
- **Seeking Allāh's ﷻ Protection from Another**
- **Seeking Refuge from Misguidance, Abuse and Foolish Behaviour**
- **Seeking Allāh's ﷻ Protection**
- **Seeking Protection from the Persecution of People**
- **Seeking Protection from Calamities and Malicious Enemies**
- **Lightening the World's Hardships and Achieving Victory Over a Hostile Person**
- **Seeking Retribution for Hurting, Hitting or Cursing Another Believer**

CHAPTER 16

Iniquity [Baghy] البَغْي

Iniquity or baghy is when one harms anything in creation without right or just cause, usually because one is entrapped and infatuated by the love of this world and of worldly position. With this hard crust over the heart, there is no moral barrier preventing one from wronging others. However, as Allāh ﷻ promises in His Qur'ān, the iniquity and injustice that people aim at others ultimately works its way back to them:

"O humanity! Your transgression is only against your own souls." [Yūnus 10:23]

The Prophet ﷺ said, "After I am gone you will experience discrimination and will observe things that you will disapprove of." **Someone asked,** "O Messenger of Allāh, what do you command us to do then?" **He ﷺ said,** "Discharge your obligations and supplicate to Allāh for your rights." [Ṣaḥīḥ Al-Bukhārī 7052]

Iniquity

Invoking Allāh's ﷻ Names

الْمَلِكُ	الرَّحْمَانُ	الرَّحِيمُ	الْمُؤْمِنُ
Al-Malik The Absolute Ruler	Ar-Raḥmān - The All Compassionate	Ar-Raḥīm The All Merciful	Al-Mumin - The One Who Gives Security
الْمُهَيْمِنُ	الرَّقِيبُ	الْوَلِيُّ	الْعَدْلُ
Al-Muhaymin The Guardian	Ar-Raqīb The Watchful	Al-Waliyy The Protecting Friend	Al-'Adl The Just
الْبَصِيرُ	الْخَبِيرُ	الْمُقْسِطُ	الْمُنْتَقِمُ
Al-Baṣīr The Seer of All (The All-Seeing)	Al-Khabīr The All-Aware	Al-Muqsiṭ The Requiter	Al-Muntaqim The Avenger
الْمُجِيبُ	الْقَوِيُّ	الْمَتِينُ	الْوَالِي
Al-Mujīb The Responsive One	Al-Qawiyy The All-Strong	Al-Matīn The Most Firm	Al-Wālī The Governor

Iniquity

Contemplation and Reflection on Allāh's ﷻ Blessed Names

- You remember that Allāh ﷻ alone is the true and Absolute Ruler and we, being His subjects, are obliged to abide by His commands.
- You understand the importance of demonstrating justice with others, which consists of putting passion and anger under the guidance of reason and religion.
- You appreciate that your very existence and survival is due to Allāh's ﷻ care, His protection, His safety and His security, reminding you to demonstrate these virtues with others.
- You realise your duties in utmost kindness, justice and forgiveness towards your family and relatives, or concerning those under your authority or responsibility.
- You remind yourself that Allāh ﷻ witnesses and sees in such a way that nothing is remote from Him. He sees your deepest insecurities and what makes you vulnerable. You come to the awareness that He will relieve you of the threats to your well-being on all levels, and thus there is no need for you to lash out at others or deprive any people of what is rightfully theirs.
- You refrain from acting unjustly because you realise that Allāh ﷻ will exact retribution by severely punishing the oppressive after giving them all the means to repentance.
- You are inspired with more conviction, sincerity and fervour that Allāh ﷻ will respond to your prayer (your worry or distress) in a way that suits you best.
- You understand that every friend of Allāh ﷻ who divorces himself from immoral or grossly unfair behaviour, especially when it appears that there is some sort of fleeting benefit to be derived from carrying it through, will see a greater gain in trusting the reward from Allāh ﷻ on the Day of Reckoning.
- You recognise that peace of mind and moral perfection lies with he who demands justice for the wronged from the wrongdoer: that is the ultimate in justice and equity.
- You study the life of the Prophet Muhammad ﷺ and his rightly guided followers: in their lives and in their legal decrees they upheld justice by insisting first of all on justice from themselves for others.

Iniquity

Aṣ-Ṣalāh Al-Ibrāhīmiyyah

اَللّٰهُمَّ صَلِّ عَلَى مُحَمَّدٍ وَعَلَى آلِ مُحَمَّدٍ كَمَا صَلَّيْتَ عَلَى
إِبْرَاهِيمَ وَآلِ إِبْرَاهِيمَ إِنَّكَ حَمِيدٌ مَجِيدٌ وَبَارِكْ عَلَى
مُحَمَّدٍ وَعَلَى آلِ مُحَمَّدٍ كَمَا بَارَكْتَ عَلَى إِبْرَاهِيمَ وَآلِ
إِبْرَاهِيمَ إِنَّكَ حَمِيدٌ مَجِيدٌ

Allāhumma ṣalli 'alā Muḥammadin wa 'alā āli Muḥammadin kamā ṣ allayta 'alā Ibrāhīm wa āli Ibrāhīm innaka ḥamīdum majīd, wa bārik 'alā Muḥammadin wa 'alā āli Muḥammadin kamā bārakta 'alā Ibrāhīm wa āli Ibrāhīm innaka ḥamīdum majīd

O Allāh, send peace upon Muḥammad and upon the family of Muḥammad, as You sent peace upon Ibrāhīm and the family of Ibrāhīm, and send blessings upon Muḥammad and upon the family of Muḥammad as You sent blessings upon Ibrāhīm and the family of Ibrāhīm. You are indeed praiseworthy, the most honourable. [Sunan An-Nasaī 1290]

Iniquity

Seeking Help

أَنِّي مَغْلُوبٌ فَٱنتَصِرْ

Annī maghlūbun fantaṣir

I am helpless, so help (me)! [Al-Qamar 54:10]

Placing Trust in Allāh ﷻ Alone

حَسْبُنَا ٱللَّهُ وَنِعْمَ ٱلْوَكِيلُ

Ḥasbunallāhu wa ni'mal wakīl

Allāh (alone) is sufficient (as an aid) for us and (He) is the best Protector. [Āli 'Imrān 3:173]

Seeking Strength in the Pursuit of Allāh's ﷻ Pleasure

اَللّٰهُمَّ إِنِّي ضَعِيفٌ فَقَوِّ فِي رِضَاكَ ضَعْفِي ، وَخُذْ إِلَى الْخَيْرِ بِنَاصِيَتِي ، وَاجْعَلِ الْإِسْلَامَ مُنْتَهَى رِضَائِي ، اللَّهُمَّ إِنِّي ضَعِيفٌ فَقَوِّنِي ، وَإِنِّي ذَلِيلٌ فَأَعِزَّنِي ، وَإِنِّي فَقِيرٌ فَاغْنِنِي

Allāhumma innī ḍa'īfun fa qawwi fi riḍāka ḍa'fi, wa khudh ilal khayri bi nāṣiyatī, waj'alil Islāma muntahā riḍā-ī, Allāhumma innī ḍa'īfun fa qawwinī wa innī dhalīlun fa a-'izzanī wa innī faqīrun faghninī

O Allāh, I am weak; replace my weakness with strength in my pursuits of Your pleasure. Pull me by my forelocks toward good. Make Islām the ultimate object of my pleasure. O Allāh, I am weak, so strengthen me. I am lowly, so give me honour. And I am needy, so provide for me. [Aṭ-Ṭabarānī in Al-Mu'jam Al-Awṣaṭ 6575]

Iniquity

Seeking the Removal of Worry and Distress

اَللّٰهُمَّ فَارِجَ الْهَمِّ، كَاشِفَ الْغَمِّ، مُجِيبَ دَعْوَةِ الْمُضْطَرِّينَ، رَحْمَانَ الدُّنْيَا وَالْآخِرَةِ وَرَحِيمَهُمَا، أَنْتَ تَرْحَمُنِي، فَارْحَمْنِي بِرَحْمَةٍ تُغْنِينِي بِهَا عَنْ رَحْمَةِ مَنْ سِوَاكَ

Allāhumma fārijal hammi kāshifal ghammi mujīb da'watil muḍṭarrīn, raḥmānad dunyā wal ākhirati wa raḥīmahumā, anta tarḥamunī farḥamnī bi raḥmatin tughnīnī bihā 'an raḥmati man siwāk

O Allāh, Who relieves worry and removes distress, Who answers the call of the desperate, the All Compassionate and the All Merciful in this world and the hereafter, You are the One who could bestow mercy on me, so bestow mercy on me, so that I will have no need of mercy from anyone else. [Al-Ḥākim 1898]

Seeking Refuge from Committing Oppression or Being Oppressed

بِسْمِ اللّٰهِ تَوَكَّلْتُ عَلَى اللّٰهِ اللّٰهُمَّ إِنَّا نَعُوذُ بِكَ مِنْ أَنْ نَزِلَّ أَوْ نَضِلَّ أَوْ نَظْلِمَ أَوْ نُظْلَمَ أَوْ نَجْهَلَ أَوْ يُجْهَلَ عَلَيْنَا

Bismillāhi tawakkaltu 'alAllāhi Allāhumma innī a'ūdhu bika min an nazilla aw naḍilla aw naẓlima aw nuẓlama aw najhala aw yujhala 'alaynā

O Allāh! We seek refuge in You from slipping unintentionally or becoming misguided, or committing oppression or being oppressed, or acting ignorantly or being treated ignorantly. [Jāmi` At-Tirmidhī 3427]

Iniquity

Seeking Refuge from Being Overpowered

اَللّٰهُمَّ إِنِّي أَعُوذُ بِكَ مِنَ الْهَمِّ وَالْحَزَنِ وَالْعَجْزِ وَالْكَسَلِ وَالْجُبْنِ وَالْبُخْلِ وَضَلَعِ الدَّيْنِ وَغَلَبَةِ الرِّجَالِ

Allāhumma innī a'ūdhu bika minal hammi wal ḥazani wal 'ajzi wal kasali wal jubni wal bukhli wa ḍala'id dayni wa ghalabatir rijāl

O Allāh, I seek refuge in you from anxiety and sadness, weakness and laziness, miserliness and cowardice, the burden of debts and from being overpowered by men. [Ṣaḥīḥ Al-Bukhārī 6369]

Seeking Refuge from the Evil of Others

اَللّٰهُمَّ إِنَّا نَجْعَلُكَ فِي نُحُورِهِمْ وَنَعُوذُ بِكَ مِنْ شُرُورِهِمْ

Allāhumma innā naj'aluka fī nuḥūrihim wa na'ūdhu bika min shurūrihim

O Allāh, we ask You to restrain them by their necks, and we seek refuge in You from their evil. [Sunan Abī Dawūd 1537]

Iniquity

Seeking Allāh's ﷻ Protection from Another

رَبِّ أَعِنِّي وَلَا تُعِنْ عَلَيَّ وَانْصُرْنِي وَلَا تَنْصُرْ عَلَيَّ وَامْكُرْ لِي وَلَا تَمْكُرْ عَلَيَّ
وَاهْدِنِي وَيَسِّرْ هُدَايَ إِلَيَّ وَانْصُرْنِي عَلَى مَنْ بَغَى عَلَيَّ

Rabbi a-'innī wa la tu'in 'alyya wanṣurnī wa lā tanṣur 'alayya wamkur lī wa lā tamkur 'alayya wahdinī wa yassir hudāya ilayya wanṣurnī 'alā man baghā 'alayya

My Lord, help me and do not help anyone against me, support me and do not support anyone against me, plan for me and do not plan against me. Guide me and make guidance easy for me. Support me against those who transgress against me. [Sunan Abī Dawūd 1510]

Seeking Refuge from Misguidance, Abuse and Foolish Behaviour

اَللّٰهُمَّ إِنِّي أَعُوذُ بِكَ أَنْ أَضِلَّ أَوْ أُضَلَّ أَوْ أَزِلَّ أَوْ أُزَلَّ أَوْ أَظْلِمَ أَوْ أُظْلَمَ أَوْ
أَجْهَلَ أَوْ يُجْهَلَ عَلَيَّ

Allāhumma innī a-'ūdhu bika an aḍilla, aw uḍalla, aw azilla, aw uzalla, aw aẓlima, aw uẓlama, aw ajhala aw yujhala 'alayya

O Allāh, I seek refuge in You lest I misguide others, or I am misguided by others, lest I cause others to err or I am caused to err, lest I abuse others or be abused, and lest I behave foolishly or meet with the foolishness of others. [Sunan Abī Dawūd 5094]

Iniquity

Seeking Allāh's ﷻ Protection

اَللّٰهُمَّ وَاقِيَةً كَوَاقِيَةِ الْوَلِيدِ

Allāhumma wāqiyatan kawāqiyatil walīd

O Allāh, I seek protection the way You protect a little baby. [Musnad Abī Ya'lā 5527]

Seeking Protection from the Persecution of People

رَبَّنَا لَا تَجْعَلْنَا فِتْنَةً لِّلْقَوْمِ ٱلظَّٰلِمِينَ وَنَجِّنَا بِرَحْمَتِكَ مِنَ ٱلْقَوْمِ ٱلْكَٰفِرِينَ

Rabbanā lā taj'alnā fitnatal lil qawmiẓ ẓālimīn wa najjinā bi raḥmatika minal qawmil kāfirīn

Our Lord! Do not subject us to the persecution of the oppressive people, and deliver us by Your mercy from the disbelieving people. [Yūnus 10:85-86]

Iniquity

Seeking Protection from Calamities and Malicious Enemies

اَللّٰهُمَّ إِنِّي أَعُوذُ بِكَ مِنْ جَهْدِ الْبَلَاءِ، وَدَرَكِ الشَّقَاءِ، وَسُوءِ الْقَضَاءِ، وَشَمَاتَةِ الْأَعْدَاءِ

Allāhumma innī a'ūdhu bika min jahdil balā-i wa darakish shaqā-i wa sū-il qaḍā-i wa shamātatil a'dā

O Allāh, I seek refuge in You from the difficulties of severe calamities, from having an evil end and a bad fate and from the malicious joy of enemies. [Ṣaḥīḥ Al-Bukhārī 6616]

Lightening the World's Hardships and Achieving Victory Over a Hostile Person

اَللّٰهُمَّ اقْسِمْ لَنَا مِنَ الْيَقِينِ مَا تُهَوِّنُ بِهِ عَلَيْنَا مُصِيبَاتِ الدُّنْيَا وَانْصُرْنَا عَلَى مَنْ عَادَانَا وَلاَ تُسَلِّطْ عَلَيْنَا مَنْ لاَ يَرْحَمُنَا

Allāhummaqsim lanā minal yaqīni ma tuhawwinu bihī 'alaynā muṣīybatid dunya, wanṣurnā 'alā man 'ādānā wa lā tusalliṭ 'alaynā man lā yarḥamunā

O Allāh, Give us that faith with which You will lighten the worldly hardships for us. Help us to victory over the one who displays enmity to us. And do not impose over us one who shows no mercy to us. [Jāmi` At-Tirmidhī 3502]

Iniquity

Seeking Retribution for Hurting, Hitting or Cursing Another Believer

اَللّٰهُمَّ إِنِّي أَتَّخِذُ عِنْدَكَ عَهْدًا لَنْ تُخْلِفَنِيهِ فَإِنَّمَا أَنَا بَشَرٌ فَأَيُّ الْمُؤْمِنِينَ آذَيْتُهُ شَتَمْتُهُ لَعَنْتُهُ جَلَدْتُهُ فَاجْعَلْهَا لَهُ صَلاَةً وَزَكَاةً وَقُرْبَةً تُقَرِّبُهُ بِهَا إِلَيْكَ يَوْمَ الْقِيَامَةِ

Allāhumma innī attakhidhu 'indaka 'ahdan lan tukhlifanīhi fa innamā ana basharun fa ayyul mu-minīna ādhaytuhū shatamtuhū la'antuhū jaladtuhū faj'alhā lahū ṣalātan wa zakātan wa qurbatan tuqarribuhū bihā ilayka yawmal qiyāmah

O Allāh, I seek from you an unbreakable promise. I am just a human being. So whichever believer I hurt or rebuke or hit or curse then change that for him into mercy, purification, and a means of closeness to You on the Day of Judgement. [Ṣaḥīḥ Muslim 2601b]

حُبُّ الدُّنيَا

Love of the World

RELATED EMOTIONS

Forgetful | Insecure | Vain | Addicted | Distracted | Deluded
Covetous | Excessive | Ignorant | Immature | Immoderate | Lazy
Oblivious | Overwhelmed | Self-absorbed | Worthless | Lustful
Deceitful | Inadequate

INVOKING NAMES OF ALLĀH ﷻ

- **Al-Bāqī - The Everlasting**
- **Al-Bā'ith - The Resurrector**
- **Al-Khāfiḍ - the Abaser**
- **Al-Qābiḍ - The Withholder**
- **Al-Khabīr - the All-Aware**
- **Al-Wārith - The Inheritor**
- **As-Shakūr - the Most Appreciative**

AṢ-ṢALĀH AL-IBRĀHĪMIYYAH

ACCEPTED PRAYERS

- **Seeking Protection from Punishing Wealth**
- **Seeking Refuge from Making This World Our Greatest Concern**
- **Seeking Protection from Worldly Trials**
- **Seeking for Good in All Sustenance**
- **Seeking for Contentment in Provision and Good in Everything**
- **Making Allāh's Love the Dearest and Cutting Off Worldly Needs**

CHAPTER 17

Love of the World

[Ḥubb ad-Dunyā] حُبُّ الدُّنيَا

Any concept, 'thing' or person that provides benefit in the Hereafter is worthy of attachment in this earthly life. Indeed, love of the world is praised if it leads to spiritual elevation and healing of the heart, or if attaining wealth and position are for the benefit of the needy. Anything that is obtained from the necessities of living on earth - food, housing, shelter, and the like - is beneficial and is not considered "worldly" per se.

However, what scholars have traditionally warned against, with regard to attaining wealth, is the danger of transgression. The more wealth one acquires, the higher the probability one will become preoccupied with other than Allāh ﷻ.

'Īsā ﵇ is reported to have said "Love of this world is the root of all evil." [Al-Bayhaqī in Shu'ab Al-Imān 9974]

It is the action of clinging to the world's 'glittering distractions', paying excessive attention to the 'things' that benefit the lower self, that ties somebody to blameworthy love of the world (ḥubb al-dunyā). The manifestation of this misdirected love includes greediness and arrogance, as well as burdening (and depending on) others with your needs. The compulsion is a desire for provision in this world only, and the salvation in the next world is dismissed in some measure. Attaining prohibited wealth and power for power's sake is normalised by the individual sufferer. Finally, it is worth remarking that 'love of wealth' (ḥubb al-māl) is undoubtedly a branch of ḥubb ad-dunyā.

Allāh ﷻ says: "Indeed, those who do not expect to meet Us, being pleased and content with this worldly life, and who are heedless of Our signs, they will have the Fire as a home because of what they have committed." [Yūnus 10: 7-8]

The Prophet ﷺ said:

- "Two hungry wolves let loose in a flock of sheep do not cause as much harm as the harm to a man's religion wrought by his desire for wealth and fame" [At-Tirmidhī 2376]
- "Whoever makes the Hereafter his goal, Allāh makes his heart rich, and organizes his affairs, and the world comes to him whether it wants to or not. And whoever makes the world his goal, Allāh puts his poverty right before his eyes, and disorganises his affairs, and the world does not come to him, except what has been decreed for him" [At-Tirmidhī 2465]
- "If the son of Ādam had two valleys of money, he would wish for a third, for nothing can fill the mouth of the son of Ādam except dust" [Ṣaḥīḥ Al-Bukhārī 6436, Ṣaḥīḥ Muslim 1048:116]

Love of the world falls under 5 categories of classical legal rulings: obligatory (wājib), recommended (mandūb), permissible (mubāḥ), reprehensible (makrūh), or forbidden (ḥarām).

Love of the World

Invoking Allāh's ﷻ Names

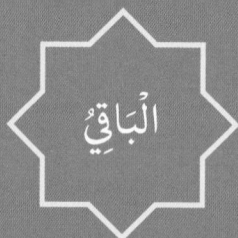

الْبَاقِي

Al-Bāqī
The Everlasting

الْبَاعِثُ

Al-Bā'ith
The Resurrector

الْخَافِضُ

Al-Khāfiḍ
The Abaser

الْقَابِضُ

Al-Qābiḍ
The Withholder

الْخَبِيرُ

Al-Khabīr
The All-Aware

الْوَارِثُ

Al-Wārith
The Inheritor

الشَّكُورُ

As-Shakūr
The Most Appreciative

Love of the World

Contemplation and Reflection on Allāh's ﷻ Blessed Names

- You realise that the root of any heartbreak is attachment to that which does not last, in stark contrast to His permanence, because when everything else leaves or dies, Allāh ﷻ is with you, so you attach your love to Him.
- You remind yourself that this worldly life is mere play and amusement, which spawns most of the evil spiritual traits and characteristics (pride, hatred, jealousy, boasting, greed, etc.) and that your true objective of this life is to make sufficient arrangements for your travels to the Hereafter.
- You see wealth and rank as two 'wolves' which tear your faith to pieces.
- Seeing the energy expended by so many men and women in gaining the 'pleasures and delights' of this world, you turn upon yourself and say: 'I cannot afford to lose myself in those trivialities.'
- You see clearly the ceaseless difficulties which strike those who love this world and are addicted to it. They become insecure, alienated from happiness and tranquillity.
- You remind yourself of the interaction between the Mother of the Believers, 'Ā-ishah ﷺ and her father, Abu Bakr ﷺ. Putting on a new dress, she became fascinated by her own good looks. Abu Bakr ﷺ asked her what she was looking at, saying, 'Surely Allāh is not looking at you... do you not realise that when someone becomes captivated by the beauty of this world, Allāh ﷻ hates him until he separates himself from this beauty?' 'Ā-ishah ﷺ then took off the dress and gave it away. From this interchange [Abū Nu'aym Al-Aṣbahānī in Ḥilyah Al-Awliyā' v.1 pg.37] you conclude that it is not a wrong action to wear handsome new clothing, but that there are trials and distractions to be found in the beauty of the life of this world.
- You learn to realise that Allāh ﷻ is the Inheritor of all that exists, and you only draw temporarily on what you possess. You begin to regard yourself only as a trustee of your belongings and instead give out of your wealth what is due to the poor and needy, remembering that you will be called to account one day.
- You don't allow the beginnings of vain pride to swell within yourself because you keep in mind that Allāh ﷻ shaped and fashioned you in the womb. Since He is the source of your being, He ﷻ is also the fount of all your wealth and well-being. Equally, He ﷻ could test you by depriving you of all physical and material goodness in a flash.
- You appreciate that Allāh ﷻ knows the full extent of your wealth and rank and that the way to draw close to Allāh ﷻ is to use the influence and bounties in your hands to please Him. You purify your wealth by giving in charity and you realise full well when extravagances or luxuries start to 'tip the scales'.
- You understand that whatever blessings come to you (night and day), are from Allāh ﷻ, and are beyond numeration, so you employ with great appreciation the use of your eyes, your ears, your tongue and your limbs correctly, to obtain His good pleasure.

Love of the World

Aṣ-Ṣalāh Al-Ibrāhīmiyyah

اَللّٰهُمَّ صَلِّ عَلَى مُحَمَّدٍ وَعَلَى آلِ مُحَمَّدٍ كَمَا صَلَّيْتَ عَلَى
إِبْرَاهِيمَ وَآلِ إِبْرَاهِيمَ إِنَّكَ حَمِيدٌ مَجِيدٌ وَبَارِكْ عَلَى
مُحَمَّدٍ وَعَلَى آلِ مُحَمَّدٍ كَمَا بَارَكْتَ عَلَى إِبْرَاهِيمَ وَآلِ
إِبْرَاهِيمَ إِنَّكَ حَمِيدٌ مَجِيدٌ

Allāhumma ṣalli ʿalā Muḥammadin wa ʿalā āli Muḥammadin kamā ṣallayta ʿalā Ibrāhīm wa āli Ibrāhīm innaka ḥamīdum majīd, wa bārik ʿalā Muḥammadin wa ʿalā āli Muḥammadin kamā bārakta ʿalā Ibrāhīm wa āli Ibrāhīm innaka ḥamīdum majīd

O Allāh, send peace upon Muḥammad and upon the family of Muḥammad, as You sent peace upon Ibrāhīm and the family of Ibrāhīm, and send blessings upon Muḥammad and upon the family of Muḥammad as You sent blessings upon Ibrāhīm and the family of Ibrāhīm. You are indeed praiseworthy, the most honourable. [Sunan An-Nasaī 1290]

Love of the World

Seeking Protection from Punishing Wealth

اَللّٰهُمَّ إِنِّي أَعُوذُ بِكَ مِنْ مَالٍ يَكُونُ عَلَيَّ عَذَابًا

Allāhumma innī a'ūdhu bika min mālin yakūnu 'alayya 'adhābā

O Allāh, I seek Your protection from the wealth that will turn into punishment for me. [Aṭ-Ṭabarānī in Ad-Du'ā 1339]

Seeking Refuge from Making This World Our Greatest Concern

اَللّٰهُمَّ لاَ تَجْعَلِ الدُّنْيَا أَكْبَرَ هَمِّنَا وَلاَ مَبْلَغَ عِلْمِنَا

Allāhumm lā taj'alid dunyā akbara hamminā wa lā mablagha 'ilminā

O Allāh, do not make this world our greatest concern and the sum total of our knowledge. [Jāmi` At-Tirmidhī 3502]

Seeking Protection from Worldly Trials

اَللّٰهُمَّ إِنِّي أَعُوذُ بِكَ مِنَ الْبُخْلِ، وَأَعُوذُ بِكَ مِنَ الْجُبْنِ، وَأَعُوذُ بِكَ أَنْ أُرَدَّ
إِلَى أَرْذَلِ الْعُمُرِ، وَأَعُوذُ بِكَ مِنْ فِتْنَةِ الدُّنْيَا وَأَعُوذُ بِكَ مِنْ عَذَابِ الْقَبْرِ

Allāhumma 'innī a-`ūdhu bika minal bukhli, wa a-`ūdhu bika minal jubni, wa a-`ūdhu bika min an uradda ilā ardhalil `umur, wa a-`ūdhu bika min fitnatid dunyā wa a-`ūdhu bika min`adhābil qabr

O Allāh, I seek Your protection from miserliness, I seek Your protection from cowardice, and I seek Your protection from being returned to feeble old age. I seek Your protection from the trials of this world and from the torment of the grave. [Ṣaḥīḥ Al-Bukhārī 6365]

Love of the World

Seeking Good in All Sustenance

اَللّٰهُمَّ اجْعَلْ سَرِيرَتِي خَيْرًا مِنْ عَلاَنِيَتِي وَاجْعَلْ عَلاَنِيَتِي صَالِحَةً
اَللّٰهُمَّ إِنِّي أَسْأَلُكَ مِنْ صَالِحِ مَا تُؤْتِي النَّاسَ مِنَ الْمَالِ وَالأَهْلِ وَالْوَلَدِ غَيْرِ
الضَّالِّ وَلاَ الْمُضِلِّ

Allāhummaj'al sarīratī khayran min 'alāniyatī waj'al 'alāniyatī ṣāliḥah, Allāhumma innī as-aluka min ṣāliḥi mā tu-tin nāsa minal māli wal ahli wal waladi ghayriḍ ḍālli wa lal muḍill

O Allāh, make my secret better than my apparent condition, and make my apparent condition righteous. O Allāh, I ask You for the good of what you give to the people, of wealth, wives, and children, not (to be) misguided, nor misguiding. [Jāmi` At-Tirmidhī 3586]

Seeking Contentment in Provision and Good in Everything

اَللّٰهُمَّ قَنِّعْنِي بِمَا رَزَقْتَنِي، وَبَارِكْ لِي فِيهِ، وَاخْلُفْ عَلَى كُلِّ غَائِبَةٍ لِي بِخَيْرٍ

Allāhumma qanni'nī bimā razaqtanī wa bārik lī fīh, wakhluf 'alā kulli ghā-ibatin lī bi khayr

O Allāh, make me content with the provision You have given me and bless me in it and appoint good for me in every thing which I do not have. [Al-Ḥākim 1878]

Love of the World

Making Allāh's Love the Dearest and Cutting Off Worldly Needs

اَللّٰهُمَّ اجْعَلْ حُبَّكَ أَحَبَّ الْأَشْيَاءِ إِلَيَّ وَاجْعَلْ خَوْفَكَ أَخْوَفَ الْأَشْيَاءِ إِلَيَّ وَاقْطَعْ عَنِّي حَاجَاتِ الدُّنْيَا بِالشَّوْقِ إِلَى لِقَائِكَ وَإِذَا أَقْرَرْتَ أَعْيُنَ أَهْلِ الدُّنْيَا مِنْ دُنْيَاهُمْ فَأَقِرَّ عَيْنِي مِنْ عِبَادَتِكَ

Allāhummaj'al ḥubbaka aḥabbal ashyā-a ilayya waj'al khawfaka akhwafal ash'yā-a ilayya waq-ṭa' 'annī ḥājātid dunyā bish shawqi ilā liqā-ik wa idhā aqrartu -a'yuna ahlid dunyā min dunyāhum fa-aqirra 'aynī min 'ibādatik

O Allāh, make Your love the dearest and make Your fear the most frightening of all things to me. Cut off worldly needs from me by giving me the longing to meet You. And as You bring comfort to the eyes of the men of the world with their worldly possessions, bring comfort to my eyes with Your obedience and worship. [Abū Nu'aym Al-Aṣbahānī in Ḥilyah Al-Awliyā' v.8 pg.282]

البُخل

Miserliness

RELATED EMOTIONS

Indifferent | Insecure | Anxious | Fearful | Cynical | Obstinate
Self-absorbed | Apathetic | Callous | Cruel | Doubtful | Excessive
Grudging | Neglectful | Reluctant | Resistant | Uncharitable | Unkind
Apprehensive | Cowardly

INVOKING NAMES OF ALLĀH

- **Al-Karīm - The Most Generous**
- **Ar-Razzāq - The Provider**
- **Al-Wahhāb - The Giver of Gifts**
- **Al-Waliyy - The Protecting Friend**
- **Al-Qayyūm - The Sustainer**
- **Dhul Jalāli wal Ikrām - the Lord of Majesty and Generosity**
- **Ar-Ra-uf - the Most Kind**
- **Ar-Raḥmān - the All Compassionate**
- **Ar-Raḥīm - the All Merciful**
- **Al-Khabīr - The All-Aware**

AṢ-ṢALĀH AL-IBRĀHĪMIYYAH

ACCEPTED PRAYERS

- **Relying on Allāh**
- **Showing Gratitude, and Worshipping with the Best Devotion**
- **Seeking Love for the Poor**
- **Seeking Refuge from Anxiety, Miserliness and Cowardice**
- **Seeking Protection from Miserliness, and the Trials of this World and the Grave**
- **Seeking Inspiration to do Good Deeds as a Sign of Gratitude**
- **Seeking Contentment with Provisions**

CHAPTER 18

Miserliness [Bukhl] البُخل

Miserliness is when one refuses to give what is required by Sacred Law (the necessary rights due to Allāh ﷻ and to His creation) or denies the merits of giving in general. This is usually as a result of a love for the wealth of this world (ḥubb al-māl for its own sake), and the dunyā, which weakens the bond of love with Allāh ﷻ.

The Messenger of Allāh ﷺ exhorted:

- "Save yourself from miserliness, for it has destroyed nations before you" [Ṣaḥīḥ Muslim 2578:56]
- "There are two habits which are never present in a believer: miserliness and bad manners" [At-Tirmidhī 1962]

Miserliness

Invoking Allāh's ﷻ Names

الْكَرِيمُ
Al-Karīm
The Most Generous

الرَّزَّاقُ
Ar-Razzāq
The Provider

الْوَهَّابُ
Al-Wahhāb
The Giver of Gifts

الْوَالِيُ
Al-Waliyy
The Protecting Friend

الْقَيَّومُ
Al-Qayyūm
The Sustainer

ذُو الْجَلَالِ وَالْإِكْرَام
Dhul Jalāli wal Ikrām
The Lord of Majesty and Generosity

الرَّؤُوفُ
Ar-Ra-uf
The Most Kind

الرَّحْمَانُ
Ar-Raḥmān - the All Compassionate

الرَّحِيمُ
Ar-Raḥīm
The All Merciful

الْخَبِيرُ
Al-Khabīr
The All-Aware

Miserliness

Contemplation and Reflection on Allāh's ﷻ Blessed Names

- You remind yourself that Allāh ﷻ is the Giver of Gifts and the Provider without a partner and sometimes we forget the scale of His benevolence in this regard.
- You make 'muḥāsabah' (take stock) of your intentions and actions. This spurs you towards genuine gratitude for what Allāh ﷻ has bestowed (more lavishly) upon you.
- You overcome any anxiety or fear of loss of wealth by helping those in need, sharing with them what Allāh ﷻ has blessed you with.
- You understand that a generous soul is one who gives to everyone what he needs, neither for recompense nor out of interest, either now or later.
- You are not indifferent or apathetic to the difficulties of others. Instead, you meet their needs graciously and to the best of your ability.
- You are sympathetic and loving toward needy people around you, offering them company and raising their esteem with positive words and kind actions.
- Knowing that Allāh ﷻ will show mercy to the merciful of His creation, you never deal in denigration or mockery. You also work hard to avoid time-wasting arguments.
- You are ultimately mindful that Allāh ﷻ is aware of all that you do.

Miserliness

Aṣ-Ṣalāh Al-Ibrāhīmiyyah

اَللّٰهُمَّ صَلِّ عَلَى مُحَمَّدٍ وَعَلَى آلِ مُحَمَّدٍ كَمَا صَلَّيْتَ عَلَى
إِبْرَاهِيمَ وَآلِ إِبْرَاهِيمَ إِنَّكَ حَمِيدٌ مَجِيدٌ وَبَارِكْ عَلَى
مُحَمَّدٍ وَعَلَى آلِ مُحَمَّدٍ كَمَا بَارَكْتَ عَلَى إِبْرَاهِيمَ وَآلِ
إِبْرَاهِيمَ إِنَّكَ حَمِيدٌ مَجِيدٌ

Allāhumma ṣalli 'alā Muḥammadin wa 'alā āli Muḥammadin kamā ṣ allayta 'alā Ibrāhīm wa āli Ibrāhīm innaka ḥamīdum majīd, wa bārik 'alā Muḥammadin wa 'alā āli Muḥammadin kamā bārakta 'alā Ibrāhīm wa āli Ibrāhīm innaka ḥamīdum majīd

O Allāh, send peace upon Muḥammad and upon the family of Muḥammad, as You sent peace upon Ibrāhīm and the family of Ibrāhīm, and send blessings upon Muḥammad and upon the family of Muḥammad as You sent blessings upon Ibrāhīm and the family of Ibrāhīm. You are indeed praiseworthy, the most honourable. [Sunan An-Nasaī 1290]

Miserliness

Relying on Allāh ﷻ

اَللّٰهُمَّ أَنْتَ رَبِّي لَا إِلَهَ إِلَّا أَنْتَ، عَلَيْكَ تَوَكَّلْتُ، وَأَنْتَ رَبُّ الْعَرْشِ الْعَظِيمِ

Allāhumma anta rabbī lā ilāha illā anta, 'alayka tawakkaltu wa anta rabbul 'arshil 'aẓīm

O Allāh! You are my Lord, there is no god but You. Upon You I rely, and You are the Lord of the Glorious Throne. [Ibn As-Sunnī in 'Amal Al-Yawm wa Al-Laylah 57]

Showing Gratitude, and Worshipping with the Best Devotion

اَللّٰهُمَّ إِنِّي أَسْأَلُكَ الثَّبَاتَ فِي الأَمْرِ وَأَسْأَلُكَ عَزِيمَةَ الرُّشْدِ وَأَسْأَلُكَ شُكْرَ نِعْمَتِكَ وَحُسْنَ عِبَادَتِكَ

Allāhumma innī as-alukath thabāta fil amri wa as-aluka 'azīmatar rushdi wa as-aluka shukra ni'matika wa ḥusna 'ibādatik

O Allāh, I beg You for steadfastness in religious affairs. I beg You for determination to follow the guidance. I beg You to enable me to show gratitude for Your bounties and to worship You with the best devotion. [Jāmi` At-Tirmidhī 3407]

Miserliness

Seeking Love for the Poor

اَللّٰهُمَّ إِنِّي أَسْأَلُكَ فِعْلَ الْخَيْرَاتِ وَتَرْكَ الْمُنْكَرَاتِ وَحُبَّ الْمَسَاكِينِ وَإِذَا
أَرَدْتَ فِي النَّاسِ فِتْنَةً فَاقْبِضْنِي إِلَيْكَ غَيْرَ مَفْتُونٍ

Allāhumma innī as-aluka fi'lal khayrāti wa tarkal munkarāti wa ḥubbal masākīni wa idhā aradta fin nāsi fitnatan faqbiḍnī ilayka ghayra maftūn

O Allāh, I beg You to enable me to do good deeds, to shun bad deeds, and to love the poor. (I beg You to) forgive me and have mercy on me. And when You plan tribulations for a people cause me to die without being put to trial. [Al-Muwaṭṭa 836]

Seeking Refuge from Anxiety, Miserliness and Cowardice

اَللّٰهُمَّ إِنِّي أَعُوذُ بِكَ مِنَ الْهَمِّ وَالْحَزَنِ وَالْعَجْزِ وَالْكَسَلِ وَالْجُبْنِ وَالْبُخْلِ
وَضَلَعِ الدَّيْنِ وَغَلَبَةِ الرِّجَالِ

Allāhumma innī a'ūdhu bika minal hammi wal ḥazani wal 'ajzi wal kasali wal jubni wal bukhli wa ḍala'id dayni wa ghalabatir rijāl

O Allāh, I seek refuge in you from anxiety and sadness, weakness and laziness, miserliness and cowardice, the burden of debts and from being overpowered by men. [Ṣaḥīḥ Al-Bukhārī 6369]

Miserliness

Seeking Protection from Miserliness, and the Trials of this World and the Grave

اَللّٰهُمَّ إِنِّي أَعُوذُ بِكَ مِنَ الْبُخْلِ، وَأَعُوذُ بِكَ مِنَ الْجُبْنِ، وَأَعُوذُ بِكَ أَنْ أُرَدَّ إِلَى أَرْذَلِ الْعُمُرِ، وَأَعُوذُ بِكَ مِنْ فِتْنَةِ الدُّنْيَا وَأَعُوذُ بِكَ مِنْ عَذَابِ الْقَبْرِ

Allāhumma 'innī a-`ūdhu bika minal bukhli, wa a-`ūdhu bika minal jubni, wa a-`ūdhu bika min an uradda ilā ardhalil `umur, wa a-`ūdhu bika min fitnatid dunyā wa a-`ūdhu bika min `adhābil qabr

O Allāh, I seek Your protection from miserliness, I seek Your protection from cowardice, and I seek Your protection from being returned to feeble old age. I seek Your protection from the trials of this world and from the torment of the grave. [ṢaḥīḥAl-Bukhārī 6365]

Seeking Inspiration to do Good Deeds as a Sign of Gratitude

رَبِّ أَوْزِعْنِيٓ أَنْ أَشْكُرَ نِعْمَتَكَ ٱلَّتِيٓ أَنْعَمْتَ عَلَيَّ وَعَلَىٰ وَٰلِدَيَّ وَأَنْ أَعْمَلَ صَٰلِحًا تَرْضَىٰهُ وَأَدْخِلْنِي بِرَحْمَتِكَ فِي عِبَادِكَ ٱلصَّٰلِحِينَ

Rabbi awzi'nī an ashkura ni'matikallatī an'amta 'alayya wa 'alā wālidayya wa an -a'mala ṣāliḥan tarḍāhu wa adkhilnī bi raḥmatika fī 'ibādikaṣ ṣāliḥīn

My Lord! Inspire me to (always) be thankful for Your favours which You have blessed me and my parents with, and to do good deeds that please you. Admit me, by Your mercy, into (the company of) Your righteous servants. [An-Naml 27:19]

Miserliness

Seeking Contentment with Provisions

اَللّٰهُمَّ قَنِّعْنِي بِمَا رَزَقْتَنِي، وَبَارِكْ لِي فِيهِ، وَاخْلُفْ عَلَيَّ كُلَّ غَائِبَةٍ بِخَيْرٍ

Allāhumma qanna'nī bimā razaqtanī wa bārik lī fīh wakhluf 'alayya kulla ghā-ibatin bi khayr

O Allāh, make me content with the provision You have given me and bless me in it and appoint good for me in every thing which I do not have. [Al-Adab Al-Mufrad 681]

السُخْرِيَّة

Mockery

RELATED EMOTIONS

Ignorant | Immature | Dismissive | Pessimistic | Cynical
Contemptuous | Harsh | Hostile | Malicious | Addicted | Callous
Careless | Cruel | Depressed | Distressed | Egotistic | Excessive
Insensitive | Insincere | Judgemental | Offended | Thoughtless
Undignified | Unkind | Wound up

INVOKING NAMES OF ALLĀH سبحانه وتعالى

- **As-Samī' - All Hearing**
- **Al-Baṣīr - The Seer of All (The All-Seeing)**
- **Ash-Shahīd - The Witness**
- **Ar-Raqīb - the Watchful**
- **Al-Mu'izz - the Honourer**
- **Al-Mudhil - The Humiliator**
- **Al-Ḥalīm - the Most Forbearing**

AṢ-ṢALĀH AL-IBRĀHĪMIYYAH

ACCEPTED PRAYERS

- **Seeking Forgiveness for Actions in Jest**
- **Seeking Forgiveness for Hurting, Rebuking or Cursing a Believer**
- **Seeking Refuge from Committing Oppression or Being Oppressed**
- **Seeking Refuge from the Malicious Joy of Enemies**
- **Seeking Refuge from the Mischief of Senses**
- **Seeking Refuge from Abusing Others, and Behaving Foolishly**

CHAPTER 19

Mockery [Sukhriyyah] السُّخرِيَّة

Mockery is when one ridicules people (making jest at their expense) with the purpose of humiliation. This is often because the one who is quick to ridicule most likely sees himself either as superior to his victim or, in fact, envious of what they possess.

The Prophet ﷺ said, "The whole of a Muslim is sanctified for another Muslim with regards to his blood, his property and his honour." [Ṣaḥīḥ Muslim 2564:32]

Humour and lightheartedness are important in human life. But humour as a way of life harms the spiritual heart. And laughter and amusement at the expense of the dignity of others is wholly inappropriate.

Mockery

Invoking Allāh's ﷻ Names

السَّمِيعُ

As-Samīʿ
All Hearing

الْبَصِيرُ

**Al-Baṣīr – The Seer of All
(The All-Seeing)**

الشَّهِيدُ

Ash-Shahīd
The Witness

الرَّقِيبُ

Ar-Raqīb
The Watchful

الْمُعِزُّ

Al-Muʿizz
The Honourer

الْمُذِلُّ

Al-Mudhil
The Humiliator

الْحَلِيمُ

Al-Ḥalīm
The Most Forbearing

Mockery

Contemplation and Reflection on Allāh's ﷻ Blessed Names

- You appreciate that Allāh ﷻ knows every sneer or snort of ridicule that arises in the mind of the mocking. You feel better within yourself for resisting the urge to speak dismissively or engage in condescending cynical humour. Indeed, you train yourself to use your speech for the benefit of divine guidance and obedience.
- You find yourself in the habit of (perhaps even addicted to) looking down upon others. You however decide to stop judging people, and become a sweeter human being in the eyes of others. People start to warm to you and want to remain in your company, merely because you refrain from running commentaries on behaviour or perceived faults in others.
- You remind yourself that every person who helps others to maintain their honour is indeed an honourable person.
- You remember that mildness (forbearance not harshness) is among the finest qualities of mankind.

Mockery

Aṣ-Ṣalāh Al-Ibrāhīmiyyah

اَللّٰهُمَّ صَلِّ عَلَى مُحَمَّدٍ وَعَلَى آلِ مُحَمَّدٍ كَمَا صَلَّيْتَ عَلَى
إِبْرَاهِيمَ وَآلِ إِبْرَاهِيمَ إِنَّكَ حَمِيدٌ مَجِيدٌ وَبَارِكْ عَلَى
مُحَمَّدٍ وَعَلَى آلِ مُحَمَّدٍ كَمَا بَارَكْتَ عَلَى إِبْرَاهِيمَ وَآلِ
إِبْرَاهِيمَ إِنَّكَ حَمِيدٌ مَجِيدٌ

Allāhumma ṣalli 'alā Muḥammadin wa 'alā āli Muḥammadin kamā ṣ allayta 'alā Ibrāhīm wa āli Ibrāhīm innaka ḥamīdum majīd, wa bārik 'alā Muḥammadin wa 'alā āli Muḥammadin kamā bārakta 'alā Ibrāhīm wa āli Ibrāhīm innaka ḥamīdum majīd

O Allāh, send peace upon Muḥammad and upon the family of Muḥammad, as You sent peace upon Ibrāhīm and the family of Ibrāhīm, and send blessings upon Muḥammad and upon the family of Muḥammad as You sent blessings upon Ibrāhīm and the family of Ibrāhīm. You are indeed praiseworthy, the most honourable. [Sunan An-Nasaī 1290]

Mockery

Seeking Forgiveness for Actions in Jest

اَللّٰهُمَّ اغْفِرْ لِي خَطِيئَتِي وَجَهْلِي وَإِسْرَافِي فِي أَمْرِي، وَمَا أَنْتَ أَعْلَمُ بِهِ مِنِّي، اَللّٰهُمَّ اغْفِرْ لِي هَزْلِي وَجِدِّي وَخَطَايَ وَعَمْدِي، وَكُلُّ ذَلِكَ عِنْدِي

Allāhummaghfirlī khatī-atī wa jahlī wa isrāfī fī amrī, wa mā anta a'lamu bihī minnī, Allāhummaghfirlī hazlī wa jiddī wa khatāya wa 'amdī wa kullu dhālika 'indī

O Allāh, forgive my errors, my ignorance and my extravagance in my affairs and what You know better than I do. O Allāh, forgive me what I do both in jest and seriousness, my errors and what I do intentionally and all that I do. [Ṣaḥīḥ Al-Bukhārī 6399]

Seeking Forgiveness for Hurting, Rebuking or Cursing a Believer

اَللّٰهُمَّ إِنِّي أَتَّخِذُ عِنْدَكَ عَهْدًا لَنْ تُخْلِفَنِيهِ فَإِنَّمَا أَنَا بَشَرٌ فَأَيُّ الْمُؤْمِنِينَ آذَيْتُهُ شَتَمْتُهُ لَعَنْتُهُ جَلَدْتُهُ فَاجْعَلْهَا لَهُ صَلَاةً وَزَكَاةً وَقُرْبَةً تُقَرِّبُهُ بِهَا إِلَيْكَ يَوْمَ الْقِيَامَةِ

Allāhumma innī attakhidhu 'indaka 'ahdan lan tukhlifanīhi fa innamā ana basharun fa ayyul mu-minīna ādhaytuhū shatamtuhū la'antuhū jaladtuhū faj'alhā lahū ṣalātan wa zakātan wa qurbatan tuqarribuhū bihā ilayka yawmal qiyāmah

O Allāh, I seek from you an unbreakable promise. I am just a human being. So whichever believer I hurt or rebuke or hit or curse then change that for him into mercy, purification, and a means of closeness to You on the Day of Judgement. [Ṣaḥīḥ Muslim 2601b]

Mockery

Seeking Refuge from Committing Oppression or Being Oppressed

بِسْمِ اللهِ تَوَكَّلْتُ عَلَى اللهِ اللَّهُمَّ إِنَّا نَعُوذُ بِكَ مِنْ أَنْ نَزِلَّ أَوْ نَضِلَّ أَوْ نَظْلِمَ أَوْ نُظْلَمَ أَوْ نَجْهَلَ أَوْ يُجْهَلَ عَلَيْنَا

Bismillāhi tawakkaltu 'alAllāhi Allāhumma innī a'ūdhu bika min an nazilla aw naḍilla aw naẓlima aw nuẓlama aw najhala aw yujhala 'alaynā

O Allāh! We seek refuge in You from slipping unintentionally or becoming misguided, or committing oppression or being oppressed, or acting ignorantly or being treated ignorantly. [Jāmi` At-Tirmidhī 3427]

Seeking Refuge from the Malicious Joy of Enemies

أَعُوذُ بِاللهِ مِنْ جَهْدِ الْبَلاَءِ، وَدَرَكِ الشَّقَاءِ، وَسُوءِ الْقَضَاءِ، وَشَمَاتَةِ الأَعْدَاءِ

A'ūdhu billāhi min jahdil balā-i wa darakish shiqā-i wa sū-il qa ā-i wa shamātatil -a'dā-i

I seek refuge with Allāh from the difficulties of severe calamities, from having an evil end and a bad fate and from the malicious joy of enemies. [Ṣaḥīḥ Al-Bukhārī 6616]

Mockery

Seeking Refuge from the Mischief of Senses

اَللّٰهُمَّ إِنِّي أَعُوذُ بِكَ مِنْ شَرِّ سَمْعِي وَمِنْ شَرِّ بَصَرِي وَمِنْ شَرِّ لِسَانِي وَمِنْ شَرِّ قَلْبِي وَمِنْ شَرِّ مَنِيِّي

Allāhumma innī a'ūdhu bika min sharri sam'ī wa min sharri baṣarī wa min sharri lisānī wa min sharri qalbī wa min sharri maniyyī

O Allāh, I seek refuge in You from the mischief of my hearing, sight, speech, heart and seed (sexual passion). [Sunan Abī Dawūd 1551]

Seeking Refuge from Abusing Others, and Behaving Foolishly

اَللّٰهُمَّ إِنِّي أَعُوذُ بِكَ أَنْ أَضِلَّ أَوْ أُضَلَّ أَوْ أَزِلَّ أَوْ أُزَلَّ أَوْ أَظْلِمَ أَوْ أُظْلَمَ أَوْ أَجْهَلَ أَوْ يُجْهَلَ عَلَيَّ

Allāhumma innī a-'ūdhu bika an aḍilla, aw uḍalla, aw azilla, aw uzalla, aw aẓlima, aw uẓlama, aw ajhala aw yujhala 'alayya

O Allāh, I seek refuge in You lest I misguide others, or I am misguided by others, lest I cause others to err or I am caused to err, lest I abuse others or be abused, and lest I behave foolishly or meet with the foolishness of others. [Sunan Abī Dawūd 5094]

الأَفْكَارُ السَّلْبِيَّة

Negative Feelings

RELATED EMOTIONS

Resentful | Frustrated | Anxious | Suspicious | Guilty | Depressed | Bitter | Malicious | Obstinate | Pessimistic | Worthless | Annoyed Cynical | Distressed | Insincere | Unkind | Vindictive

INVOKING NAMES OF ALLĀH

- **Al-Malik - The Absolute Ruler**
- **Ar-Raḥmān - The All Compassionate**
- **Ar-Raḥīm - The All Merciful**
- **Al-Mumin - The One Who Gives Security**
- **Al-Muhaymin - The Guardian**
- **Ar-Raqīb - The Watchful**
- **Al-Waliyy - The Protecting Friend**
- **Al-'Adl - The Just**
- **Al-Baṣīr - The Seer of All (The All-Seeing)**
- **Al-Khabīr - the All-Aware**
- **Al-Muqsi - The Requiter**
- **Al-Muntaqim - The Avenger**
- **Al-Mujīb - The Responsive One**
- **Al-Qawiyy - The All-Strong**
- **Al-Matīn - The Most Firm**
- **Al-Wālī - The Governor**

AṢ-ṢALĀH AL-IBRĀHĪMIYYAH

ACCEPTED PRAYERS

- **Admitting Wrongful Doing**
- **Seeking Relief from Worry and the Removal of Distress**
- **Seeking the Most Merciful Times of Distress**
- **Seeking Protection from Doubts, and Attaining Conviction**
- **Seeking Mercy and Purification for Those Whom you Hurt**
- **Seeking Refuge from Severe Difficulties and the Malicious Joy of Enemies**
- **Seeking to Mend Relationships and Guidance to Peaceful Paths**
- **Seeking Relief from Distress**
- **Seeking a Truthful Tongue Protection from Evil**
- **Seeking Refuge from Anxiety and Sadness**
- **Seeking Peacefulness**
- **Seeking Constant Mercy and Protection**
- **Protecting the Heart from Bitterness towards Believers**
- **Making the Qur'ān the Life of the Heart and a Remover of Sadness and Anxiety**
- **Seeking Pleasure with Allāh's Decree**

CHAPTER 20

Negative Feelings

[Al-Afkār as-Salbiyyah] الأفْكارُ السَّلْبِيَّة

For the purposes of this book, 'negative feelings' are those that a person harbours toward someone behaving in a righteous way. One has become bothered by the positive words or deeds of another, and has judged that person based on the heart's suspicions (ẓann) without proof. By far the most likely root cause of these negative feelings is jealousy, fed by pride of course, but there are a variety of accessories to this disease: weakness of faith and a lack of consciousness of Allāh ﷻ; the frustrated venting of anger; unfounded dislike and unjustified animosity toward the other person; and the desire to elevate oneself by declaring the faults of others.

Allāh ﷻ says, "O believers! Avoid many suspicions, (for) indeed, some suspicions are sinful." [Al-Hujurāt 49:12]

The Messenger of Allāh ﷺ said, "Allāh says, 'I am as My servant thinks of Me. If he thinks good of Me then so it shall be, and if he thinks ill of Me then so it shall be.'" [Musnad Aḥmad 9076]

Imām As-Shafi'ī said in one of his poems: "Let not your tongue mention the shame of another, for you yourself are covered in shame and all men have tongues. If your eye falls upon the sins of your brother, shield them and say: 'O my eye! All men have eyes!'" [Dīwān As-Shafi'ī, p.144]

We need to distinguish between these negative feelings that stem from a certain inadequacy of character, and the socially constructive mechanism which allows for relevant evidence to be shown against someone for their negative actions, in order that further damage can be prevented.

Negative Feelings

Invoking Allāh's ﷻ Names

الْمَلِكُ
Al-Malik
The Absolute Ruler

الرَّحْمَانُ
Ar-Raḥmān - The All Compassionate

الرَّحِيمُ
Ar-Raḥīm
The All Merciful

الْمُؤْمِنُ
Al-Mumin - The One Who Gives Security

الْمُهَيْمِنُ
Al-Muhaymin
The Guardian

الرَّقِيبُ
Ar-Raqīb
The Watchful

الْوَلِيُّ
Al-Waliyy
The Protecting Friend

الْعَدْلُ
Al-'Adl
The Just

الْبَصِيرُ
Al-Baṣīr
The Seer of All
(The All-Seeing)

الْخَبِيرُ
Al-Khabīr
The All-Aware

الْمُقْسِطُ
Al-Muqsi
The Requiter

الْمُنْتَقِمُ
Al-Muntaqim
The Avenger

الْمُجِيبُ
Al-Mujīb
The Responsive One

الْقَوِيُّ
Al-Qawiyy
The All-Strong

الْمَتِينُ
Al-Matīn
The Most Firm

الْوَالِي
Al-Wālī
The Governor

Negative Feelings

Contemplation and Reflection on Allāh's Blessed Names

- You understand that one of the many causes of negative feelings is jealousy, which in turn breeds resentment. From your studies of the 99 Names of Allāh you know that it is befitting for Allāh alone to be afforded the title of 'Al-Mutakabbir', the Supreme. Hence it is not becoming, even permissible, for anyone to have such a degree of pride in his or her heart that leads them to hold negative feelings for others.
- The smile that you wear on your face is placed there purposefully out of a genuine desire to make people feel better about the world around them. Essentially, you have grasped the idea that a smile is a simple but effective gift of charity.
- You are aware that Satan is your enemy and that he takes every opportunity to prompt you to negativity and disobedience. Instead of lingering on darker thoughts or niggling anxieties, you remember Allāh as your comforter and guide. This way, no matter what tribulation comes your way, you find that you never wallow in feelings of sorrow or self-pity.
- You understand that every servant who erases resentment and suspicion from their heart, retiring to bed each night free from anxiety in these regards, will not only live a life of cheerfulness but will please Allāh such that he will enjoy elevation of rank in the next world.
- You feel a remarkable degree of comfort and companionship. In your du'ā', your conversation with Allāh, you gain a sense of inspiration and you are convinced that Allāh will respond to your prayer in a way that suits you best.
- You remind yourself that Allāh is the perfect companion with whom the depressed or anxious person can confide. Frustrations and woes are shaken off quite quickly when you praise Allāh or ask for calmness of the heart.
- You realise that the root of any heartbreak is attachment to that which does not last, in stark contrast to His permanence, because when everything else leaves or dies, Allāh is with you, so you attach your love to Him.
- You never reveal the sins or perceived shortcomings of others except in situations when you need to warn a third party or ward off danger; you do not let your tongue mention the shame of another, for you know that you yourself are covered in shame and all men have tongues!
- When you see anxiety or depression in other people, particularly believers, you feel it is your duty to offer words of comfort or simply to raise a smile. You will use words that encourage the person in their own faith and feeling of security within their way of life.
- You place trust in the constant protection that Allāh affords to His followers. For you, He is the first stop in stepping up to the battlefield where we fight in the daily round against defeatist thoughts and negativity.
- There are a multitude of ways to dispel your self-doubts and woes, and you are improving in your du'ā', remembrances and recitation of Qur'ān for the sake of Allāh, since you have found that your happiness rests in these good practices.
- You approach Allāh alone for the development and maintenance of all of your faculties, for your health, happiness and well-being.

Negative Feelings

Aṣ-Ṣalāh Al-Ibrāhīmiyyah

اَللّٰهُمَّ صَلِّ عَلَى مُحَمَّدٍ وَعَلَى آلِ مُحَمَّدٍ كَمَا صَلَّيْتَ عَلَى
إِبْرَاهِيمَ وَآلِ إِبْرَاهِيمَ إِنَّكَ حَمِيدٌ مَجِيدٌ وَبَارِكْ عَلَى
مُحَمَّدٍ وَعَلَى آلِ مُحَمَّدٍ كَمَا بَارَكْتَ عَلَى إِبْرَاهِيمَ وَآلِ
إِبْرَاهِيمَ إِنَّكَ حَمِيدٌ مَجِيدٌ

Allāhumma ṣalli 'alā Muḥammadin wa 'alā āli Muḥammadin kamā ṣ allayta 'alā Ibrāhīm wa āli Ibrāhīm innaka ḥamīdum majīd, wa bārik 'alā Muḥammadin wa 'alā āli Muḥammadin kamā bārakta 'alā Ibrāhīm wa āli Ibrāhīm innaka ḥamīdum majīd

O Allāh, send peace upon Muḥammad and upon the family of Muḥammad, as You sent peace upon Ibrāhīm and the family of Ibrāhīm, and send blessings upon Muḥammad and upon the family of Muḥammad as You sent blessings upon Ibrāhīm and the family of Ibrāhīm. You are indeed praiseworthy, the most honourable. [Sunan An-Nasaī 1290]

Negative Feelings

Admitting Wrongful Doing

لَّآ إِلَٰهَ إِلَّآ أَنتَ سُبۡحَٰنَكَ إِنِّي كُنتُ مِنَ ٱلظَّٰلِمِينَ

Lā ilāha illā anta subḥānaka innī kuntu minaẓ ẓālimīn

There is no god (worthy of worship) except You. Glory be to You! I have certainly done wrong. [Al-Anbiyā 21:87]

Seeking Relief from Worry and the Removal of Distress

اَللّٰهُمَّ فَارِجَ الْهَمِّ، كَاشِفَ الْغَمِّ، مُجِيبَ دَعْوَةِ الْمُضْطَرِّينَ، رَحْمَانَ الدُّنْيَا وَالْآخِرَةِ وَرَحِيمَهُمَا، أَنْتَ تَرْحَمُنِي، فَارْحَمْنِي بِرَحْمَةٍ تُغْنِينِي بِهَا عَنْ رَحْمَةِ مَنْ سِوَاكَ

Allāhumma fārijal hammi kāshifal ghammi mujīb da'watil muḍṭarrīn, raḥmānad dunyā wal ākhirati wa raḥīmahumā, anta tarḥamunī farḥamnī bi raḥmatin tughnīnī bihā 'an raḥmati man siwāk

O Allāh, Who relieves worry and removes distress, Who answers the call of the desperate, the All Compassionate and the All Merciful in this world and the hereafter, You are the One who could bestow mercy on me, so bestow mercy on me, so that I will have no need of mercy from anyone else. [Al-Ḥākim 1898]

Negative Feelings

Seeking the Most Merciful in Times of Distress

رَبِّ أَنِّيْ مَسَّنِيَ الضُّرُّ وَأَنْتَ أَرْحَمُ الرّٰحِمِيْنَ

(Rabbi) Annī massaniyaḍ ḍurru wa Anta Arḥamur raḥimīn

(My Lord) I have been touched with adversity, and You are the Most Merciful of the merciful. [Al-Anbiyā' 21:83]

Seeking Protection from Doubts, and Attaining Conviction

اَللّٰهُمَّ إِنِّيْ أَعُوذُ بِكَ مِنَ الشَّكِّ فِي الْحَقِّ بَعْدَ الْيَقِينِ ، وَأَعُوذُ بِكَ مِنَ
الشَّيْطَانِ الرَّجِيمِ ، وَأَعُوذُ بِكَ مِنْ شَرِّ يَوْمِ الدِّيْنِ

Allāhumma innī a'ūdhu bika minash shakki fil haqqi ba'dal yaqīn, wa a'ūdhu bika minash Shayṭānir rajīm, wa a'ūdhu bika min sharri yawmid dīn

O Allāh, I seek Your protection from harbouring any doubts about the Truth after attaining firm conviction. I seek Your protection against the cursed Shayṭān. I seek Your protection from the harm of the Day of Judgement. [Abū Nu'aym Al-Aṣbahānī in Tārīkh Aṣbahān v.2 pg.170/219/276]

Negative Feelings

Seeking Mercy and Purification for Those Whom you Hurt or Curse

اَللّٰهُمَّ إِنِّي أَتَّخِذُ عِنْدَكَ عَهْدًا لَنْ تُخْلِفَنِيهِ فَإِنَّمَا أَنَا بَشَرٌ فَأَىُّ الْمُؤْمِنِينَ آذَيْتُهُ شَتَمْتُهُ لَعَنْتُهُ جَلَدْتُهُ فَاجْعَلْهَا لَهُ صَلاَةً وَزَكَاةً وَقُرْبَةً تُقَرِّبُهُ بِهَا إِلَيْكَ يَوْمَ الْقِيَامَةِ

Allāhumma innī attakhidhu 'indaka 'ahdan lan tukhlifanīhi fa innamā ana basharun fa ayyul mu-minīna ādhaytuhū shatamtuhū la'antuhū jaladtuhū faj'alhā lahū ṣalātan wa zakātan wa qurbatan tuqarribuhū bihā ilayka yawmal qiyāmah

O Allāh, I seek from you an unbreakable promise. I am just a human being. So whichever believer I hurt or rebuke or hit or curse then change that for him into mercy, purification, and a means of closeness to You on the Day of Judgement. [Ṣaḥīḥ Muslim 2601b]

Seeking Refuge from Severe Difficulties and the Malicious Joy of Enemies

أَعُوذُ بِاللهِ مِنْ جَهْدِ الْبَلاَءِ، وَدَرَكِ الشَّقَاءِ، وَسُوءِ الْقَضَاءِ، وَشَمَاتَةِ الأَعْدَاءِ

A'ūdhu billāhi min jahdil balā-i wa darakish shiqā-i wa sū-il qaḍā-i wa shamātatil -a'dā-i

I seek refuge with Allāh from the difficulties of severe calamities, from having an evil end and a bad fate and from the malicious joy of enemies. [Ṣaḥīḥ Al-Bukhārī 6616]

Negative Feelings

Seeking Relief from Distress

اَللّٰهُمَّ إِنِّي أَسْأَلُكَ مُوجِبَاتِ رَحْمَتِكَ وَعَزَائِمَ مَغْفِرَتِكَ وَالْغَنِيمَةَ مِنْ كُلِّ بِرٍّ
وَالسَّلَامَةَ مِنْ كُلِّ إِثْمٍ أَسْأَلُكَ أَلاَّ تَدَعَ لِي ذَنْبًا إِلاَّ غَفَرْتَهُ وَلاَ هَمًّا إِلاَّ فَرَّجْتَهُ
وَلاَ حَاجَةً هِيَ لَكَ رِضًا إِلاَّ قَضَيْتَهَا لِي

Allāhumma innī as-aluka mūjibāti raḥmatika wa 'azā-ima maghfiratika wal ghanīmata min kulli birrin was salāmata min kulli ithmin as-aluka allā tada-'a lī dhanban illā ghafartahū wa lā hamman illā farrajtahū wa lā ḥājatan hiya laka riḍan illā qaḍaytahā lī

O Allāh, I ask You for the means of Your mercy and forgiveness, the benefit of every good deed and safety from all sins. I ask You not to leave any sin of mine but You forgive it, or any distress but You relieve it, or any need that is pleasing to You but You meet it. [Sunan Ibn Mājah 1384]

Negative Feelings

Seeking to Mend Relationships and Guidance to Peaceful Paths

اَللّٰهُمَّ أَلِّفْ بَيْنَ قُلُوبِنَا وَأَصْلِحْ ذَاتَ بَيْنِنَا وَاهْدِنَا سُبُلَ السَّلَامِ وَنَجِّنَا مِنَ الظُّلُمَاتِ إِلَى النُّورِ وَجَنِّبْنَا الْفَوَاحِشَ مَا ظَهَرَ مِنْهَا وَمَا بَطَنَ وَبَارِكْ لَنَا فِي أَسْمَاعِنَا وَأَبْصَارِنَا وَقُلُوبِنَا وَأَزْوَاجِنَا وَذُرِّيَّاتِنَا وَتُبْ عَلَيْنَا إِنَّكَ أَنْتَ التَّوَّابُ الرَّحِيمُ وَاجْعَلْنَا شَاكِرِينَ لِنِعْمَتِكَ مُثْنِينَ بِهَا قَابِلِيهَا وَأَتِمَّهَا عَلَيْنَا

Allāhumma allif bayna qulūbina wa aṣliḥ dhāt bayninā wahdinā subulas salāmi wa najjinā minaẓ ẓulumāti ilan nūr, wa jannibnal fawāḥisha ma ẓahara minhā wa ma baṭan, wa bārik lanā fī asmā'inā wa abṣārinā wa qulūbinā wa azwājinā wa dhurriyyātinā wa tub 'alaynā innaka antat tawwābur raḥīm, waj'alnā shākirīna li ni'matika muthnīna bihā qābilīhā wa atimmahā 'alaynā

O Allāh, join our hearts, mend our relationships, and guide us to the paths of peace. Bring us out of darkness into light and keep us away from manifest and concealed obscenities. Bless us in our ears, our eyes, our hearts, our spouses, and our offspring. Accept our repentance. Indeed, You are the Most Forgiving, the Most Merciful. Make us grateful for Your blessings, so we receive them with due praise. And perfect them for us. [Sunan Abī Dawūd 969]

Negative Feelings

Seeking a Truthful Tongue and Protection from Evil

اَللّٰهُمَّ إِنِّي أَسْأَلُكَ الثَّبَاتَ فِي الأَمْرِ وَأَسْأَلُكَ عَزِيمَةَ الرُّشْدِ وَأَسْأَلُكَ شُكْرَ نِعْمَتِكَ وَحُسْنَ عِبَادَتِكَ وَأَسْأَلُكَ لِسَانًا صَادِقًا وَقَلْبًا سَلِيمًا وَأَعُوذُ بِكَ مِنْ شَرِّ مَا تَعْلَمُ وَأَسْأَلُكَ مِنْ خَيْرِ مَا تَعْلَمُ وَأَسْتَغْفِرُكَ مِمَّا تَعْلَمُ إِنَّكَ أَنْتَ عَلاَّمُ الْغُيُوبِ

Allāhumma innī as-alukath thabāta fil amri wa as-aluka 'azīmatar rushdi wa as-aluka shukra ni'matika wa ḥusna 'ibādatik, wa as-aluka lisānan ṣādiqa, wa qalban salīma, wa a'ūdhu bika min sharri ma ta'lam, wa as-aluka min khayri ma ta'lam, wa astaghfiruka mimmā ta'lam, innaka anta 'allāmul ghuyūb

O Allāh, I beg You for steadfastness in religious affairs. I beg You for determination to follow the guidance. I beg You to enable me to show gratitude for Your bounties and to worship You with the best devotion. I beg You for a truthful tongue, a sound heart, and an upright character. I seek Your protection from the evil of all that only You are aware of. I beg You for the good that only You know. And I seek forgiveness from You for what You know (of my sins). Surely, You are the All-Knowing of the hidden. [Jāmi` At-Tirmidhī 3407]

Negative Feelings

Seeking Refuge from Anxiety and Sadness

اَللّٰهُمَّ إِنِّي أَعُوذُ بِكَ مِنَ الْهَمِّ وَالْحَزَنِ وَالْعَجْزِ وَالْكَسَلِ وَالْجُبْنِ وَالْبُخْلِ
وَضَلَعِ الدَّيْنِ وَغَلَبَةِ الرِّجَالِ

Allāhumma innī a'ūdhu bika minal hammi wal ḥazani wal 'ajzi wal kasali wal jubni wal bukhli wa ḍala'id dayni wa ghalabatir rijāl

"O Allāh, I seek refuge in you from anxiety and sadness, weakness and laziness, miserliness and cowardice, the burden of debts and from being overpowered by men." [Ṣaḥīḥ Al-Bukhārī 6369]

Seeking Peacefulness

اَللّٰهُمَّ أَنْتَ السَّلاَمُ وَمِنْكَ السَّلاَمُ تَبَارَكْتَ ذَا الْجَلاَلِ وَالإِكْرَامِ

Allāhumma antas-salām, wa minkas-salām, tabārakta yā dhal-Jalāli wal-'Ikrām.

O Allāh, You are Peace and from You comes peace. Blessed are You, O Owner of majesty and honour. [Ṣaḥīḥ Muslim 591]

Negative Feelings

Seeking Constant Mercy and Protection

اَللّٰهُمَّ رَحْمَتَكَ أَرْجُو فَلاَ تَكِلْنِي إِلَى نَفْسِي طَرْفَةَ عَيْنٍ وَأَصْلِحْ لِي شَأْنِي كُلَّهُ لاَ إِلَهَ إِلاَّ أَنْتَ

Allāhumma raḥmataka arjū, falā takilnī ilā nafsī ṭarfata 'aynin, wa aṣliḥ lī sha-nī kullah, lā ilāha illā anta

O Allāh! Your mercy is what I hope for. Do not abandon me to myself for an instant, but put all my affairs in good order for me. There is no god but You. [Sunan Abī Dawūd 5090]

Protecting the Heart from Bitterness towards Believers

رَبَّنَا ٱغْفِرْ لَنَا وَلِإِخْوَٰنِنَا ٱلَّذِينَ سَبَقُونَا بِٱلْإِيمَٰنِ وَلَا تَجْعَلْ فِى قُلُوبِنَا غِلًّا لِّلَّذِينَ ءَامَنُوا۟ رَبَّنَآ إِنَّكَ رَءُوفٌ رَّحِيمٌ

Rabbānaghfir lanā wa li ikhwāninalladhīna sabaqūnā bil īmāni wa lā taj'al fī qulūbinā ghillal lilladhīna āmanu rabbāna innaka ra-ūfur raḥīm

Our Lord! Forgive us and our fellow believers who preceded us in faith, and do not allow bitterness into our hearts towards those who believe. Our Lord! Indeed, You are Ever Gracious, Most Merciful. [Al-Ḥashr 59:10]

Negative Feelings

Making the Qur'ān the Life of the Heart and a Remover of Sadness and Anxiety

اَللّٰهُمَّ إِنِّي عَبْدُكَ، ابْنُ عَبْدِكَ، ابْنُ أَمَتِكَ نَاصِيَتِي بِيَدِكَ، مَاضٍ فِيَّ حُكْمُكَ، عَدْلٌ فِيَّ قَضَاؤُكَ، أَسْأَلُكَ بِكُلِّ اسْمٍ هُوَ لَكَ سَمَّيْتَ بِهِ نَفْسَكَ، أَوْ عَلَّمْتَهُ أَحَدًا مِنْ خَلْقِكَ، أَوْ أَنْزَلْتَهُ فِي كِتَابِكَ، أَوِ اسْتَأْثَرْتَ بِهِ فِي عِلْمِ الْغَيْبِ عِنْدَكَ، أَنْ تَجْعَلَ الْقُرْآنَ رَبِيعَ قَلْبِي، وَنُورَ صَدْرِي، وَجِلَاءَ حُزْنِي، وَذَهَابَ هَمِّي

Allāhumma innī 'abduk, ibnu 'abdik, ibnu amatik, nāṣiyatī bi yadik, māḍin fiyya ḥukmuk, 'adlun fiyya qaḍā-uk, as-aluka bi kullismin huwa lak, sammayta bihī nafsak, aw anzaltahū fī kitābik, aw 'allamtahū aḥadan min khalqik, awis-ta-tharta bihī fī 'ilmil ghaybi 'indak, an taj'alal qur-āna rabī'a qalbī, wa nūra ṣadrī, wa jalā-a ḥuznī, wa dhahāba hammī

O Allāh, I am Your slave, son of Your slave, son of Your handmaid, my forelock is in Your hand (i.e. You have total mastery over me), Your command over me is forever executed and Your decree over me is just. I ask You by every name belonging to You which You named Yourself with, or revealed in Your Book, or You taught to any of Your creation, or You have preserved in the knowledge of the unseen with You, that You make the Qur'an the life of my heart and the light of my bosom, and a departure for my sorrow and a release for my anxiety. [Musnad Aḥmad 3712]

Negative Feelings

Seeking Pleasure with Allāh's ﷻ Decree

اَللَّهُمَّ بِعِلْمِكَ الْغَيْبَ وَقُدْرَتِكَ عَلَى الْخَلْقِ أَحْيِنِي مَا عَلِمْتَ الْحَيَاةَ خَيْرًا لِي وَتَوَفَّنِي إِذَا عَلِمْتَ الْوَفَاةَ خَيْرًا لِي وَأَسْأَلُكَ الرِّضَاءَ بَعْدَ الْقَضَاءِ وَأَسْأَلُكَ بَرْدَ الْعَيْشِ بَعْدَ الْمَوْتِ وَأَسْأَلُكَ لَذَّةَ النَّظَرِ إِلَى وَجْهِكَ وَالشَّوْقَ إِلَى لِقَائِكَ فِي غَيْرِ ضَرَّاءَ مُضِرَّةٍ وَلاَ فِتْنَةٍ مُضِلَّةٍ

Allāhumma bi 'ilmikal ghayba wa qudratika 'alal khalqi aḥyinī mā 'alimtal ḥayāta khayran lī wa tawaffanī idhā 'alimtal wafāta khayran lī, wa as-alukar riḍā ba'dal qaḍ'ā, wa as'aluka bardal 'ayshi ba'dal mawti wa as-aluka ladhdhatan naẓri ilā wajhik wash shawqa ila liqā-ika fi ghayri ḍarrā-a muḍirratin wa la fitnatin muḍillatin

O Allāh, by Your knowledge of the unseen and Your power over creation, keep me alive so long as You know that living is good for me and cause me to die when You know that death is better for me. I ask You to make me pleased with that which You have decreed and for an easy life after death. I ask You for the sweetness of looking upon Your face and a longing to meet You in a manner that does not entail a calamity that will bring about harm or a trial that will cause deviation. [Sunan An-Nasaī 1305]

كُفْرَانُ النِّعَم

Obliviousness to Blessings or Ingratitude

RELATED EMOTIONS

Undignified | Indifferent | Thoughtless | Bitter | Cynical | Resistant | Hostile | Apathetic | Arrogant | Covetous | Forgetful | Grudging Immature | Insecure | Neglectful | Oblivious

INVOKING NAMES OF ALLĀH

- **Al-Laṭīf - The Subtle One**
- **Al-Karīm - The Most Generous**
- **Al-Wahhāb - The Giver of Gifts**
- **As-Shakūr - the Most Appreciative**
- **Al-Ḥakīm - The All-Wise**
- **Al-Majīd - The Most Honourable**
- **Al-Bāsiṭ - the Expander**
- **Al-Qābiḍ - the Witholder**
- **Aẓ-Ẓāhir - The Manifest**

AṢ-ṢALĀH AL-IBRĀHĪMIYYAH

ACCEPTED PRAYERS

- **Seeking Contentment with Provisions**
- **Seeking Assistance in Being Grateful to Allāh**
- **Seeking Inspiration to be Thankful for Allāh's Favours**
- **Being Thankful for All of Allāh's Favours**
- **Being Ever-Grateful and Oft-Returning**
- **Receiving Allāh's Blessings with Due Praise**
- **Thanking Allāh Greatly for His Blessings**
- **Showing Gratitude for Allāh's Bounties**
- **Acknowledging All Favours Received in the Morning**
- **Acknowledging All Favours Received in the Evening**
- **Showing Gratitude for Food, Drink and Shelter**
- **Seeking Refuge in Allāh from His Withdrawal of Protection and Blessings**

CHAPTER 21

Obliviousness to Blessings or Ingratitude

[Kufrān an-Ni'am] كُفْرَانُ النِّعَم

Allāh ﷻ states in the Qur'ān: "Whatever blessings you have are from Allāh." [An-Naḥl 16:53]

To be bitterly hostile in disregarding this blessing can be an active and obvious personal choice, a kind of barefaced 'thumbing of the nose' at Allāh's ﷻ grace. In a more passive manner, ignorance of His blessings can originate from a person's lack of understanding and realisation. Either way, this lack of acknowledgement constitutes ingratitude.

Allāh ﷻ also says:

- "And (remember) when your Lord proclaimed, 'If you are grateful, I will certainly give you more. But if you are ungrateful, surely My punishment is severe'" [Ibrāhīm 14:7]
- "Remember Me; I will remember you. And thank Me, and never be ungrateful" [Al-Baqarah 2:152]

The Prophet ﷺ said, "If happiness reaches him (the believer), he is grateful (to Allāh)." [Ṣaḥīḥ Muslim 2999:64]

Obliviousness to Blessings or Ingratitude

Invoking Allāh's ﷻ Names

اللَّطِيفُ
Al-Laṭīf
The Subtle One

الْكَرِيمُ
Al-Karīm
The Most Generous

الْوَهَّابُ
Al-Wahhāb
The Giver of Gifts

الشَّكُورُ
As-Shakūr
The Most Appreciative

الْحَكِيمُ
Al-Ḥakīm
The All-Wise

الْمَجِيدُ
Al-Majīd
The Most Honourable

الْبَاسِطُ
Al-Bāsiṭ
The Expander

الْقَابِضُ
Al-Qābiḍ
The Witholder

الظَّاهِرُ
Aẓ-Ẓāhir
The Manifest

Obliviousness to Blessings or Ingratitude

Contemplation and Reflection on Allāh's ﷻ Blessed Names

- You remind yourself that Allāh ﷻ has provided you with a variety of things that are remarkable for their beauty and exquisite design. As for your own personal physical and mental realm, when you consider the proportion, design and how you can make use of them, even if the contemplation is only momentary, you are grateful. This gratefulness is an encouragement toward spiritual action and prayer, since your discerning self wants to give good in return.
- You express gratitude at an intellectual level, which manifests in how you employ the use of your eyes, your ears, your tongue, and your limbs, realising that the best form of gratitude is to put them to use, not in disobeying, but in obeying Him.
- Your renewed wisdom teaches you to be content but also to be regular in your worship, knowing that small but regular actions will win you the pleasure of Allāh ﷻ.
- Your senses show you that Allāh's ﷻ creative wonders are undeniably everywhere.
- You revisit the words of the testification of Islāmic Tawḥīd (Oneness of God), that simple yet profound statement that shows you bear witness to the greatness and blessings of Allāh ﷻ: There is no entity worthy of worship other than Allāh ﷻ. Without Allāh ﷻ, there are no blessings. By extension, you equate dismissal of His blessings with hostility towards Him.

Obliviousness to Blessings or Ingratitude

Aṣ-Ṣalāh Al-Ibrāhīmiyyah

اَللّٰهُمَّ صَلِّ عَلَى مُحَمَّدٍ وَعَلَى آلِ مُحَمَّدٍ كَمَا صَلَّيْتَ عَلَى
إِبْرَاهِيمَ وَآلِ إِبْرَاهِيمَ إِنَّكَ حَمِيدٌ مَجِيدٌ وَبَارِكْ عَلَى
مُحَمَّدٍ وَعَلَى آلِ مُحَمَّدٍ كَمَا بَارَكْتَ عَلَى إِبْرَاهِيمَ وَآلِ
إِبْرَاهِيمَ إِنَّكَ حَمِيدٌ مَجِيدٌ

Allāhumma ṣalli 'alā Muḥammadin wa 'alā āli Muḥammadin kamā ṣallayta 'alā Ibrāhīm wa āli Ibrāhīm innaka ḥamīdum majīd, wa bārik 'alā Muḥammadin wa 'alā āli Muḥammadin kamā bārakta 'alā Ibrāhīm wa āli Ibrāhīm innaka ḥamīdum majīd

O Allāh, send peace upon Muḥammad and upon the family of Muḥammad, as You sent peace upon Ibrāhīm and the family of Ibrāhīm, and send blessings upon Muḥammad and upon the family of Muḥammad as You sent blessings upon Ibrāhīm and the family of Ibrāhīm. You are indeed praiseworthy, the most honourable. [Sunan An-Nasaī 1290]

Obliviousness to Blessings or Ingratitude

Seeking Contentment with Provisions

اَللّٰهُمَّ قَنِّعْنِي بِمَا رَزَقْتَنِي، وَبَارِكْ لِي فِيهِ، وَاخْلُفْ عَلَيَّ كُلَّ غَائِبَةٍ لِي بِخَيْرٍ

Allāhumma qanni'nī bimā razaqtanī wa bārik lī fīh, wakhluf 'alayya kulla ghā-ibatin lī bi khayr

O Allāh, make me content with what You have provided for me and bless me in it, and be my protector in everything that is out of my sight. [Al-Ḥākim 1878]

Seeking Assistance in Being Grateful to Allāh ﷻ

اَللّٰهُمَّ أَعِنِّي عَلَى ذِكْرِكَ وَشُكْرِكَ وَحُسْنِ عِبَادَتِكَ

Allāhumma a-'innī 'alā dhikrika wa shukrika wa ḥusni 'ibādatik

O Allāh, help us in Your remembrance, in gratitude to You, and in reaching excellence in Your worship. [Sunan Abī Dawūd 1522]

Obliviousness to Blessings or Ingratitude

Seeking Inspiration to be Thankful for Allāh's ﷻ Favours

رَبِّ أَوْزِعْنِىٓ أَنْ أَشْكُرَ نِعْمَتَكَ ٱلَّتِىٓ أَنْعَمْتَ عَلَىَّ وَعَلَىٰ وَٰلِدَىَّ وَأَنْ أَعْمَلَ صَٰلِحًا تَرْضَىٰهُ وَأَدْخِلْنِى بِرَحْمَتِكَ فِى عِبَادِكَ ٱلصَّٰلِحِينَ

Rabbi awzi'nī an ashkura ni'matikallatī an'amta 'alayya wa 'alā wālidayya wa an -a'mala ṣāliḥan tarḍāhu wa adkhilnī bi raḥmatika fī 'ibādikaṣ ṣāliḥīn

My Lord! Inspire me to (always) be thankful for Your favours which You have blessed me and my parents with, and to do good deeds that please you. Admit me, by Your mercy, into (the company of) Your righteous servants. [An-Naml 27:19]

Being Ever-Grateful and Oft-Returning

رَبِّ اجْعَلْنِي لَكَ شَكَّارًا لَكَ ذَكَّارًا لَكَ رَهَّابًا لَكَ مِطْوَاعًا لَكَ مُخْبِتًا إِلَيْكَ أَوَّاهًا مُنِيبًا

Rabbij`alnī laka shakkārā, laka dhakkārā, laka rahhābā, laka miṭwā`ā, laka mukhbitan ilayka awwāham munībā

My Lord, make me ever-grateful to You, ever-remembering of You, ever-fearful of You, ever-obedient to You, ever-humble to You, oft-turning and returning to You. [Jāmi` At-Tirmidhī 3551]

Receiving Allāh's ﷻ Blessings with Due Praise

اَللّٰهُمَّ اجْعَلْنَا شَاكِرِينَ لِنِعْمَتِكَ مُثْنِينَ بِهَا قَابِلِيهَا وَأَتِمَّهَا عَلَيْنَا

Allāhummaj'alnā shākirīna li ni'matika muthnīna bihā qābilīhā wa atimmahā 'alaynā

O Allāh, make us grateful for Your blessings, so we receive them with due praise. And perfect them for us. [Sunan Abī Dawūd 969]

Obliviousness to Blessings or Ingratitude

Being Thankful for All of Allāh's ﷻ Favours

اَلْحَمْدُ لِلّٰهِ الَّذِي يُطْعِمُ وَلَا يُطْعَمُ، مَنَّ عَلَيْنَا فَهَدَانَا وَأَطْعَمَنَا وَأَسْقَانَا، وَكُلَّ بَلَاءٍ حَسَنٍ أَبْلَانَا، الْحَمْدُ لِلّٰهِ غَيْرَ مُوَدَّعٍ وَلَا مُكَافِي وَلَا مَكْفُورٍ وَلَا مُسْتَغْنًى عَنْهُ، الْحَمْدُ لِلّٰهِ الَّذِي أَطْعَمَ مِنَ الطَّعَامِ، وَسَقَى مِنَ الشَّرَابِ، وَكَسَى مِنَ الْعُرْيِ، وَهَدَى مِنَ الضَّلَالَةِ، وَبَصَّرَ مِنَ الْعَمَى، وَفَضَّلَ عَلَى كَثِيرٍ مِمَّنْ خَلَقَ تَفْضِيلًا، الْحَمْدُ لِلّٰهِ رَبِّ الْعَالَمِينَ

Alḥamdu lillāhilladhī yuṭ'imu walā yuṭ'am, manna 'alaynā fa hadānā wa aṭ'amanā wa saqānā, wa kulla balā-in ḥasanin ablānā. Alḥamdu lillāhi ghayra muwadda'in walā mukāfī walā makfūrin walā mustaghnan 'anhu. Alḥamdu lillāhilladhī aṭ'ama minaṭ ṭa'āmi, wa saqā minash sharābi, wa kasā minal 'uryi, wa hadā minaḍ ḍalālati, wa baṣṣara minal 'amā, wa faḍḍala 'ala kathīrin mimman khalaqa tafḍīlā. Alḥamdu lillāhi rabbil 'ālamīn

Praise is due to Allāh Who sustains all and is not in need of sustenance, Who has favoured us; guided us, provided us with food and drink, and favoured us with every blessing. Praise is due to Allāh, which cannot be left, compensated for, ungrateful towards, nor can it be done without. Praise is due to Allāh who gave us food, provided us with drink, and has clothed us from a state of nakedness, and has guided us from misguidance, and granted us sight from a state of blindness, and has favoured greatly over (what else) He has created. All praise is due to Allāh, Lord of the Worlds.

[Ibn As-Sunnī in 'Amal Al-Yawm wa Al-Laylah 896]

Obliviousness to Blessings or Ingratitude

Thanking Allāh ﷻ Greatly for His Blessings

اَللّٰهُمَّ اجْعَلْنِي أُعَظِّمُ شُكْرَكَ وَأُكْثِرُ ذِكْرَكَ وَأَتَّبِعُ نَصِيحَتَكَ وَأَحْفَظُ وَصِيَّتَكَ

Allāhummaj'alnī u-'aẓimu shukraka wa ukthiru dhikraka wa attabi'u naṣīḥataka wa aḥfaẓu waṣiyyatak

O Allāh, make me such that I thank you greatly for Your blessings, I remember You much, I follow Your counsel, and I preserve Your commands. [Jāmi` At-Tirmidhī 3604]

Showing Gratitude for Allāh's ﷻ Bounties

اَللّٰهُمَّ إِنِّي أَسْأَلُكَ الثَّبَاتَ فِي الْأَمْرِ وَأَسْأَلُكَ عَزِيمَةَ الرُّشْدِ وَأَسْأَلُكَ شُكْرَ نِعْمَتِكَ وَحُسْنَ عِبَادَتِكَ

Allāhumma innī as-alukath thabāta fil amri wa as-aluka 'azīmatar rushdi wa as-aluka shukra ni'matika wa ḥusna 'ibādatik

O Allāh, I beg You for steadfastness in religious affairs. I beg You for determination to follow the guidance. I beg You to enable me to show gratitude for Your bounties and to worship You with the best devotion. [Jāmi` At-Tirmidhī 3407]

Obliviousness to Blessings or Ingratitude

Acknowledging All Favours Received in the Morning

اَللّٰهُمَّ مَا أَصْبَحَ بِيْ مِنْ نِّعْمَةٍ أَوْ بِأَحَدٍ مِّنْ خَلْقِكَ ، فَمِنْكَ وَحْدَكَ لَا شَرِيْكَ لَكَ ، فَلَكَ الْحَمْدُ وَلَكَ الشُّكْرُ

Allāhumma mā aṣbaḥa bī min ni'matin aw bi aḥadim min khalqik, fa minka waḥdaka lā sharīka lak, fa lakal ḥamdu wa lakash shukr

O Allāh, all the favours that I or anyone from Your creation has received in the morning, are from You Alone. You have no partner. To You Alone belong all praise and all thanks. [Sunan Abī Dawūd 5073]

Acknowledging All Favours Received in the Evening

اَللّٰهُمَّ مَا أَمْسَى بِيْ مِنْ نِّعْمَةٍ أَوْ بِأَحَدٍ مِّنْ خَلْقِكَ ، فَمِنْكَ وَحْدَكَ لَا شَرِيْكَ لَكَ ، فَلَكَ الْحَمْدُ وَلَكَ الشُّكْرُ.

Allāhumma mā amsā bī min ni'matin aw bi aḥadim min khalqik, fa minka waḥdaka lā sharīka lak, fa lakal ḥamdu wa lakash shukr

O Allāh, all the favours that I or anyone from Your creation has received in the evening, are from You Alone. You have no partner. To You Alone belong all praise and all thanks. [Sunan Abī Dawūd 5073]

Obliviousness to Blessings or Ingratitude

Showing Gratitude for Food, Drink and Shelter

اَلْحَمْدُ لِلّٰهِ الَّذِي أَطْعَمَنَا وَسَقَانَا وَكَفَانَا وَآوَانَا فَكَمْ مِمَّنْ لاَ كَافِيَ لَهُ وَلاَ مُؤْوِيَ

Alḥamdu lillāhilladhī aṭ'amanā wa saqānā, wa kafānā, wa āwānā, fakam mimman lā kāfiya lahū wa lā mu'wī.

Praise be to Allāh Who gave us food and drink, provided for us sufficiently, and gave us shelter, for how many there are who have no one to provide for them or to give them shelter.' [Ṣaḥīḥ Muslim 2715]

Seeking Refuge in Allāh ﷻ from His Withdrawal of Protection and Blessings

اَللّٰهُمَّ إِنِّي أَعُوذُ بِكَ مِنْ زَوَالِ نِعْمَتِكَ وَتَحَوُّلِ عَافِيَتِكَ وَفُجَاءَةِ نِقْمَتِكَ وَجَمِيعِ سَخَطِكَ

Allāhumma innī a'ūdhu bika min zawāl ni'matika wa taḥawwuli 'āfiyatika wa fujā-ati niqmatika wa jamī' sakhatik

O Allāh, I seek refuge in You from the withdrawal of Your blessing and the change of Your protection (of me) and from Your sudden wrath, and from every displeasure of Yours. [Ṣaḥīḥ Muslim 2739]

الرِيَاء

Ostentation or Showing Off

RELATED EMOTIONS

Excessive | Insincere | Pretentious | Self-righteous | Addicted
Judgemental | Arrogant | Immature | Lustful | Undignified | Vain
Egotistic | Vulgar

INVOKING NAMES OF ALLĀH

- **Al-Khabīr - The All-Aware**
- **Al-Ḥakīm – The Wise**
- **Al-Bā'ith - The Resurrector**
- **Al-Mudhil - The Humiliator**
- **Al-Mu'izz - The Bestower of Honour**
- **As-Samī' - All Hearing**
- **Al-Baṣīr - The Seer of All (The All-Seeing)**
- **Ar-Raqīb - the All Observant**
- **Ash-Shahīd - the Witness**
- **Al-Muḥṣī - The One Who Keeps Record**
- **Al-Ḥasīb - The Reckoner**

AṢ-ṢALĀH AL-IBRĀHĪMIYYAH

ACCEPTED PRAYERS

- **Seeking Purification of the Heart from Ostentatious and Pretentious Deeds**
- **Seeking a Better Inner Condition and More Righteous Outer Condition**
- **Seeking Protection from Seeking the Pleasure of Others**
- **Seeking Refuge from Showing Off**
- **Seeking Constant Mercy and Protection**
- **Seeking the Hereafter and Protection from the Fire**

CHAPTER 22

Ostentation or Showing Off [Riyā'a] الرِيَاء

Ostentation is when you perform an act of devotion for other than the Creator's sake, for the purpose of seeking some worldly benefit, praise or admiration from His creation. Ostentation is a branch of ḥubb al-jāh, love of fame and glory.

When you split the purpose of worship by endeavoring to attain both public acclaim as well as the pleasure of Allāh ﷻ (i.e. partnering with Allāh ﷻ), therein lies a hint of polytheism (lesser shirk).

The Messenger of Allāh ﷺ said:

- "If anyone wants to have his deeds widely publicised, Allāh will publicise (his humiliation). And if anyone makes a hypocritical display of his deeds, Allāh will make a display of him" [Ṣaḥīḥ Muslim 2986:47]
- "Verily, even a little ostentation is shirk" [Ibn Mājah 3989]
- "Shall I not tell you about what I fear for you more than the presence of the False Messiah?" We said, "Of course!" He said, "Hidden polytheism; that a man stands for prayer and beautifies his prayer because he sees another man looking at him" [Ibn Mājah 4204]

People are known to commit riyā'a due to:

- Craving praise and acclaim (the admiration of people) over the pleasure of Allāh ﷻ because their faith in Him has become weak
- Fear of criticism or humiliation, by making a display of good deeds (for example, praying in the mosque out of fear of being criticised by people for not doing so)
- An envious greed for worldly wealth: seeing the possessions of others, they hanker after them, largely in the hope that one day they will be able to parade similar trophies and trinkets

Ostentation or Showing Off

Invoking Allāh's ﷻ Names

الْخَبِيرُ

Al-Khabīr
The All-Aware

الْحَكِيمُ

Al-Ḥakīm
The Wise

الْبَاعِثُ

Al-Bā'ith
The Resurrector

الْمُذِلُّ

Al-Mudhil
The Humiliator

الْمُعِزُّ

Al-Mu'izz
The Bestower of Honour

السَّمِيعُ

As-Samī'
All Hearing

الْبَصِيرُ

Al-Baṣīr
The Seer of All Things
(The All-Seeing)

الرَّقِيبُ

Ar-Raqīb
The All Observant

الشَّهِيدُ

Ash-Shahīd
The Witness

الْمُحْصِي

Al-Muḥṣī
The One Who Keeps Record

الْحَسِيبُ

Al-Ḥasīb
The Reckoner

Ostentation or Showing Off

Contemplation and Reflection on Allāh's ﷻ Blessed Names

- You remind yourself that this worldly life is mere play and amusement, which (unless restrained) spawns most of the evil spiritual traits and characteristics (love of fame, glory, addiction to public acclaim, etc) and that your true objective of this life is to make sufficient arrangements for your travels to the Hereafter.
- Your renewed wisdom teaches you to become aware of your lower self, its deceit, its delusions and its potential to become consumed by damaging behaviour patterns: often the culmination of small (perceived to be 'harmless') steps that bear the hallmark of a tendency to lean toward extremes and addictive traits.
- You guard against becoming the wretched soul that 'knows' its own showiness yet slips into judging others for the same spiritual sickness.
- You are aware of what goes on in your world, i.e. your heart, your body, and the hidden things by which your heart is characterised: deception and treachery, preoccupation with earthly things, or harbouring evil intent while putting on a good front.
- You filter out those actions which are 'mostly for Allāh' ﷻ in your life, when you take stock. The next time around, you attempt to perform actions that are for Allāh's ﷻ pleasure alone.
- Knowing that some humans (including yourself) have 'goals' for their acts of ostentation, you don't particularly enjoy it even when a close friend says that you are a pious person. For this reason, you make sure that your public acts marry up with your private acts. Rather, your private acts exceed your public acts. For instance, your voluntary prayers when you stir from your bed in the night-time outweigh your congregational obligatory prayers performed by day.
- You are not frightened to admit to yourself that a greater effort is required.
- Subtle ostentation can be apparent (Arabic: jaliyy), hidden (khafiyy) or deeply hidden (akhfā). You know them: the first you see easily, related to the motive of the showy action; the second you feel in yourself when you find it easier to perform an act of devotion when others are watching you; and the third you observe in yourself when you merely feel pleased when others see you performing an act of worship.
- You remember your humble origins and you completely sidestep the temptation to develop jealousy or anxiety when you meet someone else who comes across as more adept, popular or competent than you. Indeed, you feel happy for them. You fail to adopt any new 'airs or graces' when in the presence of people who are esteemed in the eyes of others.
- You appreciate that Allāh ﷻ witnesses and sees all actions, and that He will be happy with you if you don't take advantage of people. This applies to situations where the 'showy' part of you raises its ugly head: the part of you that is inclined to climb on the shoulders of others for their failings, embarrassments or sins. Instead of working to gain pleasure or advancement from their negligence or misfortunes, you pray for them in private.
- This praying for other people is part of your strategy to avoid personal embarrassment and loss in the Afterlife.

Ostentation or Showing Off

Aṣ-Ṣalāh Al-Ibrāhīmiyyah

اَللّٰهُمَّ صَلِّ عَلَى مُحَمَّدٍ وَعَلَى آلِ مُحَمَّدٍ كَمَا صَلَّيْتَ عَلَى
إِبْرَاهِيمَ وَآلِ إِبْرَاهِيمَ إِنَّكَ حَمِيدٌ مَجِيدٌ وَبَارِكْ عَلَى
مُحَمَّدٍ وَعَلَى آلِ مُحَمَّدٍ كَمَا بَارَكْتَ عَلَى إِبْرَاهِيمَ وَآلِ
إِبْرَاهِيمَ إِنَّكَ حَمِيدٌ مَجِيدٌ

Allāhumma ṣalli 'alā Muḥammadin wa 'alā āli Muḥammadin kamā ṣ allayta 'alā Ibrāhīm wa āli Ibrāhīm innaka ḥamīdum majīd, wa bārik 'alā Muḥammadin wa 'alā āli Muḥammadin kamā bārakta 'alā Ibrāhīm wa āli Ibrāhīm innaka ḥamīdum majīd

O Allāh, send peace upon Muḥammad and upon the family of Muḥammad, as You sent peace upon Ibrāhīm and the family of Ibrāhīm, and send blessings upon Muḥammad and upon the family of Muḥammad as You sent blessings upon Ibrāhīm and the family of Ibrāhīm. You are indeed praiseworthy, the most honourable. [Sunan An-Nasaī 1290]

Ostentation or Showing Off

Seeking Purification of the Heart from Ostentatious and Pretentious Deeds

اَللّٰهُمَّ طَهِّرْ قَلْبِي مِنَ النِّفَاقِ وَعَمَلِي مِنَ الرِّيَاءِ وَلِسَانِي مِنَ الْكَذِبِ وَعَيْنِي مِنَ الْخِيَانَةِ، فَإِنَّكَ تَعْلَمُ خَائِنَةَ الأَعْيُنِ وَمَا تُخْفِي الصُّدُورُ

Allāhumma ṭahhir qalbī minan nifāq wa 'amalī minar riyā- wa lisānī minal kadhib wa 'aynī minal khiyānah, fa innaka ta'lamu khā-inatal a'yuni wa mā tukhfiṣ ṣudūr

O Allāh, purify my heart from hypocrisy, my deeds from ostentation and pretension, my tongue from lies, and my eyes from wrongful glances. For, indeed, You know what the eyes deceptively glance at and what the hearts conceal. [Al-Bayhaqī in Ad-Da'awāt Al-Kabīr 258]

Seeking a Better Inner Condition and More Righteous Outer Condition

اَللّٰهُمَّ اجْعَلْ سَرِيرَتِي خَيْرًا مِنْ عَلاَنِيَتِي وَاجْعَلْ عَلاَنِيَتِي صَالِحَةً اَللّٰهُمَّ إِنِّي أَسْأَلُكَ مِنْ صَالِحِ مَا تُؤْتِي النَّاسَ مِنَ الْمَالِ وَالأَهْلِ وَالْوَلَدِ غَيْرِ الضَّالِّ وَلاَ الْمُضِلِّ

Allāhummaj'al sarīratī khayran min 'alāniyatī waj'al 'alāniyatī ṣāliḥah, Allāhumma innī as-aluka min ṣāliḥi mā tu-tin nāsa minal māli wal ahli wal waladi ghayriḍ ḍālli wa lal muḍill

O Allāh, make my secret better than my apparent condition, and make my apparent condition righteous. O Allāh, I ask You for the good of what you give to the people, of wealth, wives, and children, not (to be) misguided, nor misguiding. [Jāmi' At-Tirmidhī 3586]

Ostentation or Showing Off

Seeking Protection from Seeking the Pleasure of Others

اَللّٰهُمَّ إِنِّي أَعُوذُ بِكَ أَنْ أُشْرِكَ بِكَ وَأَنَا أَعْلَمُ، وَأَسْتَغْفِرُكَ لِمَا لَا أَعْلَمُ

Allāhumma innī a'ūdhu bika an ushrika bika wa ana -a'lam, wa astaghfiruka limā lā -a'lam

O Allāh, I seek Your protection from that I should join any partner with You knowingly and I seek Your forgiveness if I have ever done so unknowingly. [Al-Adab Al-Mufrad 716]

Seeking Refuge from Showing Off

اَللّٰهُمَّ إِنِّي أَسْأَلُكَ بِحَقِّ السَّائِلِينَ عَلَيْكَ وَأَسْأَلُكَ بِحَقِّ مَمْشَايَ هٰذَا فَإِنِّي لَمْ أَخْرُجْ أَشَرًا وَلاَ بَطَرًا وَلاَ رِيَاءً وَلاَ سُمْعَةً وَخَرَجْتُ اتِّقَاءَ سُخْطِكَ وَابْتِغَاءَ مَرْضَاتِكَ فَأَسْأَلُكَ أَنْ تُعِيذَنِي مِنَ النَّارِ وَأَنْ تَغْفِرَ لِي ذُنُوبِي إِنَّهُ لاَ يَغْفِرُ الذُّنُوبَ إِلاَّ أَنْتَ

Allāhumma innī as-aluka bi ḥaqqissā-ilīna 'alayka, wa as-aluka bi ḥaqqi mamshāya hādhā, fa innī lam akhruj asharan wa lā baṭaran, wa lā riyā-an, wa la sum'atan, wa kharajtut-tiqā-a sukhtika wabtighā-a marḍātika, fa as-aluka an tu'īdhanī minan nāri wa an taghfira lī dhunūbī, innahu lā yaghfirudh dhunūba illā Anta

O Allāh, I ask You by the right that those who ask of You have over You, and I ask by virtue of this walking of mine, for I am not going out because of pride or vanity, or to show off or make a reputation, rather I am going out because I fear Your wrath and seek Your pleasure. So I ask You to protect me from the Fire and to forgive me my sins, for no one can forgive sins except You. [Sunan Ibn Mājah 778]

Ostentation or Showing Off

Seeking Constant Mercy and Protection

اَللّٰهُمَّ رَحْمَتَكَ أَرْجُو فَلاَ تَكِلْنِي إِلَى نَفْسِي طَرْفَةَ عَيْنٍ وَأَصْلِحْ لِي شَأْنِي كُلَّهُ لاَ إِلَهَ إِلاَّ أَنْتَ

Allāhumma raḥmataka arjū, falā takilnī ilā nafsī ṭarfata ʿaynin, wa aṣliḥ lī sha-nī kullah, lā ilāha illā anta

O Allāh! Your mercy is what I hope for. Do not abandon me to myself for an instant, but put all my affairs in good order for me. There is no god but You. [Sunan Abī Dawūd 5090]

Seeking the Hereafter and Protection from the Fire

رَبَّنَآ ءَاتِنَا فِى ٱلدُّنْيَا حَسَنَةً وَفِى ٱلْـَٔاخِرَةِ حَسَنَةً وَقِنَا عَذَابَ ٱلنَّارِ

Rabbanā Ātinā fid dunyā ḥasanataw wa fil Ākhirati ḥasanataw wa qinā ʿadhāban nār

"Yet there are others who say, "Our Lord! Grant us the good of this world and the Hereafter, and protect us from the torment of the Fire." [Al-Baqarah 2:201-202]

التَّوَكُّلُ علي غيرِ الله

Relying on Other than Allāh

RELATED EMOTIONS

Doubtful | Vulnerable | Apprehensive | Astray | Limited | Uninspired
Lonely | Argumentative | Arrogant | Ashamed | Brooding | Cynical
Deluded | Deceitful | Disappointed | Embarrassed | Fearful | Ignorant
Inadequate | Insincere | Neglectful | Pessimistic | Pretentious
Superstitious | Cowardly

INVOKING NAMES OF ALLĀH

- **Al-Muta'ālī - The Self Exalted**
- **Al-Khāliq - The Creator**
- **Al-Bāri' - The Incomparable Originator**
- **Al-Wāḥid - The One**
- **Al-Aḥad - The Only One**
- **Al-Awwal - The First**
- **Al-Ākhir - The Last**
- **Al-Aziz - The Victorious**
- **Al-Mu'min - The Inspirer of Faith**
- **Al-Wakīl - The Trustee**
- **Al-'Adl - the Just**
- **Al-Ḥayy - The Ever-Living**
- **Al-Razzāq - the Provider**
- **Al-Muqīt - the Nourisher**
- **Aḍ-Ḍārr - The Distresser**
- **An-Nāfi' - The Benefactor**
- **Al-Mujīb - The Responsive One**

AṢ-ṢALĀH AL-IBRĀHĪMIYYAH

ACCEPTED PRAYERS

- **Renewal of Īmān**
- **Placing Trust in Allāh Alone**
- **Placing Trust and Sufficiency in Allāh**
- **Starting the Day with Conviction**
- **Disassociating Anything with Allāh**
- **Calling on Allāh to Set Your Affairs Right**
- **Seeking Protection from Doubts About the Truth**
- **Seeking Protection from Joining Partners with Allāh Knowingly and Unknowingly**
- **Seeking Allāh for the Disposal of All Affairs**
- **Seeking the Correct Guidance Through Tribulations**
- **Seeking Guidance, Firmness, Determination, Devoutness and Sincerity in Deeds**

CHAPTER 23

Relying on Other than Allāh ﷻ

[At-Tawakkul 'ala Ghayrillāh] التَّوَكُّل علي غَيْرِ الله

Allāh ﷻ is the possessor of unlimited power and grace. Knowing this, the ideal for the believer is to have full 'tawakkul' (trust and reliance) that Allāh ﷻ is in control of mankind's affairs. When a lack of certainty is allowed to develop within the inner heart, the believer's weakened sense of faith is transformed into a reliance on created beings and the material realm.

Allāh ﷻ says, "Say, 'He is the Most Compassionate – in Him (alone) we believe, and in Him (alone) we trust. You will soon know who is clearly astray.'" [Al-Mulk 67:29]

The Prophet ﷺ said, "When you ask something then (only) ask of Allāh, and when you seek aid, then (only) seek assistance from Allāh." [At-Tirmidhī 2516]

Relying on Other than Allāh سُبْحَانَهُ وَتَعَالَى

Invoking Allāh's سُبْحَانَهُ وَتَعَالَى Names

الْمُتَعَالِي
Al-Muta'ālī
The Self Exalted

الْخَالِقُ
Al-Khāliq
The Creator

الْبَارِئُ
Al-Bāri'
The Incomparable Originator

الْوَاحِدُ
Al-Wāḥid
The One

الْأَحَدُ
Al-Aḥad
The Only One

الأَوَّلُ
Al-Awwal
The First

الْآخِرُ
Al-Ākhir
The Last

الْعَزِيزُ
Al-Aziz
The Victorious

الْمُؤْمِنُ
Al-Mu'min
The Inspirer of Faith

الْوَكِيلُ
Al-Wakīl
The Trustee

الْعَدْلُ
Al-'Adl
The Just

الْحَيُّ
Al-Ḥayy
The Ever-Living

الْرَّزَّاقُ
Al-Razzāq
The Provider

الْمُقِيتُ
Al-Muqīt
The Nourisher

الْضَّارُّ
Aḍ-Ḍārr
The Distresser

الْنَّافِعُ
An-Nāfi'
The Benefactor

الْمُجِيبُ
Al-Mujīb
The Responsive One

Relying on Other than Allāh ﷻ

Contemplation and Reflection on Allāh's ﷻ Blessed Names

- You understand that Allāh ﷻ, as the Self Exalted, is far above any association ascribed to Him.
- You realise that only He can rescue you and meet all of your needs because He enjoys absolute power and can execute all that He wills.
- You cultivate an approach whereby you are always ready to ask Allāh ﷻ for help, praying to Him to protect you from fears, harms and frustrations and to help you with the things that are obviously out of your control.
- Entirely related to that, you develop an inherent trust in the Creator alone (called tawakkul), which means that you 'act in accordance with' Allāh's ﷻ plan, i.e. you adopt the principles and commands of the sharī'ah, and place trust in Allāh ﷻ.
- You seek refuge with Him from even minor shirk, knowingly and unknowingly.
- Allāh ﷻ inspired you towards faith: you repay Him, in all your inadequacy, by entrusting your heart to Him.
- You understand that the perfection of faith consists in knowing that all happenings in the universes take place by causes subservient to Him, all players and materials arranged in the best order and direction, according to the highest standards of the most Just and All-Compassionate.
- You understand that it is Allāh ﷻ alone who benefits or harms, and this deters you from relying on anyone other than Him for help or favours.
- You turn to Him with a pure sincerity, negating your hope in all other sources.
- You understand that Allāh ﷻ knows the needs of the needy before they (even) ask; indeed He already knew them in eternity, so He arranged the sources sufficient to their needs by creating food and nourishment, and by facilitating both the causes and the means of fulfilling all these needs.
- You are inspired with more conviction, sincerity and fervour that Allāh ﷻ will respond to your prayer in a way that suits you best.

Relying on Other than Allāh ﷻ

Aṣ-Ṣalāh Al-Ibrāhīmiyyah

اَللّٰهُمَّ صَلِّ عَلَى مُحَمَّدٍ وَعَلَى آلِ مُحَمَّدٍ كَمَا صَلَّيْتَ عَلَى
إِبْرَاهِيمَ وَآلِ إِبْرَاهِيمَ إِنَّكَ حَمِيدٌ مَجِيدٌ وَبَارِكْ عَلَى
مُحَمَّدٍ وَعَلَى آلِ مُحَمَّدٍ كَمَا بَارَكْتَ عَلَى إِبْرَاهِيمَ وَآلِ
إِبْرَاهِيمَ إِنَّكَ حَمِيدٌ مَجِيدٌ

Allāhumma ṣalli 'alā Muḥammadin wa 'alā āli Muḥammadin kamā ṣ allayta 'alā Ibrāhīm wa āli Ibrāhīm innaka ḥamīdum majīd, wa bārik 'alā Muḥammadin wa 'alā āli Muḥammadin kamā bārakta 'alā Ibrāhīm wa āli Ibrāhīm innaka ḥamīdum majīd

O Allāh, send peace upon Muḥammad and upon the family of Muḥammad, as You sent peace upon Ibrāhīm and the family of Ibrāhīm, and send blessings upon Muḥammad and upon the family of Muḥammad as You sent blessings upon Ibrāhīm and the family of Ibrāhīm. You are indeed praiseworthy, the most honourable. [Sunan An-Nasaī 1290]

Relying on Other than Allāh ﷻ

Renewal of Īmān

اَللّٰهُمَّ جَدِّدِ الإِيْمَانَ فِي قَلْبِي

Allāhumma jaddidil īmāna fī qalbī

O Allāh keep faith rejuvenated in my heart. [Al-Ḥākim 5]

Placing Trust in Allāh ﷻ Alone

حَسْبِيَ اللّٰهُ لآ إِلَهَ إِلاَّ هُوَ، عَلَيْهِ تَوَكَّلتُ، وَهُوَ رَبُّ الْعَرْشِ الْعَظِيمِ

ḤasbiyAllāhu lā ilāha illā hū, 'alayhi tawakkaltu wa huwa rabbul 'arshil 'aẓīm

Allāh is sufficient for me. There is none worthy of worship but Him. I have placed my trust in Him, and He is the lord of the Majestic Throne. [Sunan Abī Dawūd 5081]

Placing Trust and Sufficiency in Allāh ﷻ

اَللّٰهُمَّ اجْعَلْنِي مِمَّنْ تَوَكَّلَ عَلَيْكَ فَكَفَيْتَهُ، وَاسْتَهْدَاكَ فَهَدَيْتَهُ، وَاسْتَنْصَرَكَ فَنَصَرْتَهُ

Allāhummaj'alnī mimman tawakkala 'alayka fa kafaytah, wastahdāka fa hadaytah, wastanṣaraka fa naṣartah

O Allāh, make me from those who put their trust in You and You became sufficient for them, who sought guidance from You and You guided them, and who sought help from You and You helped them. [At-Tawakkul 'alā Allāh Ibn Abī Dunyā 4]

Relying on Other than Allāh ﷻ

Starting the Day with Conviction

اَللّٰهُمَّ إِنِّي أَصْبَحْتُ أُشْهِدُكَ وَأُشْهِدُ حَمَلَةَ عَرْشِكَ وَمَلاَئِكَتَكَ وَجَمِيعَ خَلْقِكَ أَنَّكَ أَنْتَ اللّٰهُ لاَ إِلَهَ إِلاَّ أَنْتَ وَحْدَكَ لاَ شَرِيكَ لَكَ وَأَنَّ مُحَمَّدًا عَبْدُكَ وَرَسُولُكَ

Allāhumma innī aṣbaḥtu ush-hiduk, wa ush-hidu ḥamalata 'arshik wa malā-ikataka wa jamī'a khalqik, annaka antAllāhu lā ilāha illā anta waḥdaka lā sharīka lak, wa anna Muḥammadan 'abduka wa rasūluk

O Allāh! As morning comes upon me, I bear witness before You, the Bearers of Your Throne, Your angels, and all Your creation - that You are Allāh, there is no god but You, alone with no partners, and that Muḥammad is Your slave and messenger. [Sunan Abī Dawūd 5078]

Disassociating Anything with Allāh ﷻ

اللّٰهُ اللّٰهُ رَبِّي لاَ أُشْرِكُ بِهِ شَيْئًا

Allāhu Allāhu rabbī lā ushriku bihī shay-ā

Allāh, Allāh is my Lord, I do not associate anything as a partner with Him. [Sunan Abī Dawūd 1525]

Relying on Other than Allāh ﷻ

Calling on Allāh ﷻ to Set Your Affairs Right

يَا حَيُّ يَا قَيُّومُ بِرَحْمَتِكَ أَسْتَغِيثُ، أَصْلِحْ لِي شَأْنِي كُلَّهُ، وَلَا تَكِلْنِي إِلَى نَفْسِي طَرْفَةَ عَيْنٍ

Yā ḥayyu yā Qayyūm, bi raḥmatika astaghīth, aṣliḥ lī sha-nī kullah, wa lā takilnī ilā nafsī ṭarafata 'ayn

O Ever-Living One, O Eternal One, by Your mercy I call on You to set right all my affairs. Do not place me in charge of my soul even for the blinking of an eye (i.e. a moment). [Al-Ḥākim 2000]

Seeking Protection from Doubts About the Truth

اَللّٰهُمَّ إِنِّي أَعُوذُ بِكَ مِنَ الشَّكِّ فِي الْحَقِّ بَعْدَ الْيَقِينِ ، وَأَعُوذُ بِكَ مِنَ الشَّيْطَانِ الرَّجِيمِ ، وَأَعُوذُ بِكَ مِنْ شَرِّ يَوْمِ الدِّينِ

Allāhumma innī a'ūdhu bika minash shakki fil haqqi ba'dal yaqīn, wa a'ūdhu bika minash Shayṭānir rajīm, wa a'ūdhu bika min sharri yawmid dīn

O Allāh, I seek Your protection from harbouring any doubts about the Truth after attaining firm conviction. I seek Your protection against the cursed Shayṭān. I seek Your protection from the harm of the Day of Judgement. [Abū Nu'aym Al-Aṣbahānī in Tārīkh Aṣbahān v.2 pg.170/219/276]

Relying on Other than Allāh ﷻ

Seeking Protection from Joining Partners with Allāh ﷻ Knowingly and Unknowingly

اَللّٰهُمَّ إِنِّي أَعُوذُ بِكَ أَنْ أُشْرِكَ بِكَ وَأَنَا أَعْلَمُ، وَأَسْتَغْفِرُكَ لِمَا لاَ أَعْلَمُ

Allāhumma innī a'ūdhu bika an ushrika bika wa ana -a'lam, wa astaghfiruka limā lā -a'lam

O Allāh, I seek Your protection from that I should join any partner with You knowingly and I seek Your forgiveness if I have ever done so unknowingly. [Al-Adab Al-Mufrad 716]

Seeking Allāh ﷻ for the Disposal of All Affairs

اَللّٰهُمَّ لَكَ الْحَمْدُ كُلُّهُ، وَلَكَ الْمُلْكُ كُلُّهُ، وَلَكَ الْخَلْقُ كُلُّهُ، وَإِلَيْكَ يَرْجِعُ الْأَمْرُ كُلُّهُ، أَسْأَلُكَ مِنَ الْخَيْرِ كُلِّهِ وَأَعُوذُ بِكَ مِنَ الشَّرِّ كُلِّهِ

Allāhumma lakal ḥamdu kulluh, wa lakal mulku kulluh, wa lakal khalqu kuluh, wa ilayka yarji'ul amru kuluh, as-aluka minal khayri kullih, wa a'ūdhu bika minash sharri kullih

O Allāh, for You alone is all praise. Yours alone is the entire dominion. To You alone belongs the entire creation. And the disposal of all matters ultimately rests in You alone. I beg You for all good and seek protection in You from all evil. [Al-Bayhaqī in Shu'ab Al-Īmān 4088]

Seeking the Correct Guidance Through Tribulations

رَبَّنَآ ءَاتِنَا مِن لَّدُنكَ رَحْمَةً وَهَيِّئْ لَنَا مِنْ أَمْرِنَا رَشَدًا

Rabbanā ātinā min ladunka raḥmatan wa hayyi- lanā min amrinā rashadā

Our Lord! Grant us mercy from Yourself and guide us rightly through our ordeal. [Al-Kahf 18:10]

Relying on Other than Allāh ﷻ

Seeking Guidance, Firmness, Determination, Devoutness and Sincerity in Deeds

اَللّٰهُمَّ إِنِّي أَسْأَلُكَ تَوْفِيقَ أَهْلِ الْهُدَى ، وَأَعْمَالَ أَهْلِ الْيَقِينِ ، وَمُنَاصَحَةَ أَهْلِ التَّوْبَةِ ، وَعَزْمَ أَهْلِ الصَّبْرِ ، وَحَذَرَ أَهْلِ الْخَشْيَةِ ، وَتَعَبُّدَ أَهْلِ الْوَرَعِ ، وَعُرْفَانَ أَهْلِ الْعِلْمِ ، حَتَّى أَخَافَكَ . اَللّٰهُمَّ إِنِّي أَسْأَلُكَ مَخَافَةً تَحْجُزُنِي عَنْ مَعَاصِيكَ ، وَحَتَّى أَعْمَلَ بِطَاعَتِكَ عَمَلًا أَسْتَحِقُّ بِهِ الرِّضَا ، وَحَتَّى أُنَاصِحَكَ فِي التَّوْبَةِ خَوْفًا مِنْكَ ، وَحَتَّى أُخْلِصَ لَكَ النَّصِيحَةَ حُبًّا لَكَ ، وَحَتَّى أَتَوَكَّلَ عَلَيْكَ فِي الْأُمُورِ كُلِّهَا حُسْنَ الظَّنِّ بِكَ ، سُبْحَانَ خَالِقِ النُّورِ

Allāhumma innī as-aluka tawfīqa ahlil hudā, wa a'māla ahlil yaqīn, wa munāṣahata ahlit tawbah, wa 'azma ahliṣ ṣabr, wa ḥadhra ahlil khasyah wa ta'abbuda ahlil war', wa 'urfān ahlil 'ilm ḥattā a-khāfak. Allāhumma innī as-aluka makhāfatan tuḥjizunī 'an ma'āsīk, wa ḥattā a'malu biṭā'atika 'amalan astaḥiqqu bihir riḍā, wa ḥattā unāṣiḥaka fit tawbati khawfan mink, wa ḥattā akhluṣu lakan naṣīḥata ḥubban lak, wa ḥattā atawakkalu 'alayka fil umūri kullihā ḥusnaẓ ẓanni bik, subḥāna khāliqin nūr

O Allāh, I beseech You for the inspiration of the guided, the deeds of the firm believers, the sincerity of the repenters, the determination of the patient, the effort of the God fearing, the aspirations of the enthusiasts, the devoutness of the pious, and the cognition of the knowledgeable-so that I fear You. O Allāh, I beg You for such fear that will restrain me from Your disobedience so that I may act in obedience to You earning Your pleasure. And so that I may repent sincerely out of Your fear. And so that I may achieve sincerity to You to avoid embarrassment before You. And so that I may put my trust totally in You. (And I beg You for having) the best expectations from You, O the Glorified, the Creator of light. [Al-Khaṭīb Al-Baghdādī in Ṣalāh At-Tasbīḥ 10]

السُّمْعَة

Seeking Reputation

RELATED EMOTIONS

Worthless | Insecure | Vain | Addicted | Insincere | Egotistic
Arrogant | Covetous | Deceitful | Disappointed | Immoderate
Harsh | Inadequate | Insensitive | Judgemental | Lustful | Manipulative
Oblivious | Pretentious | Self-absorbed | Overwhelmed

INVOKING NAMES OF ALLĀH

- **Al-Mudhil - The Humiliator**
- **Al-Jalīl - The Majestic**
- **Al-Mu'izz - The Honourer**
- **Al-Khāfiḍ - The Abaser**
- **Ar-Rāfi' - The Exalter**
- **Ar-Raqīb - The Watchful**
- **Al-Ḥaqq - The Truth**
- **Aḍ-Ḍārr - The Distresser**
- **An-Nāfi' - The Benefactor**

AṢ-ṢALĀH AL-IBRĀHĪMIYYAH

ACCEPTED PRAYERS

- **Seeking Purification from Hypocrisy, Ostentation & Pretension**
- **Seeking Betterment in Both Our Secret and Apparent Conditions**
- **Seeking Protection from Joining Partners with Allāh Knowingly and Unknowingly**
- **Seeking Refuge from Seeking Reputation and Ultimately Allāh's Wrath**
- **Making Allāh's Love the Dearest and Cutting Off Worldly Needs**
- **Avoiding Allāh's Displeasure**

CHAPTER 24

Seeking Reputation

[Sum'a] السُمْعَة

Islām is a 'transactional' way of life. The mature believer accepts that ultimate success is dependant on Allāh's ﷻ favour: the Almighty looks at all words, deeds, sacrifices and relationships, and rewards or penalizes them accordingly, with His perfect justice. An individual who outwardly professes that they wish to seek Allāh's ﷻ pleasure, yet inwardly they crave admiration, respect and honour from others in humanity, is walking a dangerous high-wire of hypocrisy. They long to be in a permanent state of 'high profile', tiptoeing across the peaks of spiritual or material endeavour, their hearts cheered by the feeling that others are marvelling at their progress.

While walking this tightrope, they communicate their achievements 'back to ground level' by all manner of modes of communication, whether obvious or underhand. People come to know about them, and the hunger for 'sum'a' is fulfilled when tongues start chattering, and compliments come cascading. Because of the 'show' of it all, the seeking of reputation is the close cousin of 'riyā'a', or ostentation. The person who suffers from the affliction of 'sum'a' is often sadly unaware or even dismissive of the fact that their position on the high-wire is not secure, and that they can take a tumble at any time.

The Prophet ﷺ however said:

- "Know that if the nation were to gather to benefit you with anything, it would only benefit you with something that Allāh has already prescribed for you, and that if they gather to harm you with anything, they would only harm you with something Allāh has already prescribed for you. The pen has been lifted and the pages have dried" [At-Tirmidhī 2516]
- "If the son of Ādam had two valleys of money, he would wish for a third, for nothing can fill the mouth of the son of Ādam except dust" [Ṣaḥīḥ Al-Bukhārī 6436]
- "Two hungry wolves let loose in a flock of sheep do not cause as much harm as the harm to a man's religion wrought by his desire for wealth and fame" [At-Tirmidhī 2376]

Seeking Reputation

Invoking Allāh's ﷻ Names

الْمُذِلُّ
Al-Mudhil
The Humiliator

الْجَلِيلُ
Al-Jalīl
The Majestic

الْمُعِزُّ
Al-Mu'izz
The Honourer

الْخَافِضُ
Al-Khāfiḍ
The Abaser

الرَّافِعُ
Ar-Rāfi'
The Exalter

الرَّقِيبُ
Ar-Raqīb
The Watchful

الْحَقُّ
Al-Ḥaqq
The Truth

الضَّارُّ
Aḍ-Ḍārr
The Distresser

النَّافِعُ
An-Nāfi'
The Benefactor

Seeking Reputation

Contemplation and Reflection on Allāh's ﷻ Blessed Names

- You restrain and control your proud desires to become anything 'majestic' in this world, since you appreciate that Allāh ﷻ is Majestic, beyond compare. He is Mighty, All-Knowing and it is therefore from Him you should be seeking approval and reputation.
- This is not to say that you give up striving for achievement in this world: you know that the majestic and beautiful among mankind are the ones who seek the pleasure of Allāh ﷻ by observing His commands, avoiding His prohibitions, and promoting His religion.
- Islām is the source of truth and Allāh ﷻ calls all its adherents to uphold truth and give up falsehood; you turn to Him ﷻ with humility and a sincere intention, realising that this is the only way to gain His ultimate pleasure.
- You remind yourself that Allāh ﷻ alone delegates power and dominion. In absolutely the same fashion, He withdraws authority from whomever He wills, whenever He wills.
- You realise that seeking reputation from others eventually leads to humiliation and in the end will deprive you of the very thing you long for.
- You remember your humble origins, ignoring the status of your family name and the wealth you might have been born into. You recognise from your reading of the Qur'ān that the dominion (al-Mulk) consists of the owner (al-Mālik), the property (al-Milk) that he deals with and the king (al-Malik) who rules these owners. Allāh ﷻ owns all the kings, owners and properties. As long as the dominion is in Allāh's ﷻ hands, you are certain of your priorities. You seek help and guidance from Allāh ﷻ alone, and seek refuge with Him from even minor shirk, knowingly and unknowingly.
- You are ever-conscious that this worldly life is mere play and amusement, and when left unbridled this over-gratification of the self spawns most of the evil spiritual traits, addictions and vain characteristics (self-interest, arrogance, etc) that benefit nobody in the afterlife. Knowing this, you see your true objective being to make sufficient arrangements for your travels to the Hereafter, beginning with your time in the grave.

Seeking Reputation

Aṣ-Ṣalāh Al-Ibrāhīmiyyah

اَللّٰهُمَّ صَلِّ عَلَى مُحَمَّدٍ وَعَلَى آلِ مُحَمَّدٍ كَمَا صَلَّيْتَ عَلَى
إِبْرَاهِيمَ وَآلِ إِبْرَاهِيمَ إِنَّكَ حَمِيدٌ مَجِيدٌ وَبَارِكْ عَلَى
مُحَمَّدٍ وَعَلَى آلِ مُحَمَّدٍ كَمَا بَارَكْتَ عَلَى إِبْرَاهِيمَ وَآلِ
إِبْرَاهِيمَ إِنَّكَ حَمِيدٌ مَجِيدٌ

Allāhumma ṣalli 'alā Muḥammadin wa 'alā āli Muḥammadin kamā ṣ allayta 'alā Ibrāhīm wa āli Ibrāhīm innaka ḥamīdum majīd, wa bārik 'alā Muḥammadin wa 'alā āli Muḥammadin kamā bārakta 'alā Ibrāhīm wa āli Ibrāhīm innaka ḥamīdum majīd

O Allāh, send peace upon Muḥammad and upon the family of Muḥammad, as You sent peace upon Ibrāhīm and the family of Ibrāhīm, and send blessings upon Muḥammad and upon the family of Muḥammad as You sent blessings upon Ibrāhīm and the family of Ibrāhīm. You are indeed praiseworthy, the most honourable. [Sunan An-Nasaī 1290]

Seeking Reputation

Seeking Purification from Hypocrisy, Ostentation and Pretension

اَللّٰهُمَّ طَهِّرْ قَلْبِي مِنَ النِّفَاقِ وَعَمَلِي مِنَ الرِّيَاءِ وَلِسَانِي مِنَ الْكَذِبِ وَعَيْنِي مِنَ الْخِيَانَةِ، فَإِنَّكَ تَعْلَمُ خَائِنَةَ الأَعْيُنِ وَمَا تُخْفِي الصُّدُورُ

Allāhumma ṭahhir qalbī minan nifāq wa 'amalī minar riyā- wa lisānī minal kadhib wa 'aynī minal khiyānah, fa innaka ta'lamu khā-inatal a'yuni wa mā tukhfiṣ ṣudūr

O Allāh, purify my heart from hypocrisy, my deeds from ostentation and pretension, my tongue from lies, and my eyes from wrongful glances. For, indeed, You know what the eyes deceptively glance at and what the hearts conceal. [Al-Bayhaqī in Ad-Da'awāt Al-Kabīr 258]

Seeking Betterment in Both Our Secret and Apparent Conditions

اَللّٰهُمَّ اجْعَلْ سَرِيرَتِي خَيْرًا مِنْ عَلاَنِيَتِي وَاجْعَلْ عَلاَنِيَتِي صَالِحَةً اَللّٰهُمَّ إِنِّي أَسْأَلُكَ مِنْ صَالِحِ مَا تُؤْتِي النَّاسَ مِنَ الْمَالِ وَالأَهْلِ وَالْوَلَدِ غَيْرِ الضَّالِّ وَلاَ الْمُضِلِّ

Allāhummaj'al sarīratī khayran min 'alāniyatī waj'al 'alāniyatī ṣāliḥah, Allāhumma innī as-aluka min ṣāliḥi mā tu-tin nāsa minal māli wal ahli wal waladi ghayriḍ ḍālli wa lal muḍill

O Allāh, make my secret better than my apparent condition, and make my apparent condition righteous. O Allāh, I ask You for the good of what you give to the people, of wealth, wives, and children, not (to be) misguided, nor misguiding. [Jāmi` At-Tirmidhī 3586]

Seeking Reputation

Seeking Protection from Joining Partners with Allāh ﷻ Knowingly and Unknowingly

اَللّٰهُمَّ إِنِّي أَعُوذُ بِكَ أَنْ أُشْرِكَ بِكَ وَأَنَا أَعْلَمُ، وَأَسْتَغْفِرُكَ لِمَا لاَ أَعْلَمُ

Allāhumma innī a'ūdhu bika an ushrika bika wa ana -a'lam, wa astaghfiruka limā lā -a'lam

O Allāh, I seek Your protection from that I should join any partner with You knowingly and I seek Your forgiveness if I have ever done so unknowingly. [Al-Adab Al-Mufrad 716]

Seeking Refuge from Seeking Reputation and Ultimately Allāh's ﷻ Wrath

اَللّٰهُمَّ إِنِّي أَسْأَلُكَ بِحَقِّ السَّائِلِينَ عَلَيْكَ وَأَسْأَلُكَ بِحَقِّ مَمْشَايَ هَذَا فَإِنِّي لَمْ أَخْرُجْ أَشَرًا وَلاَ بَطَرًا وَلاَ رِيَاءً وَلاَ سُمْعَةً وَخَرَجْتُ اتِّقَاءَ سُخْطِكَ وَابْتِغَاءَ مَرْضَاتِكَ فَأَسْأَلُكَ أَنْ تُعِيذَنِي مِنَ النَّارِ وَأَنْ تَغْفِرَ لِي ذُنُوبِي إِنَّهُ لاَ يَغْفِرُ الذُّنُوبَ إِلاَّ أَنْتَ

Allāhumma innī as-aluka bi ḥaqqissā-ilīna 'alayka, wa as-aluka bi ḥaqqi mamshāya hādhā, fa innī lam akhruj asharan wa lā baṭaran, wa lā riyā-an, wa la sum'atan, wa kharajtut-tiqā-a sukhtika wabtighā-a mar ātika, fa as-aluka an tu'īdhanī minan nāri wa an taghfira lī dhunūbī, innahu lā yaghfirudh dhunūba illā Anta

O Allāh, I ask You by the right that those who ask of You have over You, and I ask by virtue of this walking of mine, for I am not going out because of pride or vanity, or to show off or make a reputation, rather I am going out because I fear Your wrath and seek Your pleasure. So I ask You to protect me from the Fire and to forgive me my sins, for no one can forgive sins except You. [Sunan Ibn Mājah 778]

Seeking Reputation

Making Allāh's ﷻ Love the Dearest and Cutting Off Worldly Needs

اَللّٰهُمَّ اجْعَلْ حُبَّكَ أَحَبَّ الْأَشْيَاءِ إِلَيَّ وَاجْعَلْ خَوْفَكَ أَخْوَفَ الْأَشْيَاءِ إِلَيَّ وَاقْطَعْ عَنِّي حَاجَاتِ الدُّنْيَا بِالشَّوْقِ إِلَى لِقَائِكَ وَإِذَا أَقْرَرْتَ أَعْيُنَ أَهْلِ الدُّنْيَا مِنْ دُنْيَاهُمْ فَأَقِرَّ عَيْنِي مِنْ عِبَادَتِكَ

Allāhummaj'al ḥubbaka aḥabbal ashyā-a ilayya waj'al khawfaka akhwafal ash'yā-a ilayya waq-ṭa' 'annī ḥājātid dunyā bish shawqi ilā liqā-ik wa idhā aqrartu -a'yuna ahlid dunyā min dunyāhum fa-aqirra 'aynī min 'ibādatik

O Allāh, make Your love the dearest and make Your fear the most frightening of all things to me. Cut off worldly needs from me by giving me the longing to meet You. And as You bring comfort to the eyes of the men of the world with their worldly possessions, bring comfort to my eyes with Your obedience and worship. [Abū Nu'aym Al-Aṣbahānī in Ḥilyah Al-Awliyā' v.8 pg.282]

Avoiding Allāh's ﷻ Displeasure

اَللّٰهُمَّ إِنِّي أَعُوذُ بِكَ مِنْ زَوَالِ نِعْمَتِكَ وَتَحَوُّلِ عَافِيَتِكَ وَفُجَاءَةِ نِقْمَتِكَ وَجَمِيعِ سَخَطِكَ

Allāhumma innī a'ūdhu bika min zawāl ni'matika wa taḥawwuli 'āfiyatika wa fujā-ati niqmatika wa jamī' sakhatik

O Allāh, I seek refuge in You from the withdrawal of Your blessing and the change of Your protection (of me) and from Your sudden wrath, and from every displeasure of Yours. [Ṣaḥīḥ Muslim 2739]

العُجب

Vanity

RELATED EMOTIONS

Insecure | Oblivious | Self-righteous | Egotistic | Addicted
Undignified | Aggressive | Deluded | Disappointed | Excessive
Forgetful | Ignorant | Immature | Inadequate | Fantasizing | Pretentious
Self-absorbed | Vain | Insincere

INVOKING NAMES OF ALLĀH ﷻ

- **Al-Jalīl - the Majestic**
- **Al-Mutakabbir - The Supreme**
- **Dhul-Jalāli Wal-Ikrām - Lord of Majesty and Bounty**
- **Al-Mājid - The Illustrious**
- **Al-Bā'ith - The Resurrector**
- **Al-Muḥyī, Al-Mumīt - The Giver of Life, the Slayer**
- **Ar-Raqīb - The Watchful**
- **Al-Mudhil - The Humiliator**
- **An-Nāfi' - The Benefactor**

AṢ-ṢALĀH AL-IBRĀHĪMIYYAH

ACCEPTED PRAYERS

- **Seeking Protection from the Evil of Ourselves**
- **Seeking Refuge from being Under the Control of Ego**
- **Seeking Refuge from Vanity and Ultimately Allāh's ﷻ Wrath**
- **Seeking the Best Moral Characteristics**
- **Seeking Improvement in Both Our Secret and Apparent States**
- **Showing Gratitude for a Beautiful Internal and External Condition**

CHAPTER 25

Vanity [Ujub] العُجب

Vanity is to attribute one's excellence to oneself while forgetting that it came from Allāh ﷻ and being oblivious of the possibility of such excellence being snatched away by Allāh ﷻ. The vain person labours under the notion that these bounties they have accrued are everlasting and noteworthy. The word 'vanity' comes from the Latin word 'vanus', which means 'empty', implying that the source of our vanity is devoid of substance, and will vanish.

The Prophet ﷺ said, "On the Day of Resurrection, the man of vanity, strutting about in overconfidence, will meet Allāh, and He (Allāh) will be irate." [Al-Adab Al-Mufrad 549]

Vanity is related to arrogance, which - it is said - requires two people for its outward manifestation: the arrogant one and the one to whom the arrogance is shown. Contrastingly, the vain person is always preoccupied with the agony of wondering what other people think of him, yet this worry continues regardless of whether there are any other people passing judgement on him. In other words, vanity does not need a second person. In a very similar vein, in the case of the close cousin, pride (takabbur), the proud person must be noticeably superior to the other(s). With vanity, this does not apply: there can be a fluctuating sense of inferiority with the insecure and vain individual.

Vanity

Invoking Allāh's ﷻ Names

الْجَلِيلُ

Al-Jalīl
The Majestic

الْمُتَكَبِّرُ

Al-Mutakabbir
The Supreme

ذُو الْجَلَالِ وَالْإِكْرَام

Dhul-Jalāli Wal-Ikrām
Lord of Majesty and Bounty

الْمَاجِدُ

Al-Mājid
The Illustrious

الْبَاعِثُ

Al-Bā'ith
The Resurrector

الْمُحْيِي الْمُمِيت

Al-Muḥyī, Al-Mumīt
The Giver of Life, The Slayer

الرَّقِيبُ

Ar-Raqīb
The Watchful

الْمُذِلُّ

Al-Mudhil
The Humiliator

النَّافِعُ

An-Nāfi'
The Benefactor

Vanity

Contemplation and Reflection on Allāh's ﷻ Blessed Names

- You do not suffer from any delusion of greatness, no matter how many favours Allāh ﷻ has bestowed upon you, for you know that true power, greatness and glory belong only to Allāh ﷻ.
- You remind yourself that exterior beauty is of lesser worth, and that the most respected and admired among mankind is the one whose interior attributes are attractive and that give true pleasure to those that can truly distinguish between right and wrong.
- You see that it is unwise and undignified to show off anything that we have been blessed with.
- You are thankful for being a follower of the Prophet Muhammad ﷺ a man who actively chose the status of a 'slave-messenger' over that of a 'prophet-king'.
- You also consider that when you die, all that time spent in front of the mirror and the times you were locked in dreams of grandeur and self-absorption will be of no benefit: all your worldly efforts and vain addictions in this regard will have been profitless and the difficulty which you experienced in executing these acts will be confiscated and lost. You are content with the image of yourself as one in old age, with wrinkled skin and plain garments, finding comfort in your prayer beads or reading Qur'ān.
- You adopt humility and avoid self-importance by remembering Allāh ﷻ and being grateful; you realise that if you do not humble yourself, Allāh ﷻ will humble you.

Vanity

Aṣ-Ṣalāh Al-Ibrāhīmiyyah

اَللّٰهُمَّ صَلِّ عَلَى مُحَمَّدٍ وَعَلَى آلِ مُحَمَّدٍ كَمَا صَلَّيْتَ عَلَى إِبْرَاهِيمَ وَآلِ إِبْرَاهِيمَ إِنَّكَ حَمِيدٌ مَجِيدٌ وَبَارِكْ عَلَى مُحَمَّدٍ وَعَلَى آلِ مُحَمَّدٍ كَمَا بَارَكْتَ عَلَى إِبْرَاهِيمَ وَآلِ إِبْرَاهِيمَ إِنَّكَ حَمِيدٌ مَجِيدٌ

Allāhumma ṣalli ʿalā Muḥammadin wa ʿalā āli Muḥammadin kamā ṣ allayta ʿalā Ibrāhīm wa āli Ibrāhīm innaka ḥamīdum majīd, wa bārik ʿalā Muḥammadin wa ʿalā āli Muḥammadin kamā bārakta ʿalā Ibrāhīm wa āli Ibrāhīm innaka ḥamīdum majīd

O Allāh, send peace upon Muḥammad and upon the family of Muḥammad, as You sent peace upon Ibrāhīm and the family of Ibrāhīm, and send blessings upon Muḥammad and upon the family of Muḥammad as You sent blessings upon Ibrāhīm and the family of Ibrāhīm. You are indeed praiseworthy, the most honourable. [Sunan An-Nasaī 1290]

Vanity

Seeking Protection from the Evil of Ourselves

اَللّٰهُمَّ قِنِي شَرَّ نَفْسِي، وَاعْزِمْ لِي عَلَى أَرْشَدِ أَمْرِي

Allāhumma qinī sharra nafsī wa'zim lī 'alā arshadi amrī

O Allāh, protect me from the evil of myself and give me the determination to do what is most right in my affair. [Al-Ḥākim 1880]

Seeking Refuge from being Under the Control of Ego

يَا حَيُّ يَا قَيُّوم بِرَحْمَتِكَ أَسْتَغِيث ، أَصْلِحْ لِي شَأْنِي كُلَّه ، وَلَا تَكِلْنِي إِلَى نَفْسِي طَرَفَةَ عَيْنٍ

Yā ḥayyu yā qayyūm bi raḥmatika astaghīth aṣliḥ lī sha-nī kullah, wa lā takilnī ilā nafsā ṭarafata 'ayn

O the Everliving, the Eternal, I beg through Your mercy. Set right all of my affairs and do not leave me under the control of my ego (nafs) for even the blink of an eye. [Al-Ḥākim 2000]

Vanity

Seeking Refuge from Vanity and Ultimately Allāh's ﷻ Wrath

اَللّٰهُمَّ إِنِّي أَسْأَلُكَ بِحَقِّ السَّائِلِينَ عَلَيْكَ وَأَسْأَلُكَ بِحَقِّ مَمْشَايَ هَذَا فَإِنِّي لَمْ أَخْرُجْ أَشَرًا وَلاَ بَطَرًا وَلاَ رِيَاءً وَلاَ سُمْعَةً وَخَرَجْتُ اتِّقَاءَ سُخْطِكَ وَابْتِغَاءَ مَرْضَاتِكَ فَأَسْأَلُكَ أَنْ تُعِيذَنِي مِنَ النَّارِ وَأَنْ تَغْفِرَ لِي ذُنُوبِي إِنَّهُ لاَ يَغْفِرُ الذُّنُوبَ إِلاَّ أَنْتَ

Allāhumma innī as-aluka bi ḥaqqissā-ilīna 'alayka, wa as-aluka bi ḥaqqi mamshāya hādhā, fa innī lam akhruj asharan wa lā baṭaran, wa lā riyā-an, wa la sum'atan, wa kharajtut-tiqā-a sukhtika wabtighā-a mar ātika, fa as-aluka an tu'īdhanī minan nāri wa an taghfira lī dhunūbī, innahu lā yaghfirudh dhunūba illā Anta

O Allāh, I ask You by the right that those who ask of You have over You, and I ask by virtue of this walking of mine, for I am not going out because of pride or vanity, or to show off or make a reputation, rather I am going out because I fear Your wrath and seek Your pleasure. So I ask You to protect me from the Fire and to forgive me my sins, for no one can forgive sins except You. [Sunan Ibn Mājah 778]

Seeking the Best Moral Characteristics

اَللّٰهُمَّ أَحْسَنْتَ خَلْقِي، فَأَحْسِنْ خُلُقِي

Allāhumma aḥsanta khalqī fa aḥsin khuluqī

O Allāh You have made my creation perfect, so make my moral characteristics also be the best. [Musnad Aḥmad 3823]

Vanity

Seeking Improvement in Both Our Secret and Apparent States

اَللّٰهُمَّ اجْعَلْ سَرِيرَتِي خَيْرًا مِنْ عَلاَنِيَتِي وَاجْعَلْ عَلاَنِيَتِي صَالِحَةً اللَّهُمَّ إِنِّي أَسْأَلُكَ مِنْ صَالِحِ مَا تُؤْتِي النَّاسَ مِنَ الْمَالِ وَالأَهْلِ وَالْوَلَدِ غَيْرِ الضَّالِّ وَلاَ الْمُضِلِّ

Allāhummaj'al sarīratī khayran min 'alāniyatī waj'al 'alāniyatī ṣāliḥah, Allāhumma innī as-aluka min ṣāliḥi mā tu-tin nāsa minal māli wal ahli wal waladi ghayriḍ ḍālli wa lal muḍill

O Allāh, make my secret better than my apparent condition, and make my apparent condition righteous. O Allāh, I ask You for the good of what you give to the people, of wealth, wives, and children, not (to be) misguided, nor misguiding. [Jāmi` At-Tirmidhī 3586]

Showing Gratitude for a Beautiful Internal and External Condition

اَلْحَمْدُ لِلّٰهِ الَّذِي سَوَّى خَلْقِي فَعَدَلَهُ، وَصَوَّرَ صُورَةَ وَجْهِي فَحَسَّنَهَا، وَجَعَلَنِي مِنَ الْمُسْلِمِينَ

Alḥamdulillāhilladhī sawwā khalqī fa 'addalah, wa ṣawwara ṣūrata wajhī fa ḥassanahā, wa ja'alanī minal muslimīn

Praise be to Allāh, Who has fashioned my person and perfected it, and has fashioned the form of my face and beautified it, and made me one of the Muslims. [Aṭ-Ṭabarānī in Al-Mu'jam Al-Awṣaṭ 787]

البَطَر/ الحِرْص

Wantonness or Greed

RELATED EMOTIONS

Ungrateful | Reckless | Depressed | Callous | Covetous | Cruel
Deceitful | Disappointed | Excessive | Grudging | Lustful | Malicious
Manipulative | Overwhelmed

INVOKING NAMES OF ALLĀH

- **Al-Bāʿith - The Resurrector**
- **Al-Muḥyī, Al-Mumīt - The Giver of Life, the Destroyer**
- **Al-Mudhil - The Humiliator**
- **Al-Qābiḍ - The Witholder**
- **Al-Bāsiṭ - The Extender**
- **As-Shakūr - The Most Appreciative**

AṢ-ṢALĀH AL-IBRĀHĪMIYYAH

ACCEPTED PRAYERS

- **Seeking Protection from Greed**
- **Seeking Contentment from Allāh**
- **Seeking Protection from Wealth that Leads to Punishment**
- **Seeking Allāh's Love and Cutting Off Worldly Needs**
- **Seeking Contentment with Provision and Good in Everything**

CHAPTER 26

Wantonness [Baṭar] البَطَر or Greed [Ḥirṣ] الحِرْص

Wantonness or baṭar, is when one demonstrates reckless extravagance; there exists an excessive desire to need and want more, usually because one places significant value on what the fleeting things of this world have to offer, whether it is wealth, prestige, fame, or the like. Wantonness is also defined as exuberance or excessive amusement.

Something similar to wantonness is greed (ḥirṣ), stemming from the heart's obsession with wealth, which leads to people-plundering and usurping the rights of others. Something similar is covetousness (ṭama'), which is when one prefers things that conflict with the sharī'ah.

Allāh ﷻ says:

- "(Imagine) how many societies We have destroyed that had been spoiled by their (comfortable) living! Those are their residences, never inhabited after them except passingly. And We (alone) were the Successor" [Al-Qaṣaṣ 28:58]
- "(Some of) his people advised him, 'Do not be prideful! Surely Allāh does not like the prideful'" [Al-Qaṣaṣ 28:76] **(relating to wealth, status etc.)**
- "And whoever is saved from the selfishness of their own souls, it is they who are (truly) successful" [Al-Ḥashr 59:9]

The Prophet ﷺ said, "The son of Adām grows old and so also two (desires) grow old with him, love for wealth and (a wish for) a long life." [Ṣaḥīḥ Al-Bukhārī 6421]

Wantonness or Greed

Invoking Allāh's ﷻ Names

الْبَاعِثُ

Al-Bā'ith
The Resurrector

الْمُحْيِي الْمُمِيت

Al-Muḥyī, Al-Mumīt
The Giver of Life, The Slayer

الْمُذِلُّ

Al-Mudhil
The Humiliator

الْقَابِضُ

Al-Qābiḍ
The Witholder

الْبَاسِطُ

Al-Bāsiṭ
The Extender

الشَّكُورُ

As-Shakūr
The Most Appreciative

Wantonness or Greed

Contemplation and Reflection on Allāh's ﷻ Blessed Names

- Your consistent reflection upon death increases your desire to show gratitude for the things that Allāh ﷻ has given you. At the same time, your gratitude inhibits any feelings toward 'grabbing': you happily restrain your urge to accumulate 'things' for the sake of 'things'. You prefer to empathise with the needs of others and to cooperate in a way that garners social cohesion and gives you and those other people quality time. Wealth, prestige, fame: these are things that your gratitude towards Allāh ﷻ allows you to gently disregard.
- With an improving mental picture of the Afterlife as your eternal dwelling place, you convert to a conscious state where you seek 'wealth' in the setting of Paradise, and you translate worldly 'fame' into a pursuit of increased rank and status with your Lord.
- Your renewed wisdom teaches you to be content because this will make you the most grateful of people.
- You reflect on the times when your greed allowed you to exploit other people and you pray that Allāh ﷻ shows you mercy for this shortcoming. .
- You remind yourself that Allāh ﷻ will not take away a blessing unless you show ingratitude, and that gratitude to Allāh ﷻ protects one from having blessings removed.
- You understand that greed and dishonesty are loathsome qualities in the sight of both Allāh ﷻ and humankind. People too are generally aware of the unhappiness that stems from the limitless pursuit of wealth and status.

Wantonness or Greed

Aṣ-Ṣalāh Al-Ibrāhīmiyyah

اَللّٰهُمَّ صَلِّ عَلَى مُحَمَّدٍ وَعَلَى آلِ مُحَمَّدٍ كَمَا صَلَّيْتَ عَلَى
إِبْرَاهِيمَ وَآلِ إِبْرَاهِيمَ إِنَّكَ حَمِيدٌ مَجِيدٌ وَبَارِكْ عَلَى
مُحَمَّدٍ وَعَلَى آلِ مُحَمَّدٍ كَمَا بَارَكْتَ عَلَى إِبْرَاهِيمَ وَآلِ
إِبْرَاهِيمَ إِنَّكَ حَمِيدٌ مَجِيدٌ

Allāhumma ṣalli 'alā Muḥammadin wa 'alā āli Muḥammadin kamā ṣ allayta 'alā Ibrāhīm wa āli Ibrāhīm innaka ḥamīdum majīd, wa bārik 'alā Muḥammadin wa 'alā āli Muḥammadin kamā bārakta 'alā Ibrāhīm wa āli Ibrāhīm innaka ḥamīdum majīd

O Allāh, send peace upon Muḥammad and upon the family of Muḥammad, as You sent peace upon Ibrāhīm and the family of Ibrāhīm, and send blessings upon Muḥammad and upon the family of Muḥammad as You sent blessings upon Ibrāhīm and the family of Ibrāhīm. You are indeed praiseworthy, the most honourable. [Sunan An-Nasaī 1290]

Wantonness or Greed

Seeking Protection from Greed

اَللّٰهُمَّ قِنِي شُحَّ نَفْسِي

Allāhumma qinī shuḥḥa nafsī

O Allāh, protect me from the greed of my soul! [Tafsīr Aṭ-Ṭabarī 22:530 under verse 59:9]

Seeking Contentment from Allāh ﷻ

اَللّٰهُمَّ إِنِّي أَسْأَلُكَ غِنَايَ وَغِنَى مَوْلَايَ

Allāhumma innī as-aluka ghināya wa ghinā mawlāy

I seek from You my contentment and that of my family. [Aṭ-Ṭabarānī in Al-Mu'jam Al-Kabīr 828]

Seeking Protection from Wealth that Leads to Punishment

اَللّٰهُمَّ إِنِّي أَعُوذُ بِكَ مِنْ مَالٍ يَكُونُ عَلَيَّ عَذَابًا

Allāhumma innī a'ūdhu bika min mālin yakūnu 'alayya 'adhābā

O Allāh, I seek Your protection from the wealth that will turn into punishment for me. [Aṭ-Ṭabarānī in Ad-Du'ā 1339]

Wantonness or Greed

Seeking Allāh's ﷻ Love and Cutting Off Worldly Needs

اَللّٰهُمَّ اجْعَلْ حُبَّكَ أَحَبَّ الْأَشْيَاءِ إِلَيَّ وَاجْعَلْ خَوْفَكَ أَخْوَفَ الْأَشْيَاءِ إِلَيَّ وَاقْطَعْ عَنِّي حَاجَاتِ الدُّنْيَا بِالشَّوْقِ إِلَى لِقَائِكَ وَإِذَا أَقْرَرْتَ أَعْيُنَ أَهْلِ الدُّنْيَا مِنْ دُنْيَاهُمْ فَأَقِرَّ عَيْنِي مِنْ عِبَادَتِكَ

Allāhummaj'al ḥubbaka aḥabbal ashyā-a ilayya waj'al khawfaka akhwafal ash'yā-a ilayya waq-ṭa' 'annī ḥājātid dunyā bish shawqi ilā liqā-ik wa idhā aqrartu -a'yuna ahlid dunyā min dunyāhum fa-aqirra 'aynī min 'ibādatik

O Allāh, make Your love the dearest and make Your fear the most frightening of all things to me. Cut off worldly needs from me by giving me the longing to meet You. And as You bring comfort to the eyes of the men of the world with their worldly possessions, bring comfort to my eyes with Your obedience and worship. [Abū Nu'aym Al-Aṣbahānī in Ḥilyah Al-Awliyā' v.8 pg.282]

Seeking Contentment with Provision and Good in Everything

اَللّٰهُمَّ قَنِّعْنِي بِمَا رَزَقْتَنِي، وَبَارِكْ لِي فِيهِ، وَاخْلُفْ عَلَيَّ كُلَّ غَائِبَةٍ بِخَيْرٍ

Allāhumma qaani'nī bimā razaqtanī wa bārik lī fīh wakhluf 'alayya kulla ghā-ibatin bi khayr

O Allāh, make me content with the provision You have given me and bless me in it and appoint good for me in everything which I do not have. [Al-Adab Al-Mufrad 681]

Glossary of Allāh's ﷻ Beautiful Names

				Disease	Page
1	اَلرَّحْمَانُ	Ar-Raḥmān	**The All Compassionate**	Iniquity Negative Feelings	238 276
2	اَلرَّحِيمُ	Ar-Raḥīm	**The All Merciful**	Hatred Iniquity Negative Feelings	218 238 276
3	اَلْمَلِكُ	Al-Malik	**The Absolute Ruler**	Iniquity	238
4	اَلْقُدُّوسُ	Al-Quddūs	**The Pure One**	Heedlessness	226
5	اَلسَّلَامُ	As-Salām	**The Source of Peace**	Anger Envy Negative Feelings	102 150 276
6	اَلْمُؤْمِنُ	Al-Mu'min	**The Inspirer of Faith**	False Hope Relying on Other than Allāh ﷻ	168 312
7	اَلْمُهَيْمِنُ	Al-Muhaymin	**The Guardian**	Extravagance Iniquity	160 238
8	اَلْعَزِيزُ	Al-Azīz	**The Victorious**	Relying on Other than Allāh ﷻ	312
9	اَلْجَبَّارُ	Al-Jabbār	**The Compeller**	Negative Feelings	276
10	اَلْمُتَكَبِّرُ	Al-Mutakabbir	**The Supreme**	Vanity	330
11	اَلْخَالِقُ	Al-Khāliq	**The Creator**	Relying on Other than Allāh ﷻ	312

Glossary of Allāh's ﷻ Beautiful Names

				Disease	Page
12	ٱلْبَارِئ	Al-Bāri'	**The Incomparable Originator**	Boasting, Arrogance & Pride Relying on Other than Allāh ﷻ	126 312
13	ٱلْمُصَوِّر	Al-Muṣawwir	**The Fashioner**	Boasting, Arrogance & Pride	126
14	ٱلْغَفَّار	Al-Ghaffār	**The Forgiving**	Anger Hatred Negative Feelings	102 218 276
15	ٱلْقَهَّار	Al-Qahhār	**The Ever-Dominating**	Displeasure with the Divine Decree	142
16	ٱلْوَهَّاب	Al-Wahhāb	**The Giver of Gifts**	Miserliness Obliviousness to Blessings or Ingratitude	258 292
17	ٱلرَّزَّاق	Ar-Razzāq	**The Provider**	Fear of Poverty Miserliness	186 258
18	ٱلْفَتَّاح	Al-Fattāḥ	**The Opener**	Blameworthy Modesty	118
19	ٱلْعَلِيم	Al-'Alīm	**The All-Knowing**	Displeasure with the Divine Decree Fantasizing Fraud	142 176 198
20	ٱلْقَابِض	Al-Qābiḍ	**The Withholder**	Displeasure with the Divine Decree Fear of Poverty Love of the World Obliviousness to Blessings or Ingratitude Wantonness or Greed	142 186 250 292 338
21	ٱلْبَاسِط	Al-Bāsiṭ	**The Extender**	Displeasure with the Divine Decree Fear of Poverty	142 186

Glossary of Allāh's ﷻ Beautiful Names

				Disease	Page
22	ٱلْخَافِض	Al-Khāfiḍ	**The Abaser**	Blameworthy Modesty Boasting, Arrogance & Pride Displeasure with Blame or Disapproval Extravagance Love of the World Seeking Reputation	118 126 134 160 250
23	ٱلرَّافِع	Ar-Rāfi'	**The Exalter**	Blameworthy Modesty Boasting, Arrogance & Pride Displeasure with Blame or Disapproval Seeking Reputation	118 126 134 322
24	ٱلْمُعِز	Al-Mu'izz	**The Bestower of Honour**	Extravagance Ostentation or Showing Off	160 304
25	ٱلْمُذِل	Al-Mudhil	**The Humiliator**	Boasting, Arrogance & Pride Seeking Reputation	126 322
26	ٱلسَّمِيع	As-Samī'	**The Hearer of All (The All-Hearing)**	Boasting, Arrogance & Pride Fraud Negative Feelings	126 198 276
27	ٱلْبَصِير	Al-Baṣīr	**The Seer of All (The All-Seeing)**	Extravagance Fantasizing Fraud Iniquity Mockery Ostentation or Showing Off	160 176 198 238 268 304
28	ٱلْحَكَم	Al-Ḥakam	**The Judge**	Displeasure with the Divine Decree Hatred	142 218

Glossary of Allāh's ﷻ Beautiful Names

				Disease	Page
29	ٱلْعَدْل	Al-'Adl	**The Just**	Anger Blameworthy Modesty Displeasure with the Divine Decree Fraud Iniquity Relying on Other than Allāh ﷻ	102 118 134 198 238 312
30	ٱللَّطِيف	Al-Laṭīf	**The Subtle One**	Boasting, Arrogance & Pride Hard-Heartedness Obliviousness to Blessings or Ingratitude	126 208 292
31	ٱلْخَبِير	Al-Khabīr	**The All-Aware**	Fantasizing Fraud Heedlessness Iniquity Love of the World Miserliness Negative Feelings Ostentation or Showing Off	176 198 228 238 250 258 276 304
32	ٱلْحَلِيم	Al-Ḥalīm	**The Forbearing**	Anger Hard-Heartedness Hatred	102 210 218
33	ٱلْعَظِيم	Al-'Aẓīm	**The Magnificent**	Boasting, Arrogance & Pride	126
34	ٱلْغَفُور	Al-Ghafūr	**The Exceedingly Forgiving**	Hatred	218
35	ٱلشَّكُور	Ash-Shakūr	**The Most Appreciative**	Love of the World Obliviousness to Blessings or Ingratitude Wantonness or Greed	250 292 338

Glossary of Allāh's ﷻ Beautiful Names

				Disease	Page
36	اَلْعَلِي	Al-'Aliyy	**The Highest**	Boasting, Arrogance & Pride	126
37	اَلْكَبِير	Al-Kabīr	**The Greatest**	Boasting, Arrogance & Pride	126
38	اَلْحَفِيظ	Al-Ḥafīẓ	**The Preserver**	Envy Negative Feelings	150 276
39	اَلْمُقِيت	Al-Muqīt	**The Nourisher**	Fear of Poverty Negative Feelings Relying on Other than Allāh ﷻ	186 276 312
40	اَلْحَسِيب	Al-Ḥasīb	**The Reckoner**	Antipathy Towards Death Fraud Ostentation or Showing Off	110 198 304
41	اَلْجَلِيل	Al-Jalīl	**The Mighty**	Boasting, Arrogance & Pride	126
42	اَلْكَرِيم	Al-Karīm	**The Most Generous**	Extravagance Miserliness Obliviousness to Blessings or Ingratitude	160 258 292
43	اَلرَّقِيب	Ar-Raqīb	**The Watchful**	Boasting, Arrogance & Pride Fantasizing Fraud Iniquity Vanity	126 176 198 238 330
44	اَلْمُجِيب	Al-Mujīb	**The Responsive One**	Iniquity Negative Feelings Relying on Other than Allāh ﷻ	238 276 312
45	اَلْوَاسِع	Al-Wāsi'	**The All-Comprehending**	Envy	150

Glossary of Allāh's ﷻ Beautiful Names

				Disease	Page
46	اَلْحَكِيم	Al-Ḥakīm	**The All-Wise**	Antipathy Towards Death Blameworthy Modest Displeasure with Blame or Disapproval Displeasure with the Divine Decree False Hope Obliviousness to Blessings or Ingratitude	110 118 134 142 168 292
47	اَلْوَدُود	Al-Wadūd	**The Most Loving**	Anger Hard-Heartedness Negative Feelings	102 208 276
48	اَلْمَجِيد	Al-Majīd	**The Most Honourable**	Obliviousness to Blessings or Ingratitude	292
49	اَلْبَاعِث	Al-Bā'ith	**The Resurrector**	Antipathy Towards Death False Hope Heedlessness Ostentation or Showing Off Wantonness or Greed	110 168 228 304 338
50	اَلشَّهِيد	Ash-Shahīd	**The Witness**	Fantasizing Fraud Mockery Ostentation or Showing Off	176 198 268 304
51	اَلْحَق	Al-Ḥaqq	**The Truth**	Anger Displeasure with Blame or Disapproval Displeasure with the Divine Decree Fraud Seeking Reputation	102 134 142 198 322

Glossary of Allāh's سبحانه وتعالى Beautiful Names

				Disease	Page
52	ٱلْوَكِيل	Al-Wakīl	**The Trustee**	Fear of Poverty Relying on Other than Allāh سبحانه وتعالى	186 312
53	ٱلْقَوِي	Al-Qawiyy	**The All-Strong**	Blameworthy Modesty Iniquity	118 238
54	ٱلْمَتِين	Al-Matīn	**The Most Firm**	Blameworthy Modesty Iniquity	118 238
55	ٱلْوَلِي	Al-Waliyy	**The Protecting Friend**	Iniquity Miserliness	238 258
56	ٱلْحَمِيد	Al-Ḥamīd	**The Praiseworthy**	Displeasure with Blame or Disapproval	134
57	ٱلْمُحْصِي	Al-Muḥṣī	**The One Who Keeps Record**	Fantasizing Fraud Ostentation or Showing Off	176 198 304
58	ٱلْمُبْدِئ	Al-Mubdī	**The Initiator**	Boasting, Arrogance & Pride	126
59	ٱلْمُعِيد	Al-Mu'īd	**The Restorer**	Antipathy Towards Death	110
60	ٱلْمُحْيِي	Al-Muḥyī	**The Giver of Life**	Antipathy Towards Death Vanity Wantonness or Greed	110 330 338
61	ٱلْمُمِيت	Al-Mumīt	**The Destroyer**	Antipathy Towards Death False Hope Vanity Wantonness or Greed	110 168 330 338
62	ٱلْحَيّ	Al-Ḥayy	**The Ever-Living**	Relying on Other than Allāh سبحانه وتعالى	312

Glossary of Allāh's سبحانه وتعالى Beautiful Names

				Disease	PAGE
63	ٱلْقَيُّوم	Al-Qayyūm	**The Sustainer**	Fear of Poverty Miserliness	186 258
64	ٱلْوَاجِد	Al-Wājid	**The Finder**	Fear of Poverty Negative Feelings	186 276
65	ٱلْمَاجِد	Al-Mājid	**The Illustrious**	Vanity	330
66	ٱلْوَاحِد	Al-Wāḥid	**The One**	Relying on Other than Allāh سبحانه وتعالى	312
67	ٱلْأَحَد	Al-Aḥad	**The Only One**	Relying on Other than Allāh سبحانه وتعالى	312
68	ٱلصَّمَد	Aṣ-Ṣamad	**The Eternal**	Boasting, Arrogance & Pride	126
69	ٱلْقَادِر	Al-Qādir	**The All Powerful**	Fear of Poverty	186
70	ٱلْمُقْتَدِر	Al-Muqtadir	**The Omnipotent**	Fear of Poverty	186
71	ٱلْمُقَدِّم	Al-Muqaddim	**The Expediter**	Heedlessness Hard-Heartedness	228 208
72	ٱلْمُؤَخِّر	Al-Mu'akhkhir	**The Delayer**	False Hopes Fraud	168 198
73	ٱلْأَوَّل	Al-Awwal	**The First**	Relying on Other Than Allāh سبحانه وتعالى	312
74	ٱلْآخِر	Al-Ākhir	**The Last**	Relying on Other Than Allāh سبحانه وتعالى	312
75	ٱلظَّاهِر	Aṭ-Ṭāhir	**The Manifest**	Obliviousness to Blessings or Ingratitude	292

Glossary of Allāh's ﷻ Beautiful Names

				Disease	Page
76	اَلْبَاطِن	Al-Bāṭin	**The Hidden One**	Fantasizing Fraud	176 198
77	اَلْوَالِي	Al-Wālī	**The Governor**	Fear of Poverty Iniquity Negative Feelings	186 238 276
78	اَلْمُتَعَالِي	Al-Muta'ālī	**The Self Exalted**	Relying on Other than Allāh ﷻ	312
79	اَلْبَرُّ	Al-Barr	**The Source of Goodness**	Envy Hatred	150 218
80	اَلتَّوَّاب	At-Tawwāb	**The Relenting**	Anger Hatred	102 218
81	اَلْمُنْتَقِم	Al-Muntaqim	**The Avenger**	Iniquity	238
82	اَلْعَفُوُّ	Al-'Afuww	**The Pardoner**	Heedlessness	228
83	اَلرَّؤُوف	Ar-Ra-ūf	**The Most Kind**	Miserliness	258
84	مَالِكُ ٱلْمُلْك	Mālik-Ul-Mulk	**Master of the Kingdom**	Boasting, Arrogance & Pride	126
85	ذُو ٱلْجَلَالِ وَٱلْإِكْرَام	Dhul-Jalāli Wal-Ikrām	**Lord of Majesty and Bounty**	Boasting, Arrogance & Pride Vanity	126 330
86	اَلْمُقْسِط	Al-Muqsiṭ	**The Requiter**	Fraud Iniquity	198 238
87	اَلْجَامِع	Al-Jāmi'	**The Uniter**	Antipathy Towards Death	110

Glossary of Allāh's سبحانه وتعالى Beautiful Names

				Disease	Page
88	ٱلْغَنِيّ	Al-Ghaniyy	**The Wealthy**	Fear of Poverty	186
89	ٱلْمُغْنِي	Al-Mughniyy	**The Enricher**	Fear of Poverty Hard-Heartedness	186 208
90	ٱلْمَانِع	Al-Māni'	**The Preventer**	Fantasizing Fraud	176 198
91	ٱلضَّارّ	Aḍ-Ḍārr	**The Distresser**	Relying on Other than Allāh سبحانه وتعالى Seeking Reputation	312 322
92	ٱلنَّافِع	An-Nāfi'	**The Benefactor**	Displeasure with the Divine Decree Relying on Other than Allāh سبحانه وتعالى Seeking Reputation	142 312 322
93	ٱلنُّور	An-Nūr	**The Light**	Heedlessness	228
94	ٱلْهَادِي	Al-Hādī	**The Guide**	Heedlessness	228
95	ٱلْبَدِيع	Al-Badī'	**The Originator**	Boasting, Arrogance & Pride	126
96	ٱلْبَاقِي	Al-Bāqī	**The Everlasting**	Love of the World Negative Feelings	250 276
97	ٱلْوَارِث	Al-Wārith	**The Inheritor**	Love of the World	250
98	ٱلرَّشِيد	Ar-Rashīd	**The Director**	Fraud Heedlessness	198 228
99	ٱلصَّبُور	Aṣ-Ṣabūr	**The Patient**	Anger Displeasure with the Divine Decree	102 142

Glossary of Arabic Terms

Arabic Term	Definition
Adhān	The Muslim call to prayer to announce the starting of the window of time wherein prayer is allowed
Adhkār	Plural of dhikr, meaning 'litany'
Ad'iyah	Plural of du'ā, meaning 'supplications'
'Āfiyah	Protection of Allāh ﷻ, as opposed to being subject to trials and difficulty
Aḥādīth	The corpus of literature on the words and actions of the Prophet Muḥammad ﷺ
Akhfā	The arabic superlative form of the word hidden (khafiyy), meaning 'most hidden'
Al-Fātiḥah	The opening and first chapter of the Holy Qur'ān
Allāh	The sole Muslim deity
Al-Firdaws	The highest level of paradise
Al-Mālik	The owner of an item or property
Al-Marwah	A hill located in the city of Makkah which is involved in the practices surrounding the Muslim pilgrimage
Al-Masīḍ Ad-Dajjāl	The foretold figure who will appear at the end of times and be a means of tribulation for the world, before ultimately being stopped by 'Īsā ﵇
Al-Milk	The thing that is owned; property
Al-Mulk	The concept of ownership (dominion)
Āmīn	An exclamation uttered at the end of a prayer
'Aqabah	A location situated between the mountains of Makkah related to the Muslim rites of pilgrimage
'Arafah	A plain situated near Makkah where pilgrims must visit on the 9th day of the final month of the Muslim lunar calendar
'Aṣr	The daily prayer that occurs from approximately when the sun is halfway down from noon to sunset
Aṣ-Ṣafā	A hill located in the city of Makkah which is involved in the practices surrounding the Muslim pilgrimage

Glossary of Arabic Terms

Arabic Term	Definition
Astaghfirullah	"I seek forgiveness from Allāh"
Āyah	A verse of the Holy Qur'ān (lit. 'sign')
Djinn	The species of intelligent life created by Allāh from smokeless flame
Du'ā	Supplication
Farḍ	A compulsory act
Ḥadīth	A singular narration from the corpus of literature on the words and actions of the Prophet Muḥammad
Hajj	The pilgrimage to Makkah that is compulsory on every Muslim once in their lifetime if they have the means. The pilgrimage involves the carrying out of geographically specific rituals over the course of five or six days
Hijr	The semi-circular attachment that is opposite the Yemeni corner and Blackstone wall of the Kabah
Iblis	The leader of the disobedient djinn who disobeyed Allāh and whispered to Adam
Ibrāhīm	Abraham, the friend of Allāh
Imām	A senior figure in Islāmic scholarship
Īmān	Conviction in belief
Inshā'Allāh	"If Allāh wills"
Iqāmah	The call to prayer immediately before the prayer in congregation starts
Islām	A worldview based upon the principles found in the Qur'ān and taught by the Prophet Muḥammad
Istiqāmah	Steadfastness
Jaliyy	Apparent
Jamrah	The pillars located near Makkah which are pelted during the Muslim pilgrimage
Jannah	Paradise

Glossary of Arabic Terms

Arabic Term	Definition
Jumu'ah	The day of Friday; the Friday prayers
Ka'bah	The structure that is located in Makkah which determines the direction towards which Muslims pray; the House of Allāh ﷻ
Khafiyy	Hidden
Ma'arifat	Higher knowledge of Allāh ﷻ
Makkah	The city in Arabia where the Prophet Muḥammad ﷺ began his mission
MāshāAllāh	What Allāh ﷻ wills, a statement of congratulations attributing success back to Allāh ﷻ
Masjid	The public place of worship where Muslims congregate to pray; it can also serve other secondary functions
Mughaffal	Simpleton; one who has been made ignorant
Muḥāsabah	Introspection
Muḥammad	The name of the last and final Prophet of Allāh ﷻ; the Prophet of Islām ﷺ
Mukh	Essence
Mukh-ul-ibaadah	Essence of worship
Muṣalli	A praying person; the one who offers the ṣalāh (Muslim prayer)
Nafl	Supererogatory
Qadr	Fate
Qiblah	The direction towards the Ka'bah
Qur'ān	The revealed divine message to the Prophet Muḥammad ﷺ
Ramadan	The ninth month of the Muslim lunar calendar wherein fasting is obligatory
Rasūl	A messenger
Ṣadaqah	Charity

Glossary of Arabic Terms

Arabic Term	Definition
Ṣadaqah jāriyah	A continuous charity that persists in providing reward for the doer even after his death
Sajdah	Prostration
Ṣalāh	Prayer
Salām	The Muslim greeting of peace
Salawāt	Salutations and invocations of peace
Sharī'ah	The Islāmic legal system
Shayṭān	The evil and disobedient servants of Allāh ﷻ, predominantly from the djinn
Sunnah	The active practice from the corpus of literature on the words and actions of the Prophet Muḥammad ﷺ
Surah	A chapter from the Holy Qur'ān
Takbīr	To proclaim "Allāh is the Greatest" (Allāhu Akbar)
Taqwā	The awareness of Allāh ﷻ that causes one to shun his disobedience
Tashahhud	A portion of the closing words of the Muslim prayer while sitting down; also used to refer to the sitting position in prayer when the words are being recited
Tawakkul	Reliance upon Allāh ﷻ
Tawḥīd	Monotheism
'Ubūdiyyah	Servitude
Ummah	The term used to denote the collective body of Muslims that transcends ethnicity, background, culture etc.
Umrah	The voluntary pilgrimage to Makkah
Zamzam	The water from a specific well located in Makkah that miraculously sprang forth for the wife of Abraham ﷺ and his son Ismail ﷺ
Zuhr	The daily midday Muslim prayer

BIBLIOGRAPHY

Qur'ān source:

- Dr. Mustafa Khattab, The Clear Qur'ān: A Thematic English Translation of the Message of the Final Revelation, Book of Signs Foundation, 2016

Aḥādīth sources (sayings of the Prophet ﷺ):

- Imām Al-Bukhārī, Ṣaḥīḥ Al-Bukhārī using the numbering of Muhammad Fuad Abdul Baqi
- Imām Al-Bukhārī, Al-Adab Al-Mufrad, Dar Al-Bashāir Al-Islāmiyyah Beirut, 1989, Third Edition, verified by Muhammad Fuad Abdul Baqi
- Imām Muslim, Ṣaḥīḥ Muslim using the numbering of Muhammad Fuad Abdul Baqi
- Imām Nasai, Sunan An-Nasaī using the numbering of Muhammad Fuad Abdul Baqi
- Imām Abū Dāwūd, Sunan Abī Dāwūd using the numbering of Muhammad Fuad Abdul Baqi
- Imām Abū Dawūd, Marāsīl of Abū Dawūd, Muassasah Ar-Risālah Beirut, 1988, First Edition, verified by Shuaib Al Arna'ut
- Imām At-Tirmidhī, Sunan At-Tirmidhī, using the numbering of Muhammad Fuad Abdul Baqi
- Imām At-Tirmidhī, Shamāil Al-Muḥammadiyyah, Muassasah Al-Kutub At-Thaqafiyya (Cultural Books Publishing) Beirut, 1992, First Edition, verified by Sayyid Abbās Al-Jalīmī
- Imām Ibn Majah, Sunan Ibn Majah using the numbering of Muhammad Fuad Abdul Baqi

o Imām Mālik , Al-Muwaṭṭa, Zayed Foundation for Charity and Humanitarian Works Abu Dhabi, 2004, First Edition, verified by Dr. Muhammad Mustafa Azmi

o Imām Abū Dāwūd Aṭ-Ṭayālisī, Musnad Abī Dāwūd Aṭ-Ṭayālisī, Dār Hijr Egypt, 1999, First Edition, verified by Dr AbdAllāh Ben Abdel Mohsen At-Turki

o Imām 'Abd Ar-Razzāq Aṣ-Ṣan'ānī, Muṣannaf 'Abd Ar-Razzāq, Al-Majlis Al-'Ilmī India, 1983, Second Edition, verified by Ḥabībur Raḥmān Al-A'ẓamī

o Imām Aḥmad ibn Ḥanbal, Musnad Aḥmad, Mu'assasah Ar-Risalah Syria, 2001, First Edition, verified by Shuaib Al Arna'ut

o Imām Ibn As-Sunnī , 'Amal Al-Yawm wa Al-Laylah, Dār Al-Qiblah li At-Thiqāfah Al-Islāmiyyah wa Mu'assasah 'Ulūm Al-Qur'ān Jeddah/Beirut, n.d, N/A Edition, verified by Kawthar Al-Burnī

o Imām Al-Bazzār, Musnad Al-Bazzār, Maktabah Al-'Ulūm wal Ḥikam Madinah, 2009, First Edition, verified by Maḥfūdhur Raḥmān Zaynullāh, Ṣabrī 'Abdul Khāliq Ash-Shāfi'ī and 'Ādil ibn Sa'd

o Imām Aṭ-Ṭabarānī, Al-Mu'jam Aṣ-Ṣaghir, Dar Ammar Publishing & Distribution Amman, 1985, First Edition, verified by Muḥammad Shakūr Maḥmūd Al-Hajj Amrīr

o Imām Aṭ-Ṭabarānī, Al-Mu'jam Al-Awsaṭ, Dar Elharamen Cairo, 1995, First Edition, verified by Abdul Muḥsin ibn Ibrahim Al-Ḥusaini and Ṭāriq ibn 'Awaḍullāh ibn Muḥammad

o Imām Aṭ-Ṭabarānī , Al-Mu'jam Al-Kabīr, Maktaba Ibn Taymiyyah Cairo, Second Edition, verified by Ḥamdī ibn 'Abdul Majīd As-Salafī

- Imām Aṭ-Ṭabarānī , Ad-Du'ā li Aṭ-Ṭabarānī, Dar Al-Kotob Al-ilmiyah Beirut, 1992, First Edition, verified by Muṣṭafā 'Abdul Qādir 'Aṭā

- Imām Al-Bayhaqī , Ad-Da'awāt Al-Kabīr, Gheras Publishing Company, distribution and advertising Kuwait, 2009, First Edition, verified by Badr ibn 'Abdullah Al-Badr

- Imām Al-Bayhaqī, Shu'ab Al-Īmān, Al-Rushd Publishers Riyadh in collaboration with Ad-Dar As-Salafiyya Mumbai, 2003, First Edition, verified by Dr. Abdul 'Ālī Abdul Ḥamīd Ḥāmid

- Imām Al-Ḥākim, Al-Mustadrak, Dar Al-Kotob Al-ilmiyah Beirut, 1990, First Edition, verified by Muṣṭafā Abdul Qādir 'Aṭā

- Imām Abū Bakr ibn Abī Shaybah , Muṣannaf Ibn Abī Shaybah, Dar Al-Qiblah Jeddah, 2006, First Edition, verified by Muḥammad 'Awwamah

- Imām Ibn Ḥibbān, Ṣaḥīḥ Ibn ḥibbān, Muassasah Ar-Risālah Beirut, 1993, Second Edition, verified by Shuaib Al Arna'ut

- Imām Ibn Abī Dunyā , Al-Farj ba'd As-Shiddah, Dār Ar-Rayyān li At-Turāth Egypt, 1988, Second Edition, verified by Abū Ḥudhayfah 'Ubaydullāh ibn 'Āliyah

- Imām Ibn Abī Dunyā, Al-Jū'u, Dar Ibn Ḥazm Beirut, 1997, First Edition, verified by Muḥammad Khayr Ramaḍān Yūsuf

- Imām Abū 'Awānah, Mustakhraj of Abū 'Awānah, Dār Al-Ma'rifah Beirut, 1998, First Edition, verified by Ayman ibn 'Ārif Ad-Dimashqī

- Imām Abū Ya'lā, Musnad Abī Ya'lā, Dār Al-Ma-mūn lit Turāth Damascus, 1984, First Edition, verified by Ḥusayn Salīm Asad

o Imām Zakī Ad-Dīn Al-Mundhirī, At-Targhīb wa At-Tarhīb, Dar Al-Kotob Al-ilmiyah Beirut, 1996, First Edition, verified by Ibrāhīm Shams Ad-Dīn

o Imām Abū Al-Qasim Al-Aṣbahanī, At-Targhīb wa At-Tarhīb, Dar Al-Ḥadīth Cairo, 1993, First Edition, verified by Ayman ibn Ṣāliḥ ibn Sha'bān

Scholarly/Other sources:

o Imām Ibn Al-Qayyim, Ad-Dā' wa Ad-Dawā', Dār Al-Ma'rifah Morocco, 1997, First Edition

o Imām Ibn Al-Qayyim, Badā'i Al-Fawā-id, Dār 'Aṭā-ātil 'Ilm Riyadh and Dār Ibn Ḥazm Beirut, 2019, Fifth Edition, verified by 'Alī ibn Muḥammad Al-'Imrān

o Imām Ibn Al-Qayyim, Madārij As-Sālikīn, Dār Al-Kitāb Al-'Arabī Beirut, 1996, Third Edition, verified by Muḥammad Al-Mu'taṣim billāh Al-Baghdādī

o Imām Abū Nu'aym Al-Aṣbahānī, Tārīkh Aṣbahān, Dar Al-Kotob Al-ilmiyah Beirut, 1990, First Edition, verified by Sayyid Kasrawī Ḥasan

o Imām Abū Nu'aym Al-Aṣbahānī, Ḥilyah Al-Awliyā' wa Ṭabaqāt Al-Aṣfiyā', Dar Al-Kotob Al-ilmiyah Beirut, 1988, First Edition

o Imām Aṭ-Ṭabarī, Tafsīr Aṭ-Ṭabarī, Dār Hijr, 2001, First Edition, verified by Dr AbdAllāh Ben Abdel Mohsen At-Turki

o Imām Al-Qurṭubī, Al-Jāmi' li Aḥkām al-Qur'ān (Tafsīr Al-Qurṭubī), Dār Al-Kutub Miṣriyyah Cairo, 1964, Second Edition, verified by Aḥmad Al-Bardūnī and Ibrāhīm Aṭfīsh

o Imām Ibn Kathīr, Tafsīr Ibn Kathīr, Dar Taibah for Publishing and Distribution Riyadh, 1999, Second Edition, verified by Sāmī ibn Muḥammad Salāmah

- Imām Ibn Qutaybah, Gharīb Al-Ḥadīth, Maṭba'ah Al-'Āni Baghdad, 1977, First Edition, verified by Abdullah al-Jabouri
- Imām Ibn 'Asākir, Tārīkh Dimashq, Dār Al-Fikr Amman, 1995, verified by 'Umar ibn Gharāmah Al-'Umrawī
- Imām Ibn Taymiyyah, Majmū' Al-Fatāwā, King Fahd Complex for the Printing of the Holy Qur'ān Madinah, 1995, verified by 'Abdur Raḥmān ibn Muḥammad ibn Qāsim
- Imām As-Sakhāwī, Al-Qawl Al-Badī' fi Aṣ-Ṣalāti 'alā Al-Ḥabīb As-Shafī', Muassasah Ar-Rayyān, 2002, verified by Muḥammad 'Awwāmah
- Imām Al-Ghazālī, Letter to a Disciple (Ayyuhāl Walad), The Islāmic Texts Society, 2005, bilingual English-Arabic Edition
- Imām Al-Ghazālī, Iḥyā 'Ulūm Ad-Dīn, Dar ElMarefah, Beirut, 1982
- Imām Al-Ghazālī, The Beginning of Guidance (Bidāyah Al-Hidāyah), White Thread Press London, 2010, Translated by Mashad al-Allaf
- Imām Al-Ghazālī, Mīzān Al-'Amal, Dār Al-Ma'ārif Egypt, 1964, First Edition, Verified by Dr Sulaymān Dunyā
- Imām An-Nawawī, Al-Adhkār, Dar Ibn Kathīr Damascus, 1990, Second Edition, verified by Muḥiyyuddīn Mastū

DISCLAIMER
This work is a compilation of select supplications from the Qur'ān and vast corpus of ḥadīth literature that the author and academic team believe relate to the spiritual diseases and emotions outlined in this book. Throughout this work, supplications from the Qur'ān and Prophetic sayings are either wholly or partially listed in accordance to their targeted relevance to the disease or emotion in question. The decision of cropping supplications where necessary was undertaken under academic supervision in an effort to make these supplications more accessible to a wider audience. Nevertheless, the reference for the original supplication for every du'ā' listed can be found at the end of the translation if the reader wishes to locate the full supplication.

THE HANDBOOK TEAM

Author & Publisher

Ibn Daud

Director of Ibn Daud Books, Leicester, UK

Qur'ān, Ahādīth & Scholarly Referencing & Translations

Mawlānā Amaan Muhammad

Graduate of Darul Uloom Leicester, and student of Shaykh Ayyub Surti, Leicester, UK

Editing

Mustafa Abid Russell

Leicester, UK

Design & Artwork

Irfan Chhatbar

Director of Brandboard Creative, Leicester, UK

Contributions

Khaleel Kassim

Founder & Director of Eclectic House & Mental Health Consultant, Leicester, UK

Inaayat Kassim

Co-Founder & Director of Eclectic House, Leicester, UK

Muhammad Uzair Kassim & Ammarah

Research Team, Eclectic House, Leicester, UK

Tehmina Parekh & Mashal Parekh

Halifax & Cleadon, UK

Ammaarah, Hafsah & Muhammad Ali Parekh

University, College & Primary School Students, UK

Along my journey, I have received invaluable support from many other kind and generous individuals.

May Allāh compensate them all abundantly with the best of rewards in both worlds.

Āmīn.